Super Graphic

A VISUAL GUIDE TO THE COMIC BOOK UNIVERSE

Tim Leong

CHRONICLE BOOKS

SAN FRANCISCO

What's in This Book?

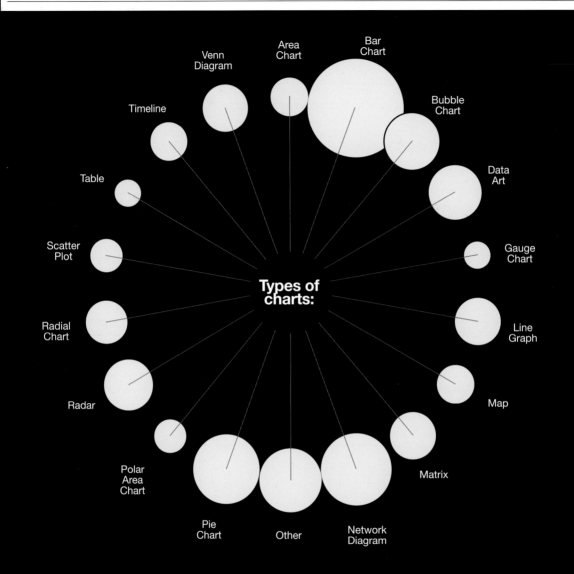

Types of charts:
Area Chart
Bar Chart
Bubble Chart
Data Art
Gauge Chart
Line Graph
Map
Matrix
Network Diagram
Other
Pie Chart
Polar Area Chart
Radar
Radial Chart
Scatter Plot
Table
Timeline
Venn Diagram

What the charts are about:

SUPERHEROES	NON-SUPERHEROES

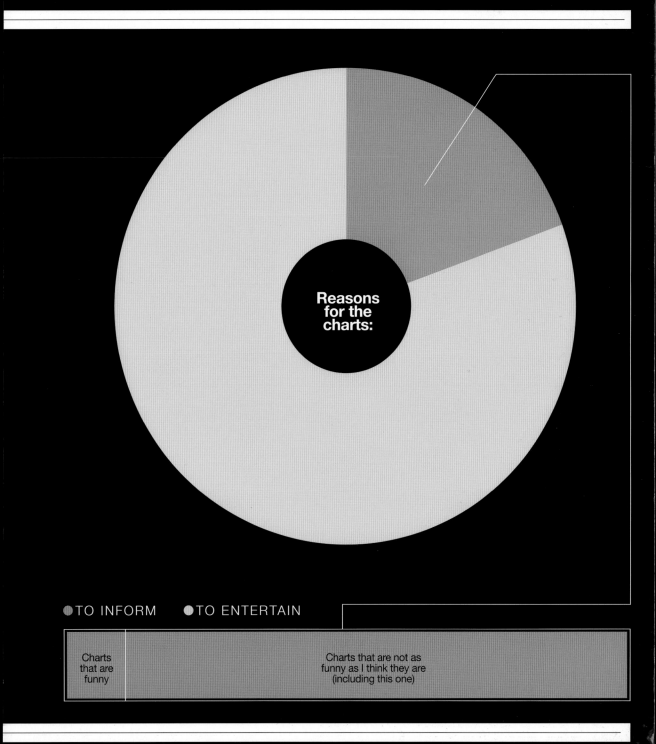

Reasons for the charts:

TO INFORM   TO ENTERTAIN

| Charts that are funny | Charts that are not as funny as I think they are (including this one) |

FULL DISCLOSURE

My Bookshelf

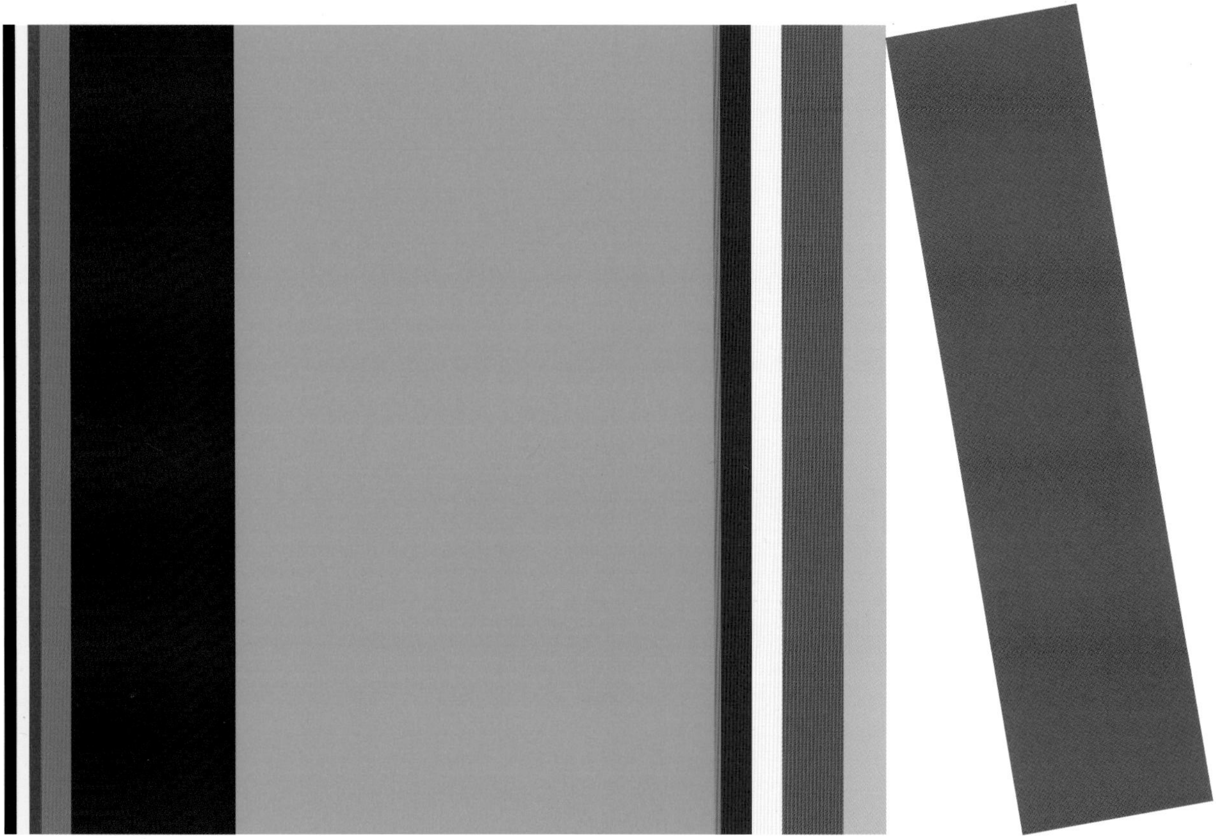

● Ad House Books ● Archaia Entertainment ● BOOM! Studios ● Drawn & Quarterly ● Dark Horse Comics ● DC Comics ● Dynamite Entertainment ● Fantagraphics Books ● First Second ● Icon ● IDW Publishing ● Image Comics

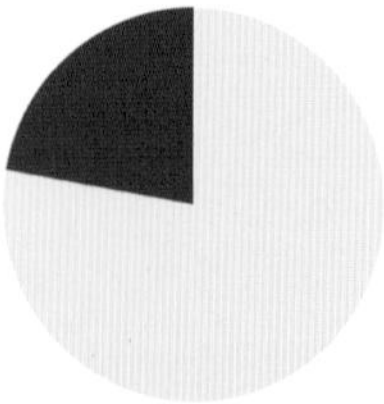

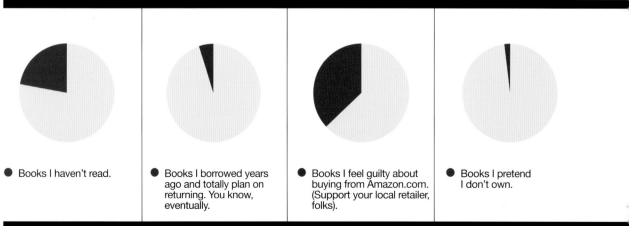

● Books I haven't read.

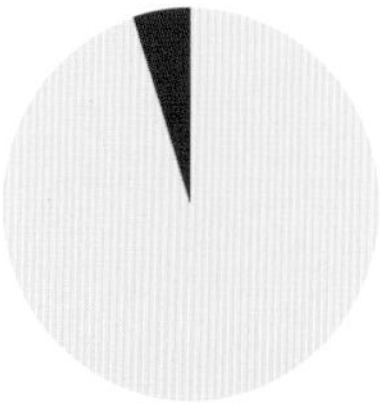

● Books I borrowed years ago and totally plan on returning. You know, eventually.

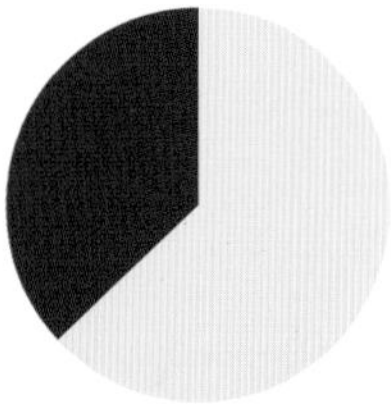

● Books I feel guilty about buying from Amazon.com. (Support your local retailer, folks).

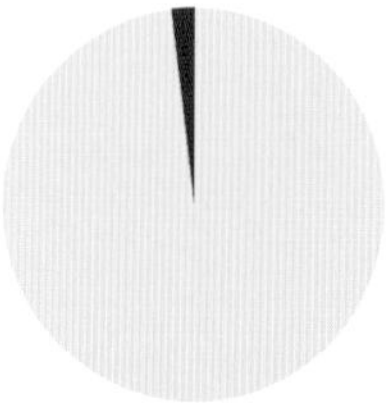

● Books I pretend I don't own.

● Marvel Comics ● MAX ● Oni Press ● Other ● Pantheon Books ● Scholastic ● SLG Publishing ● Tokyopop
● Top Shelf Productions ● Vertical, Inc. ● Vertigo ● Viz Media ● Wildstorm

● Books I've read more than once.

● Books I bought only because I like the writer.

● Books I've bought multiple copies of because I forgot that I owned them.

● Incomplete series I plan on compulsively completing.

True Colors

Crimson Cavalier	Crimson Daffodil	Scarlet Scarab	Red Ronin	Red Hulk	Pink Pearl	Green Torpedo
Crimson Dynamo	Scarlet Witch	Red Nine	Omega Red	Pink Lady	Yellow Claw	Fiddler's Green
Scarlet Spider	Red Tornado	Redwing	Percy Pinkerton	Yellow Kid	Hershel Greene	Green Turtle
Red Skull	Red Sonja	Red Hood	Pinky Pinkerton	Yellowjacket	Green Lama	Green Hornet
Red Robin	Red Ghost	Lonesome Pinky	Booster Gold	Green Arrow	Green Lantern	Blue Streak
Rose Red	Pinky	Yellow Wasp	Jade Dragon	Jade Emperor	Blue Diamond	Blue Falcon
Rose	Yellow Peri	Abe Brown	Jade	Blue Devil	Rafaella Blue	Ultra Violet
Agent Orange	Charlie Brown	Sage	Blue Beetle	Cobalt Blue	Indigo Eshun	Black Bolt
Stephanie Brown	Yorick Brown	Blue Bolt	Deep Blue	Odysseus Indigo	Black Adam	Black Panther

Green Skull	Bomo Greenbark	Green Thumb	Blue Marvel	Blue Eagle	Purple Zombie	Black Widow
Green Sorceress	Green Ghoul	Blue Shield	Norwegian Blue	Purple Claw	Black Canary	Blackheart
Green Goblin	Crazy Blue Rocket	Bluebird	Purple Phantom	Black Knight	Black Cloak	Black Goliath
Blue Blade	Boy Blue	Purple Mask	Camilla Black	Black Talon	Silver Surfer	Silver Squire
Code Blue	Purple Marauder	Black Mamba	Black Lightning	Silver Fox	Silver Sable	White Queen
Violet Grey	Black Jack	Black Spectre	Silver Samurai	Silver Racer	Ebony White	Aelfyre Whitemane
Black Tom Cassidy	Black Mantis	Silver Scorpion	Silverclaw	Jean Grey	White Dragon	White Ghost
Black Cat	Silver Dagger	Silver	Graymalkin	Whiteout	White Rabbit	White Noise
Silvermane	Silver Sentry	Nate Grey	Perry White	Whiteface	White Wolf	White Tiger

Superheroes and Primary Colors

Spider-Man

Superman

Wolverine

Iron Man

Captain
America

Thor

Flash

Beast

Doctor
Strange

Costume Color Ratio

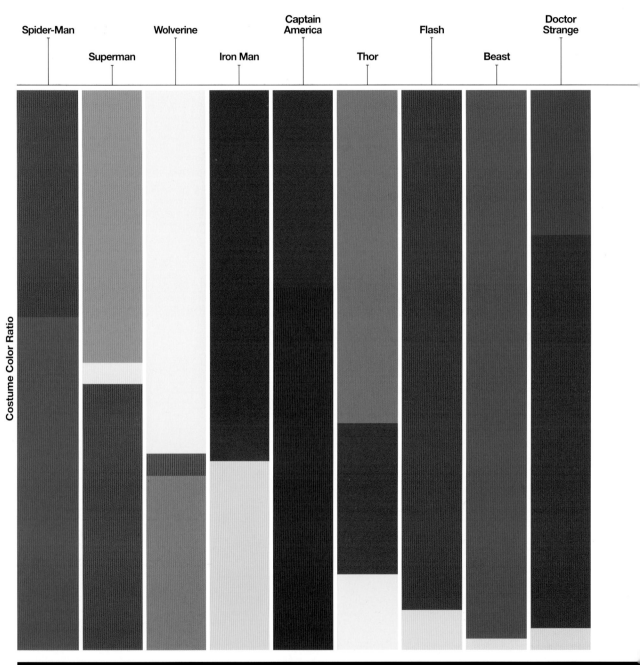

Historically, superhero costumes have been designed in reds, yellows, and blues. The decisions are about more than just what looks good; spandex in primary colors is a visual cue to the character's heroic nature.

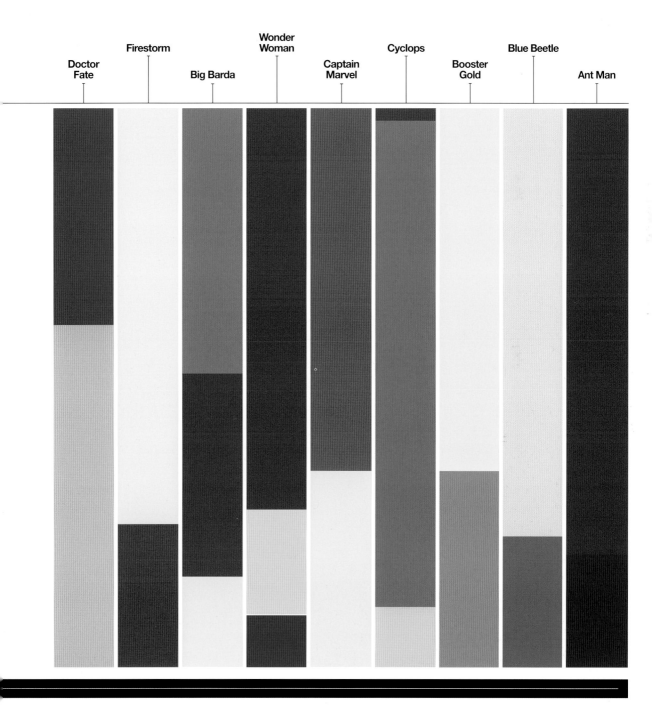

Doctor Fate

Firestorm

Big Barda

Wonder Woman

Captain Marvel

Cyclops

Booster Gold

Blue Beetle

Ant Man

Supervillains and Secondary Colors

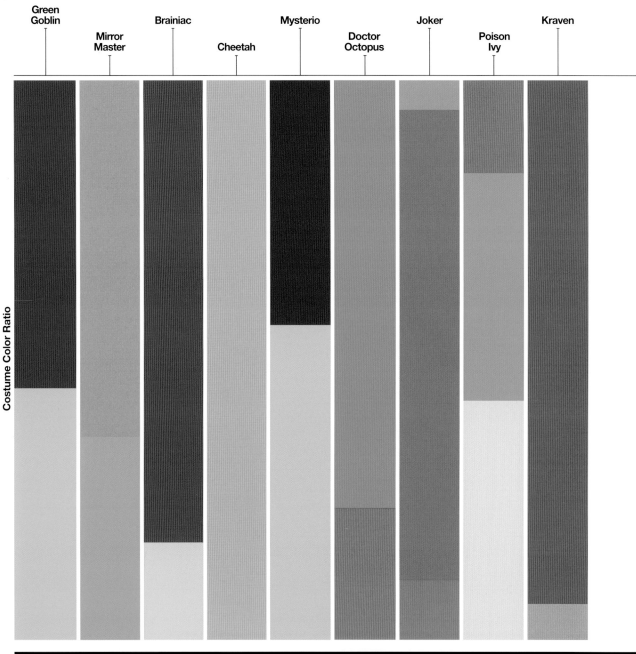

Green Goblin

Mirror Master

Brainiac

Cheetah

Mysterio

Doctor Octopus

Joker

Poison Ivy

Kraven

Costume Color Ratio

Like superheroes, supervillains developed a set of costume conventions early on, too. Orange, green, and purple are a signal of a character's evil intentions.

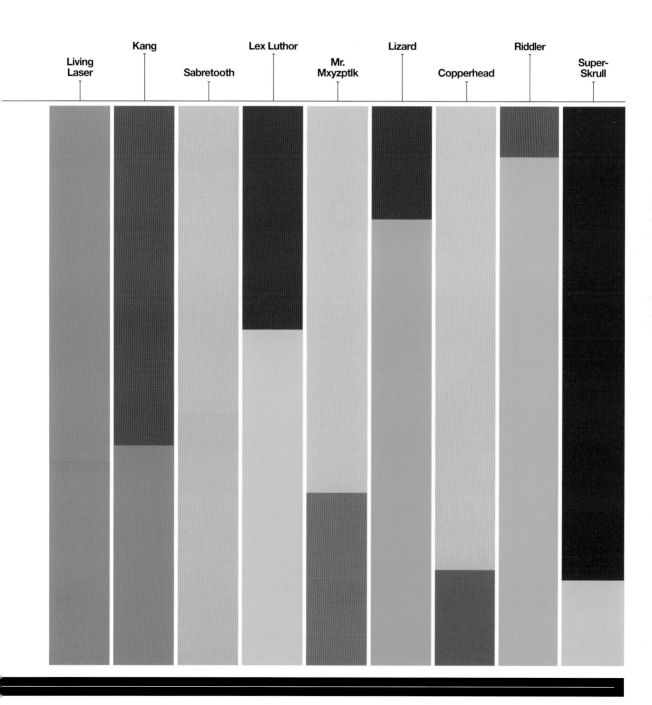

Living
Laser

Kang

Sabretooth

Lex Luthor

Mr.
Mxyzptlk

Lizard

Copperhead

Riddler

Super-
Skrull

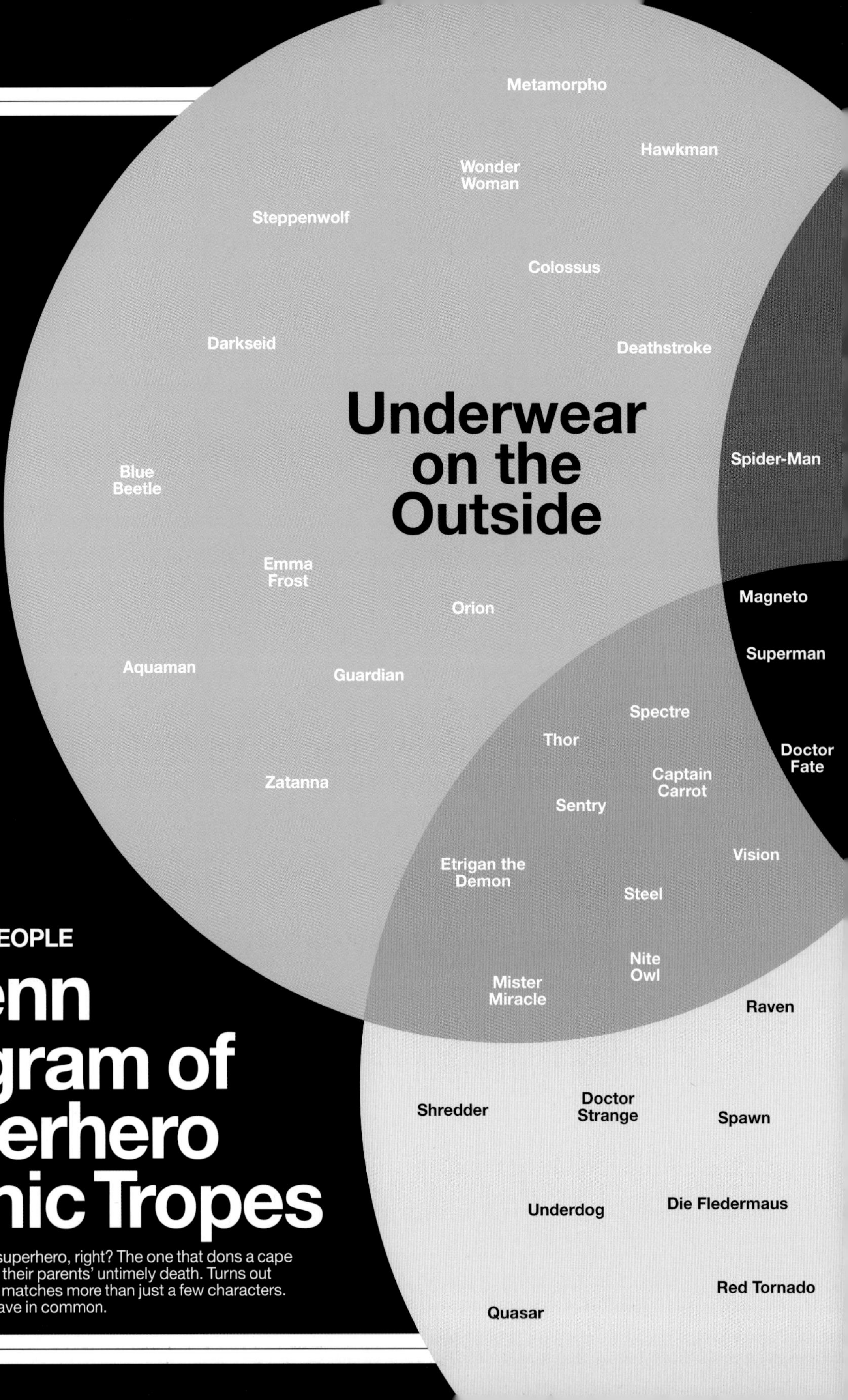
Metamorpho
Hawkman
Wonder Woman
Steppenwolf
Colossus
Darkseid
Deathstroke
Underwear on the Outside
Spider-Man
Blue Beetle
Emma Frost
Orion
Magneto
Aquaman
Guardian
Superman
Spectre
Thor
Doctor Fate
Zatanna
Captain Carrot
Sentry
Vision
Etrigan the Demon
Steel
Nite Owl
Mister Miracle
Raven
Shredder
Doctor Strange
Spawn
Underdog
Die Fledermaus
Red Tornado
Quasar

COMMON PEOPLE

A Venn Diagram of Superhero Comic Tropes

You know that one superhero, right? The one that dons a cape and tights following their parents' untimely death. Turns out that the description matches more than just a few characters. Here's what most have in common.

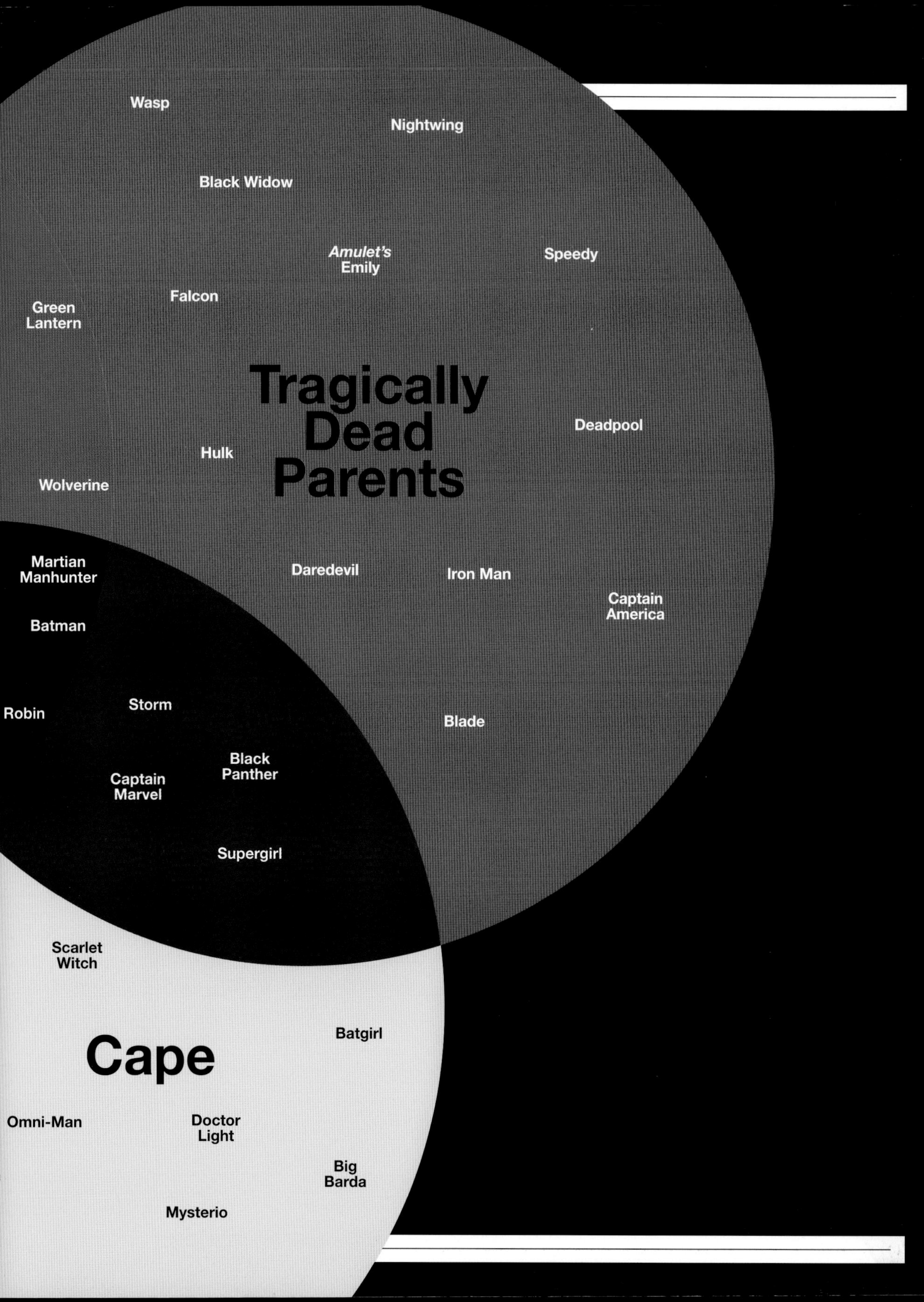
Wasp
Nightwing
Black Widow
Amulet's Emily
Speedy
Falcon
Green Lantern
Tragically Dead Parents
Deadpool
Hulk
Wolverine
Martian Manhunter
Daredevil
Iron Man
Captain America
Batman
Robin
Storm
Blade
Black Panther
Captain Marvel
Supergirl
Scarlet Witch
Batgirl
Cape
Omni-Man
Doctor Light
Big Barda
Mysterio

How to Read a Comic Book

ENGLISH

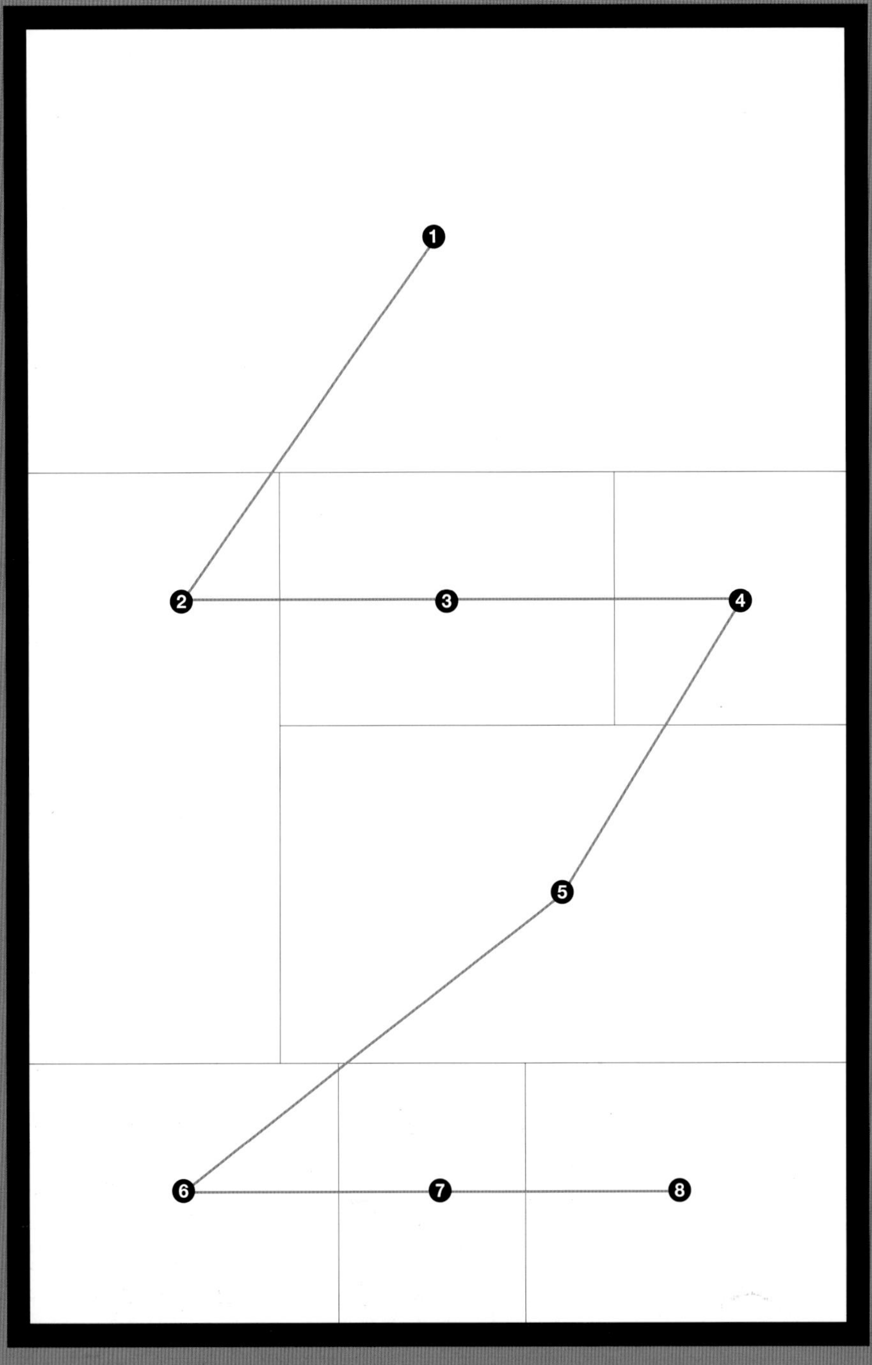
1
2
3
4
5
6
7
8

The 22 pages that are standard in American comics are read pretty much like any other book you pick up: from left to right and top to bottom. Japanese comics though, called *manga*, are bound on the other side and are read from right to left. Manga is printed on smaller-sized paper than its American counterpart and has six times the number of pages.

JAPANESE

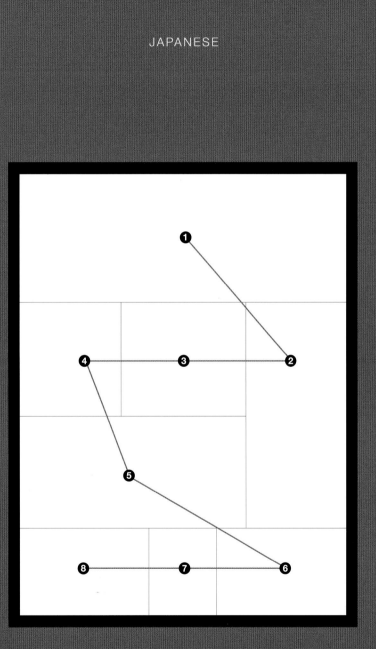

What Is Manga?

Manga is the Japanese word for comics. In Japan, it's a massive industry, making up nearly a quarter of all printed material. Typically, manga is first published in 850-page anthology magazines that serialize chapters from several different comics. Successful stories are then collected individually and sold afterward as books known as *tankobon*. Manga created in the United States is called OEL manga, or Original English-Language manga.

History

Though manga has ties to Japanese art and culture dating back to the 1800s, modern manga originated after WWII.

Around 1920, Japan started printing magazines with illustrated stories focusing on fun. In the 1930s, however, the tone shifted to military heroism and soldiers preparing for battle.

With Japan's entry into WWII, manga was limited to all-ages content, and in some cases, propaganda against the Allied forces.

After Japan's defeat and the nuclear bombing of Hiroshima and Nagasaki, the country found solace in lighter fare including:

Sazae-san (1946), the story of a resilient housewife. The creator, Machiko Hasegawa, was one of the few women working in the industry at the time.

Another success was Osamu Tezuka's manga and eventual TV show, *Astro Boy* (1951), about a super-powered robot boy. Tezuka went on to become the animation equivalent of Walt Disney in Japan.

Longest-running manga

Golgo 13 (1969 – ongoing), 160 vol.   *Dokaben* (1972 – ongoing), 165 vol.   *Kochikame* (1976 – ongoing), 176 vol.

Bestselling manga in Japan vs. worldwide bestsellers
as of 2012

■ MANGA   ■ NON-MANGA

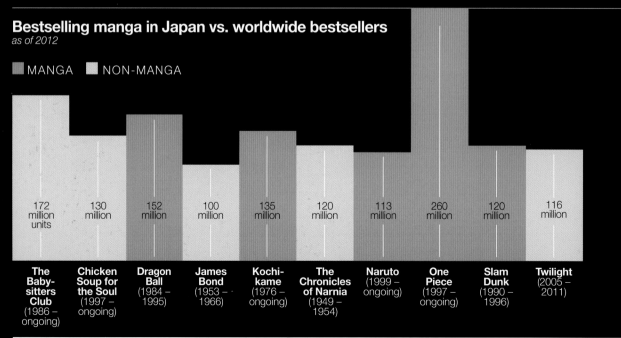

The Baby-sitters Club (1986 – ongoing)	Chicken Soup for the Soul (1997 – ongoing)	Dragon Ball (1984 – 1995)	James Bond (1953 – 1966)	Kochi-kame (1976 – ongoing)	The Chronicles of Narnia (1949 – 1954)	Naruto (1999 – ongoing)	One Piece (1997 – ongoing)	Slam Dunk (1990 – 1996)	Twilight (2005 – 2011)
172 million units	130 million	152 million	100 million	135 million	120 million	113 million	260 million	120 million	116 million

Types of manga

If this were a manga, the headline would be over here. And in Japanese.

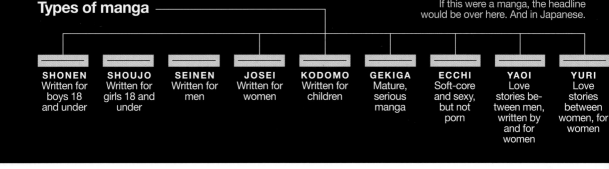

SHONEN	SHOUJO	SEINEN	JOSEI	KODOMO	GEKIGA	ECCHI	YAOI	YURI
Written for boys 18 and under	Written for girls 18 and under	Written for men	Written for women	Written for children	Mature, serious manga	Soft-core and sexy, but not porn	Love stories between men, written by and for women	Love stories between women, for women

Manga content

While superheroes dominate American comics, Japanese manga is much more diverse and without a single genre overshadowing the market.

Japan

ACTION	ADVENTURE	BUSINESS
COMEDY	FANTASY	FOOD
HORROR	MYSTERY	ROMANCE
SCIENCE FICTION	SEX	SPORTS

America

DOMINATED BY SUPERHEROES

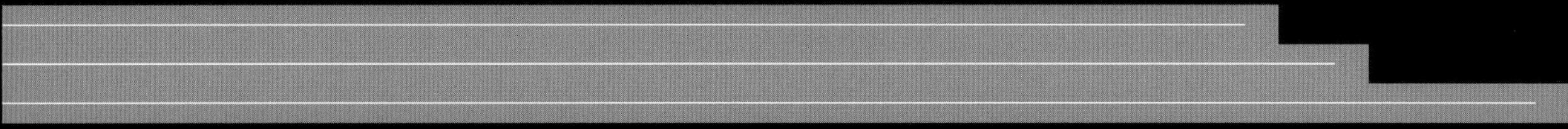

Big in Japan

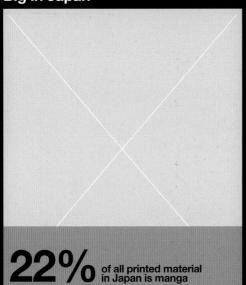

22% of all printed material in Japan is manga

Physical attributes

Some characters tend to be drawn with exaggerated eyes, a small nose, and a very expressive mouth.

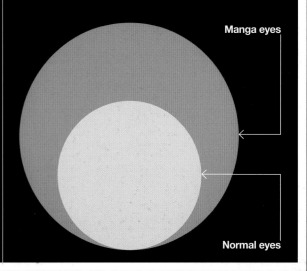

Manga eyes

Normal eyes

Character Lineup

From insect-sized to giant, this crowd is full of standouts in stature.

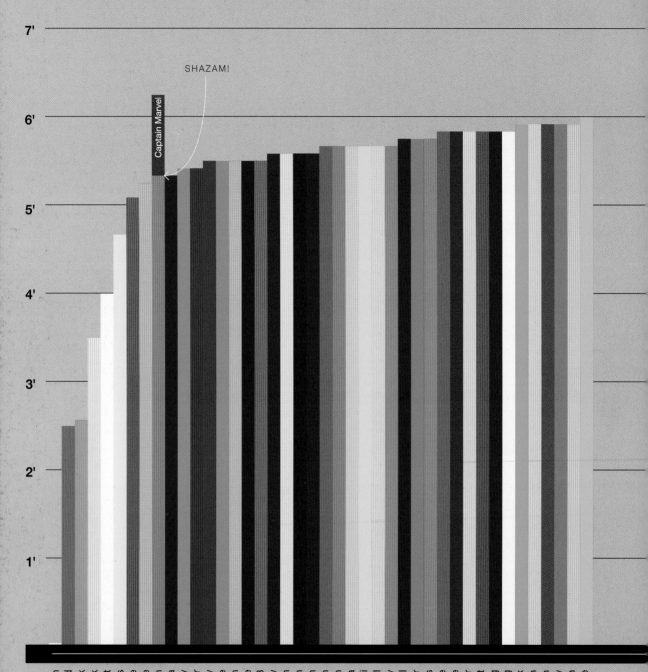

SHAZAM!

Captain Marvel

7'

6'

5'

4'

3'

2'

1'

Kandorian
Lockheed
Howard the Duck
Puck
Ganthet
Franklin Richards
Wolfsbane
Wolverine
Billy Batson
Cassandra Nova
Black Canary
Dagger
Jean Grey
Kitty Pride
Invisible Woman
Lois Lane
X-23
Black Widow
Catwoman
Scarlet Witch
Harley Quinn
Iceman
Cheetah
Renée Montoya
Kamandi
Supergirl
Bouncing Boy
Hawkgirl
Nightcrawler
Doctor Octopus
Vandal Savage
Perry White
Peter Parker
Emma Frost
Nightwing
Ambush Bug
Jonah Hex
J. Jonah Jameson
Wonder Woman
Green Arrow
Storm
Bullseye

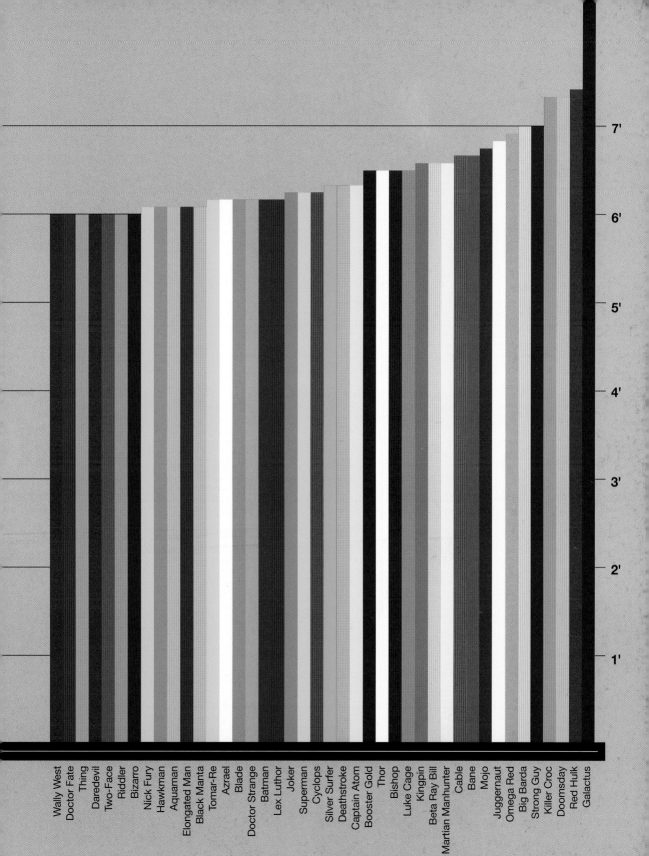

7'

6'

5'

4'

3'

2'

1'

Wally West
Doctor Fate
Thing
Daredevil
Two-Face
Riddler
Bizarro
Nick Fury
Hawkman
Aquaman
Elongated Man
Black Manta
Tomar-Re
Azrael
Blade
Doctor Strange
Batman
Lex Luthor
Joker
Superman
Cyclops
Silver Surfer
Deathstroke
Captain Atom
Booster Gold
Thor
Bishop
Luke Cage
Kingpin
Beta Ray Bill
Martian Manhunter
Cable
Bane
Mojo
Juggernaut
Omega Red
Big Barda
Strong Guy
Killer Croc
Doomsday
Red Hulk
Galactus

Character Weigh-In

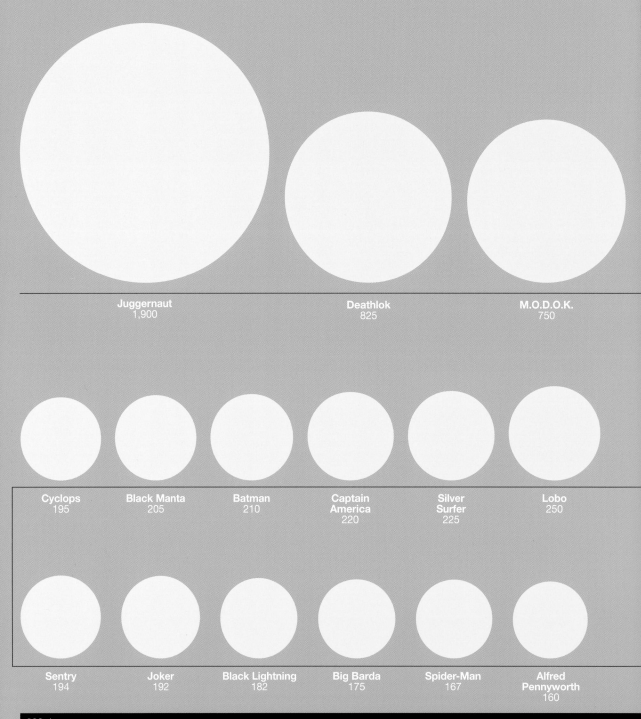

Juggernaut
1,900

Deathlok
825

M.O.D.O.K.
750

Cyclops
195

Black Manta
205

Batman
210

Captain
America
220

Silver
Surfer
225

Lobo
250

Sentry
194

Joker
192

Black Lightning
182

Big Barda
175

Spider-Man
167

Alfred
Pennyworth
160

Sometimes weight means power. You wouldn't think so by looking at him, but Kingpin is all muscle mass. The same can't be said for Chunk, who is aptly named. Here's how superheroes and villains in Marvel and DC titles compare on the scales, in pounds.

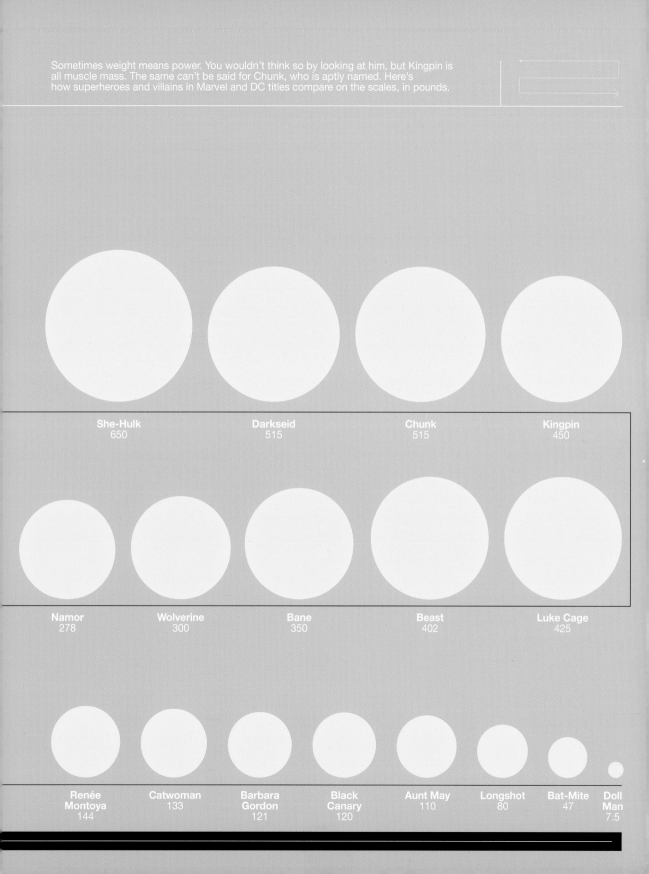

She-Hulk
650

Darkseid
515

Chunk
515

Kingpin
450

Namor
278

Wolverine
300

Bane
350

Beast
402

Luke Cage
425

**Renée
Montoya**
144

Catwoman
133

**Barbara
Gordon**
121

**Black
Canary**
120

Aunt May
110

Longshot
80

Bat-Mite
47

**Doll
Man**
7.5

Map Quest

Locating the fictional world's most important super cities and countries.

● Character lives/is from here   ○ Location referenced in character's series

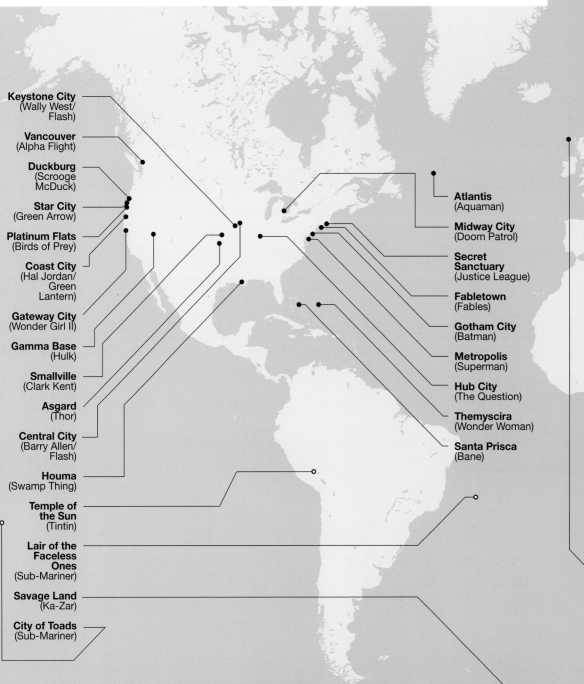

Keystone City
(Wally West/
Flash)

Vancouver
(Alpha Flight)

Duckburg
(Scrooge
McDuck)

Star City
(Green Arrow)

Platinum Flats
(Birds of Prey)

Coast City
(Hal Jordan/
Green
Lantern)

Gateway City
(Wonder Girl II)

Gamma Base
(Hulk)

Smallville
(Clark Kent)

Asgard
(Thor)

Central City
(Barry Allen/
Flash)

Houma
(Swamp Thing)

Temple of
the Sun
(Tintin)

Lair of the
Faceless
Ones
(Sub-Mariner)

Savage Land
(Ka-Zar)

City of Toads
(Sub-Mariner)

Atlantis
(Aquaman)

Midway City
(Doom Patrol)

Secret
Sanctuary
(Justice League)

Fabletown
(Fables)

Gotham City
(Batman)

Metropolis
(Superman)

Hub City
(The Question)

Themyscira
(Wonder Woman)

Santa Prisca
(Bane)

Antarctica

The Arctic

Fortress of
Solitude
(Superman)

Territory of
Polar Parasites
(Kamandi)

Monster Island
(Mole Man)

Neo-Tokyo
(Akira)

Nanda Parbat
(Deadman)

Providence
(Cable)

Gaipajama
(Tintin)

Kanga Rat
Murder Society
(Kamandi)

Slorenia
(Bloodwraith)

Rumekistan
(Cable)

Latveria
(Dr. Doom)

Genosha
(Magneto)

Wakanda
(Black
Panther)

Transia
(New Men)

Olympia
(The Eternals)

Gorilla City
(Gorilla Grodd)

Symkaria
(Silver Sable)

Markovia
(Terra/
Teen Titans)

Braddock
Lighthouse
(Excalibur)

Muir Island
(X-Men)

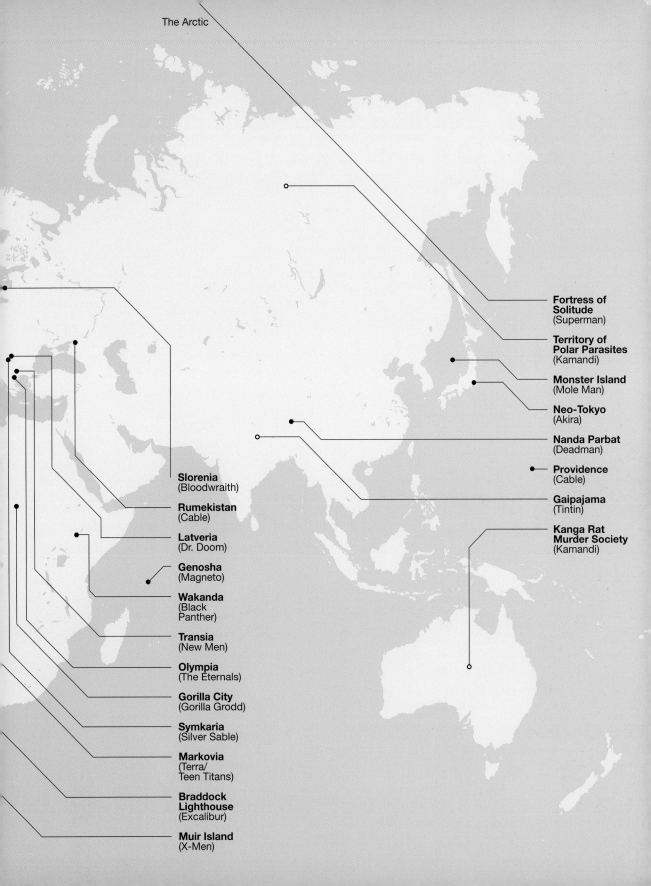

WELCOME TO THE MULTIVERSE

Wait, There's More Than One Earth?

There's no easy way to say this . . . this Earth is not the only Earth. Still with me? Okay. So, the DC Comics world you're most familiar with—the one where Superman grows up in Smallville and Bruce Wayne decides to avenge his parents by becoming Batman—(a.k.a. New Earth) is actually a part of a larger "multiverse" where there are an endless number of possible Earths. But that changed in 1985 when DC used its fiftieth anniversary to launch one of the most famous stories of all time, *Crisis on Infinite Earths*. During the 12-issue series, most of the alternate Earths are destroyed. The few that remain are pulled together to form one single Earth, destroying the multiverse in the process. This single-Earth setup lasts twenty years until the sequel, *Infinite Crisis*, relaunches the multiverse. This time around the possibilities aren't endless, as the multiverse hosts a finite number (52 at the moment) of possible Earths.

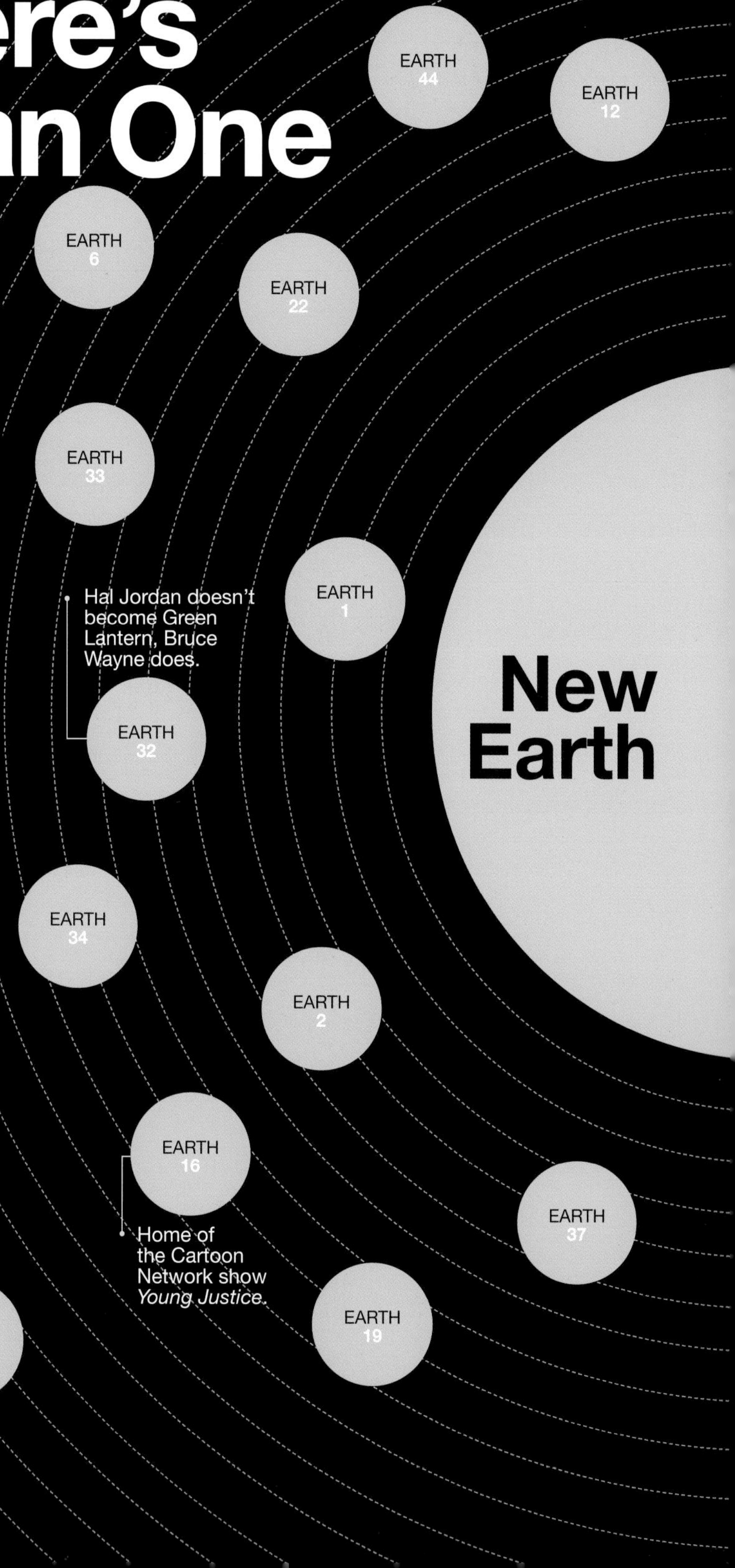

EARTH 44
EARTH 12
EARTH 6
EARTH 22
EARTH 33
EARTH 1
New Earth
Hal Jordan doesn't become Green Lantern, Bruce Wayne does.
EARTH 32
EARTH 34
EARTH 2
EARTH 16
Home of the Cartoon Network show *Young Justice*.
EARTH 37
EARTH 19
EARTH 8

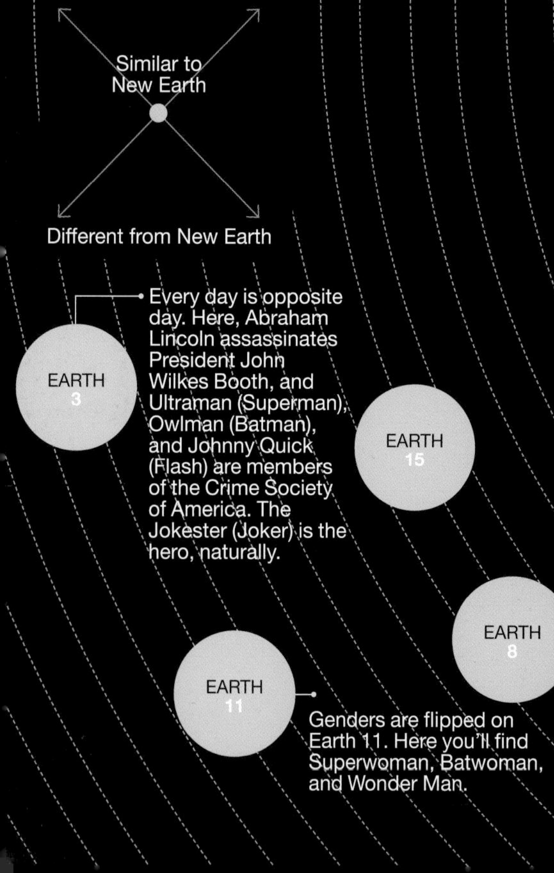

Similar to New Earth
Different from New Earth
EARTH 3
Every day is opposite day. Here, Abraham Lincoln assassinates President John Wilkes Booth, and Ultraman (Superman), Owlman (Batman), and Johnny Quick (Flash) are members of the Crime Society of America. The Jokester (Joker) is the hero, naturally.
EARTH 15
EARTH 11
Genders are flipped on Earth 11. Here you'll find Superwoman, Batwoman, and Wonder Man.

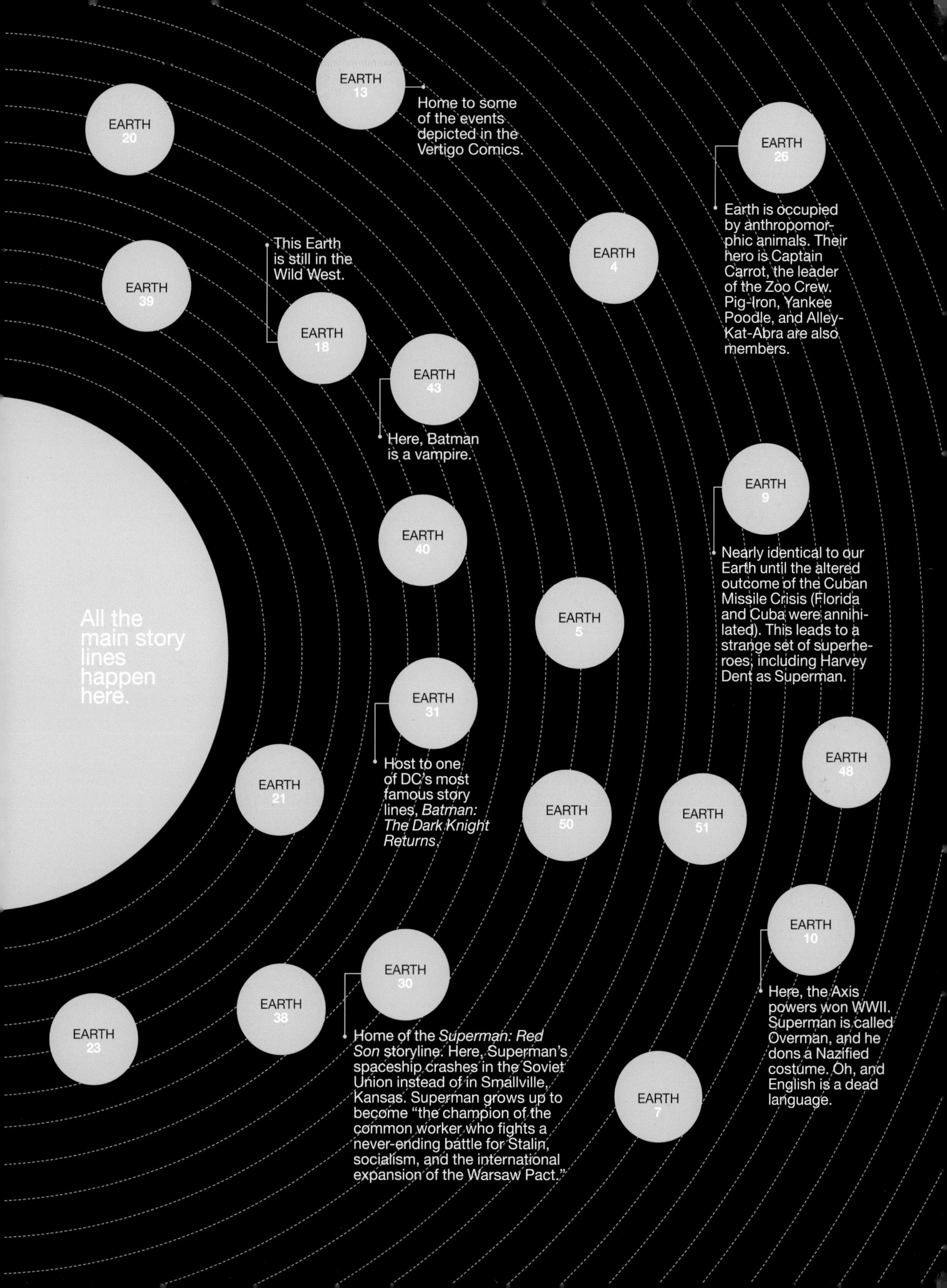
EARTH 13
Home to some of the events depicted in the Vertigo Comics.
EARTH 20
EARTH 26
Earth is occupied by anthropomorphic animals. Their hero is Captain Carrot, the leader of the Zoo Crew. Pig-Iron, Yankee Poodle, and Alley-Kat-Abra are also members.
This Earth is still in the Wild West.
EARTH 39
EARTH 4
EARTH 18
EARTH 43
Here, Batman is a vampire.
EARTH 9
Nearly identical to our Earth until the altered outcome of the Cuban Missile Crisis (Florida and Cuba were annihilated). This leads to a strange set of superheroes, including Harvey Dent as Superman.
EARTH 40
All the main story lines happen here.
EARTH 5
EARTH 31
Host to one of DC's most famous story lines, *Batman: The Dark Knight Returns*.
EARTH 48
EARTH 21
EARTH 50
EARTH 51
EARTH 10
EARTH 30
Here, the Axis powers won WWII. Superman is called Overman, and he dons a Nazified costume. Oh, and English is a dead language.
EARTH 38
EARTH 23
Home of the *Superman: Red Son* storyline. Here, Superman's spaceship crashes in the Soviet Union instead of in Smallville, Kansas. Superman grows up to become "the champion of the common worker who fights a never-ending battle for Stalin, socialism, and the international expansion of the Warsaw Pact."
EARTH 7

A History of Heroic Proportions

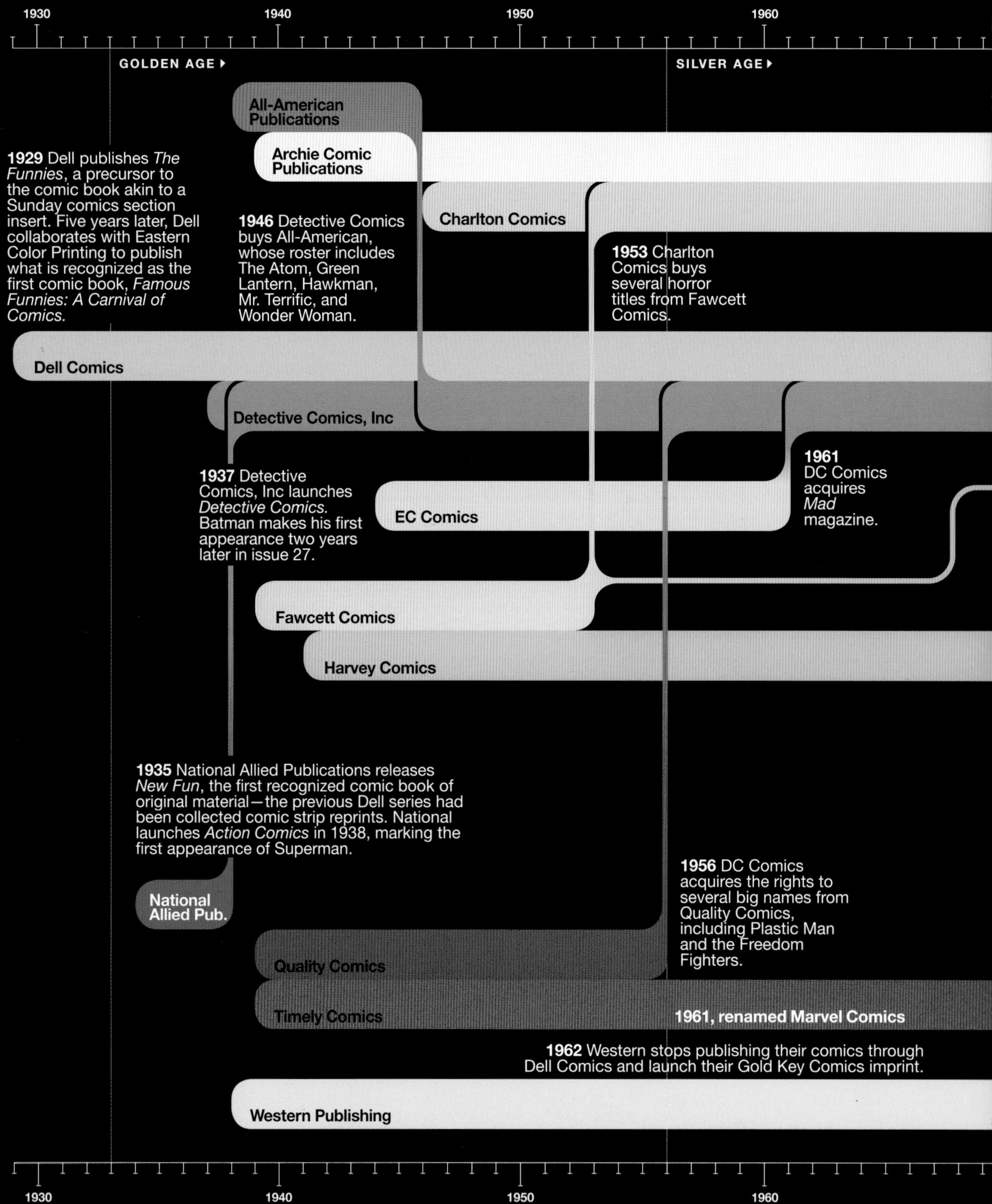
1930
1940
1950
1960
GOLDEN AGE
SILVER AGE
All-American Publications
Archie Comic Publications
1929 Dell publishes The Funnies, a precursor to the comic book akin to a Sunday comics section insert. Five years later, Dell collaborates with Eastern Color Printing to publish what is recognized as the first comic book, Famous Funnies: A Carnival of Comics.
1946 Detective Comics buys All-American, whose roster includes The Atom, Green Lantern, Hawkman, Mr. Terrific, and Wonder Woman.
Charlton Comics
1953 Charlton Comics buys several horror titles from Fawcett Comics.
Dell Comics
Detective Comics, Inc
1961 DC Comics acquires Mad magazine.
1937 Detective Comics, Inc launches Detective Comics. Batman makes his first appearance two years later in issue 27.
EC Comics
Fawcett Comics
Harvey Comics
1935 National Allied Publications releases New Fun, the first recognized comic book of original material—the previous Dell series had been collected comic strip reprints. National launches Action Comics in 1938, marking the first appearance of Superman.
National Allied Pub.
1956 DC Comics acquires the rights to several big names from Quality Comics, including Plastic Man and the Freedom Fighters.
Quality Comics
Timely Comics
1961, renamed Marvel Comics
1962 Western stops publishing their comics through Dell Comics and launch their Gold Key Comics imprint.
Western Publishing
1930
1940
1950
1960

The story behind the companies that publish your favorite comics is one of intense competition, censorship, and idea theft. Artists defected, characters were traded, and new companies were born.

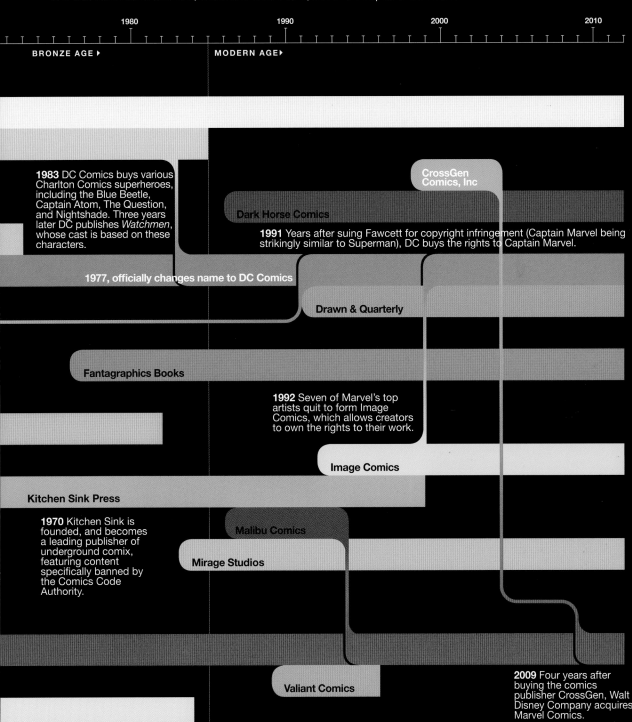

1980   1990   2000   2010

BRONZE AGE ▶   MODERN AGE ▶

1983 DC Comics buys various Charlton Comics superheroes, including the Blue Beetle, Captain Atom, The Question, and Nightshade. Three years later DC publishes *Watchmen*, whose cast is based on these characters.

CrossGen Comics, Inc

Dark Horse Comics

1991 Years after suing Fawcett for copyright infringement (Captain Marvel being strikingly similar to Superman), DC buys the rights to Captain Marvel.

1977, officially changes name to DC Comics

Drawn & Quarterly

Fantagraphics Books

1992 Seven of Marvel's top artists quit to form Image Comics, which allows creators to own the rights to their work.

Image Comics

Kitchen Sink Press

1970 Kitchen Sink is founded, and becomes a leading publisher of underground comix, featuring content specifically banned by the Comics Code Authority.

Malibu Comics

Mirage Studios

Valiant Comics

2009 Four years after buying the comics publisher CrossGen, Walt Disney Company acquires Marvel Comics.

Power Publishers

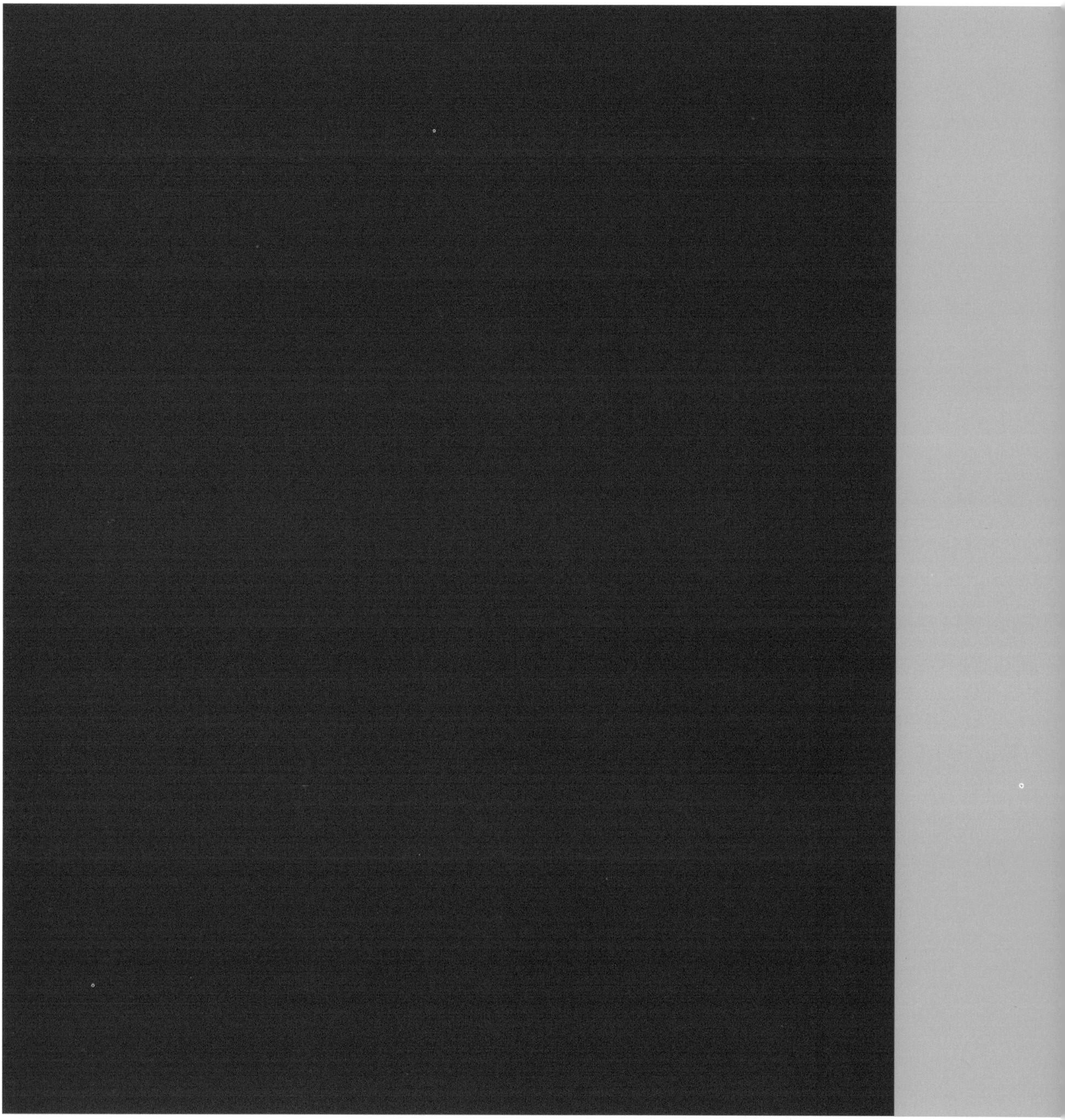

COMPANY, MARKET SHARE:
Marvel Comics, 40.93%
DC Comics, 36.77%
Image Comics, 4.71%
IDW Publishing, 3.78%
Dark Horse Comics, 3.35%
Dynamite Entertainment, 2.85%
Publishers not in the top 25, 1.79%
BOOM! Studios, 1.43%

THE REST, HAVING LESS THAN 1% EACH:
Archie Comics, 0.74%
Zenescope Entertainment, 0.64%
Avatar Press, 0.54%

Although there are dozens of independent presses and thousands of indie artists stapling together passion projects, most of what sold in comic stores in 2011 came from just a few influential paper-pushers.

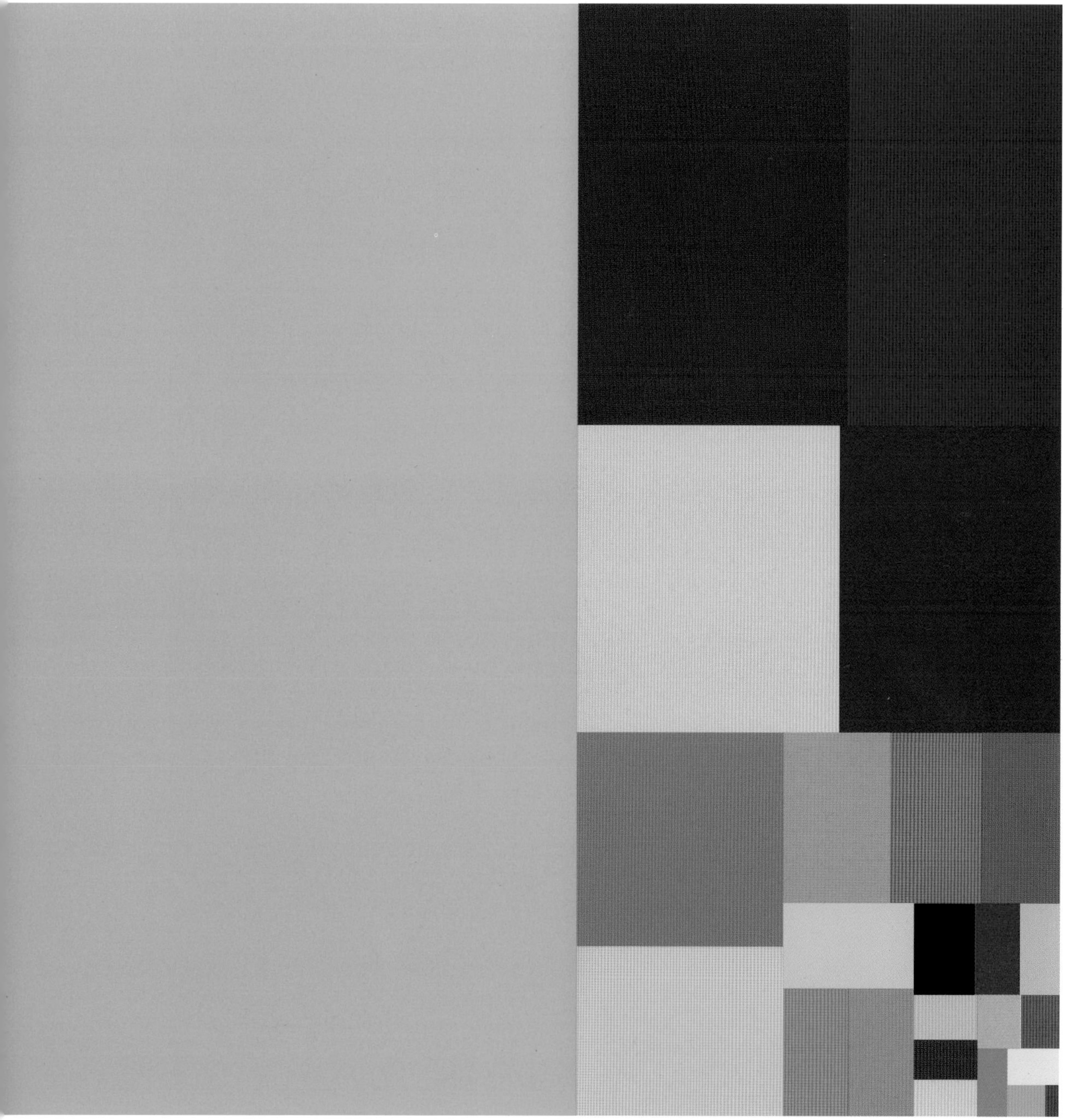

Viz Media, 0.47%
Aspen MLT, 0.35%
Bongo Comics, 0.34%
Eaglemoss Publications Ltd., 0.23%
Random House, 0.17%

Oni Press, 0.15%
Hachette Book Group USA, 0.12%
Fantagraphics Books, 0.11%
Titan, 0.10%
Abstract Studios, 0.10%

Archaia, 0.09%
Tokyopop, 0.09%
Top Shelf Productions, 0.08%
Drawn & Quarterly, 0.05%
Humanoids, 0.02%

TAKE SHAPE

Evolution of Superman's Logo

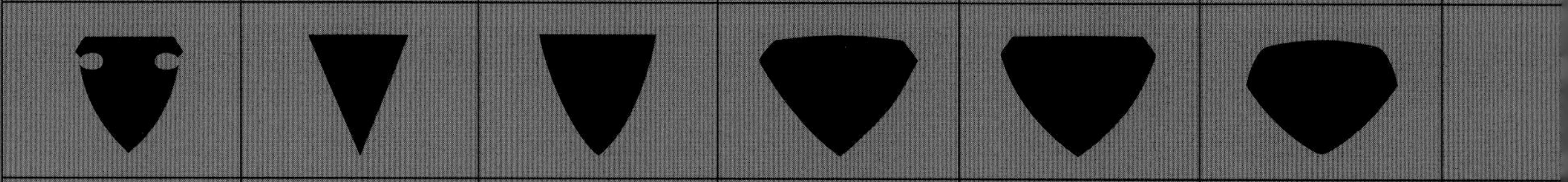

1938	1939	1939	1941	1946	1948
Akin to a police badge, the first emblem to grace Superman's chest is on the cover of *Action Comics* #1, his first appearance.	The original design doesn't last, however, and by the time *Superman* #1 debuts that next year it has already become more triangular.	The first two are blended. The bottom becomes more rounded and the shape expands.	When Max Fleischer creates his art deco Superman cartoons, the shield becomes much wider and gets notched corners.	By the time Wayne Boring becomes the comic's regular artist, the top becomes flatter and the bottom wider.	The first live-action Superman hits screens as a 15-part serial starring Kirk Alyn. The logo shrinks.

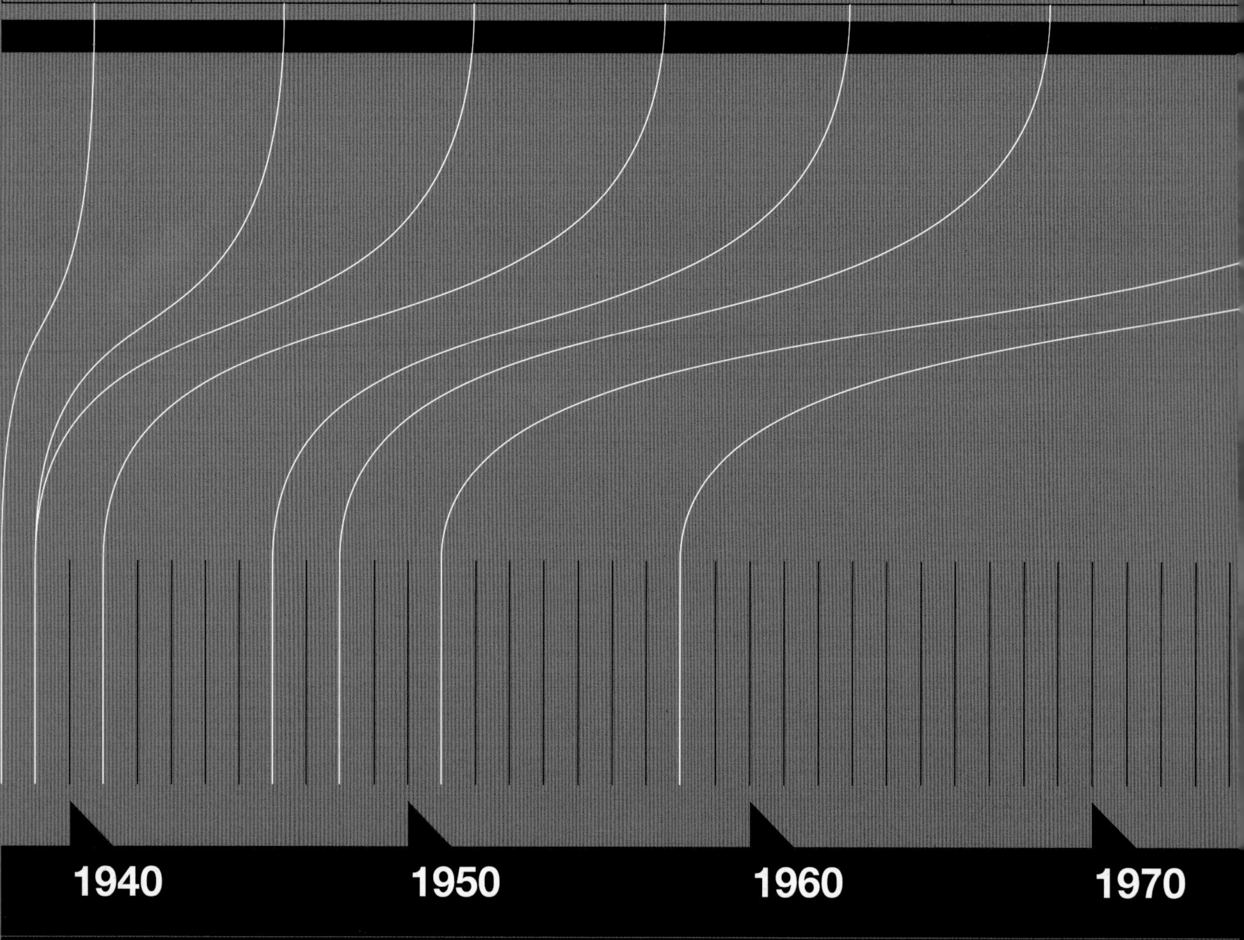
1940
1950
1960
1970

The Man of Steel was a pioneer in more ways than you probably realize. Created by Jerry Siegel and Joe Shuster, Superman is one of the first (and most successful) superheroes ever. He was also one of the first to wear a logo on his chest, which later became standard superhero fare. What was not standard, though, was what exactly appeared there. The Superman logo shape, like the stories themselves, morphed over time.

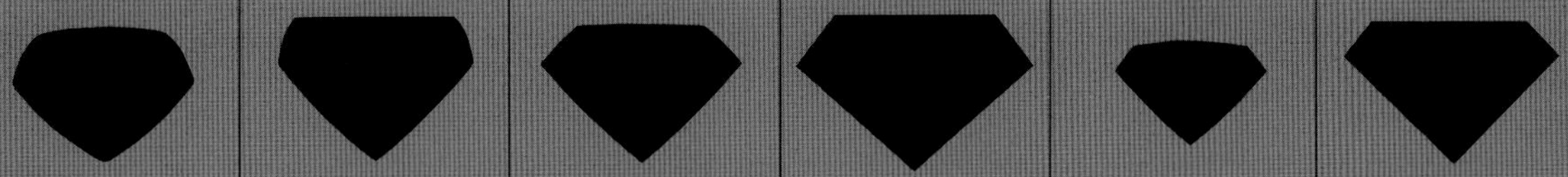

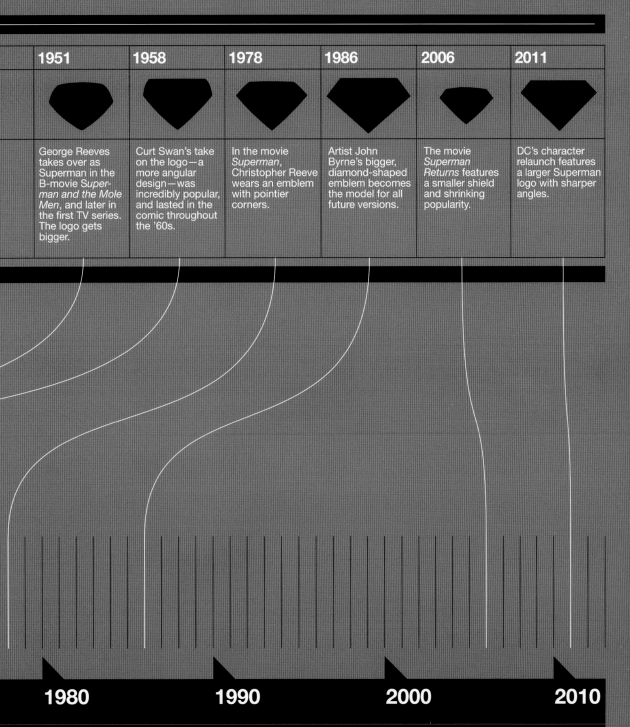

1951	1958	1978	1986	2006	2011
George Reeves takes over as Superman in the B-movie *Superman and the Mole Men*, and later in the first TV series. The logo gets bigger.	Curt Swan's take on the logo—a more angular design—was incredibly popular, and lasted in the comic throughout the '60s.	In the movie *Superman*, Christopher Reeve wears an emblem with pointier corners.	Artist John Byrne's bigger, diamond-shaped emblem becomes the model for all future versions.	The movie *Superman Returns* features a smaller shield and shrinking popularity.	DC's character relaunch features a larger Superman logo with sharper angles.

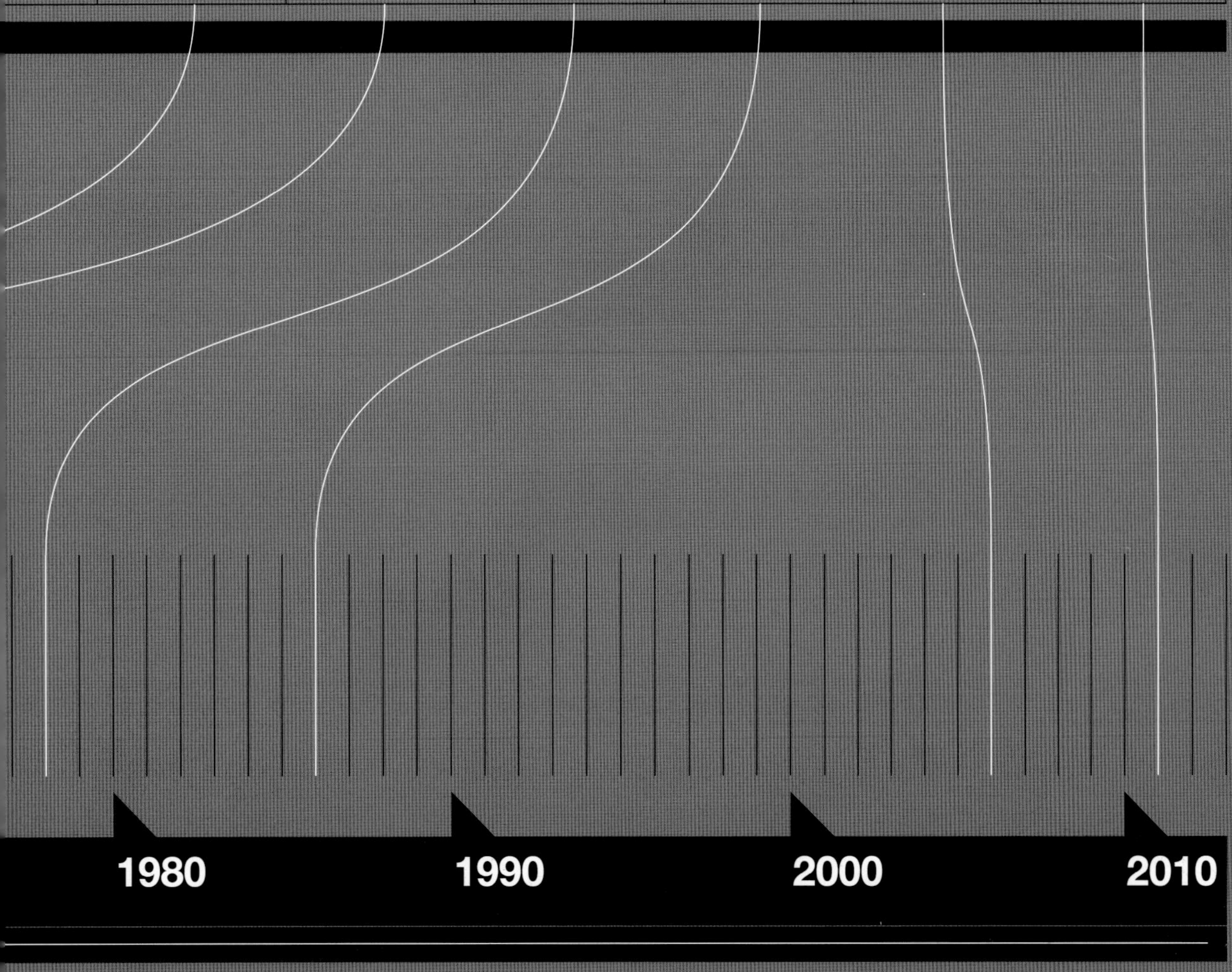
1980
1990
2000
2010

The Pizzas of the Teenage Mutant Ninja Turtles

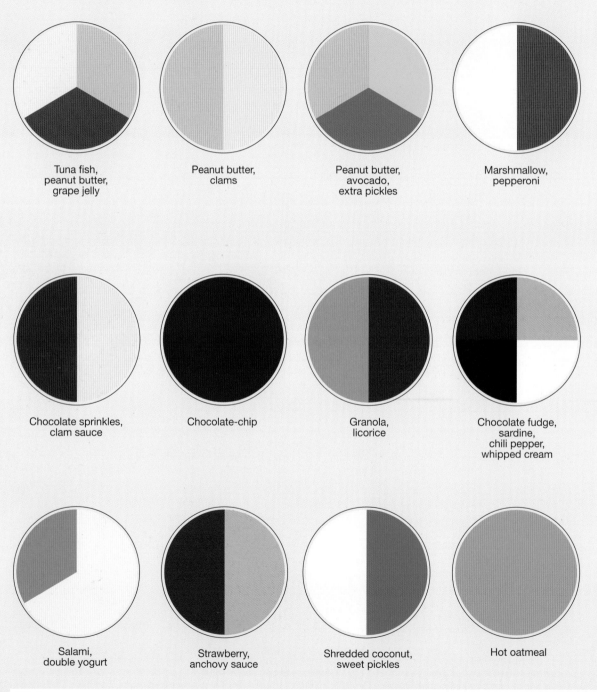

Tuna fish,
peanut butter,
grape jelly

Peanut butter,
clams

Peanut butter,
avocado,
extra pickles

Marshmallow,
pepperoni

Chocolate sprinkles,
clam sauce

Chocolate-chip

Granola,
licorice

Chocolate fudge,
sardine,
chili pepper,
whipped cream

Salami,
double yogurt

Strawberry,
anchovy sauce

Shredded coconut,
sweet pickles

Hot oatmeal

In the Teenage Mutant Ninja Turtles cartoons that aired for ten years in the '80s and '90s, the Turtles were passionate about three things: defeating the Foot Clan, saying "Cowabunga!," and eating strange, strange pizza.

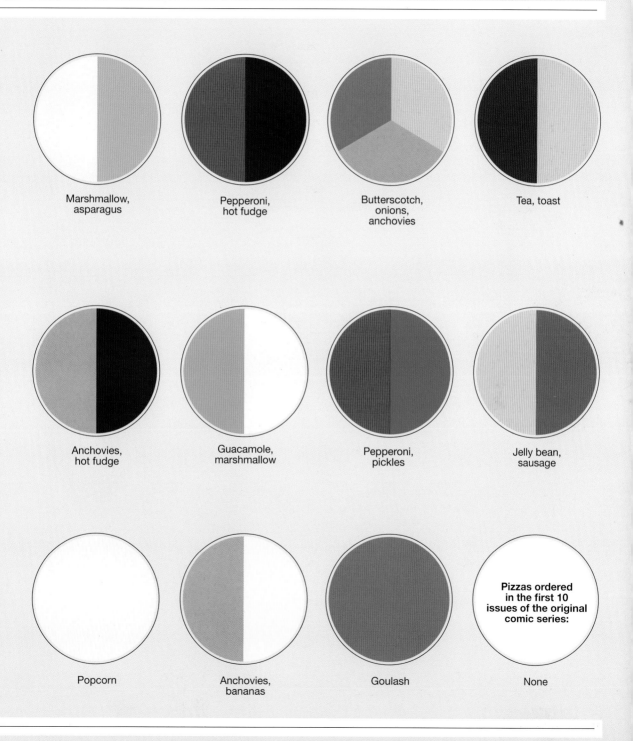

Marshmallow, asparagus

Pepperoni, hot fudge

Butterscotch, onions, anchovies

Tea, toast

Anchovies, hot fudge

Guacamole, marshmallow

Pepperoni, pickles

Jelly bean, sausage

Popcorn

Anchovies, bananas

Goulash

Pizzas ordered in the first 10 issues of the original comic series:

None

The Batman Theme Quantified

Only two words make up the popular '60s theme song.

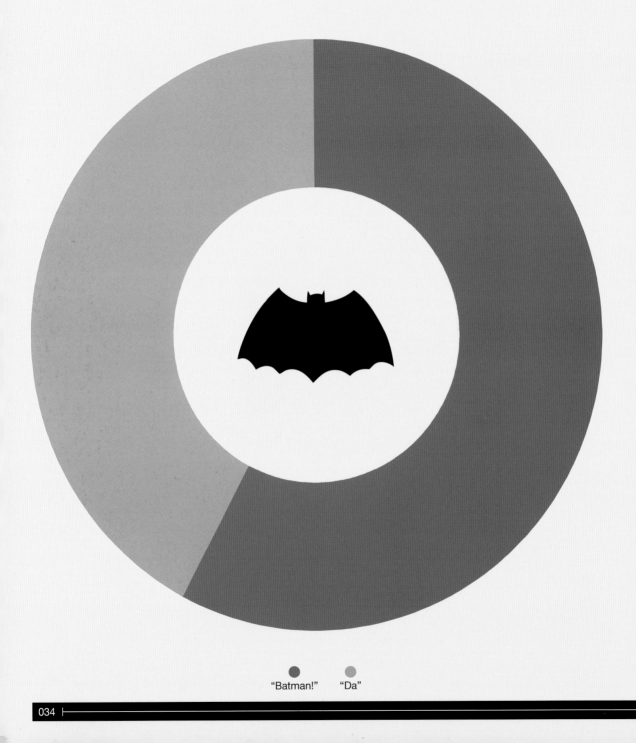

"Batman!"   "Da"

The Joker's Favorite Questions for Batman

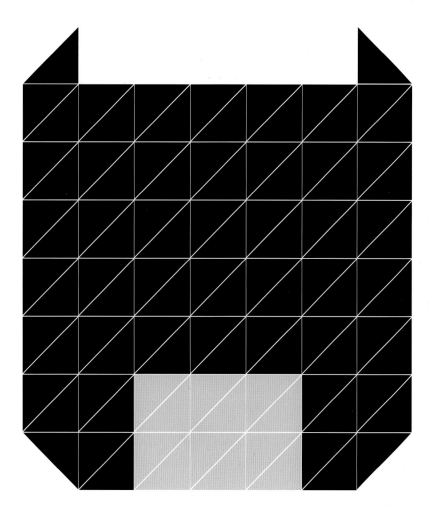

◢ Why so serious?   ◿ Where does he get those wonderful toys?

THE COLORS OF MONEY

Following Fictional Fortunes

Every year (except 2009) *Forbes* ranks the net worth of fictional characters. Criteria for inclusion mandate that characters be authored fictional creations, star in a body of work, and are known for being rich. Net worth is based on real-world economies pitted against each character's source material.

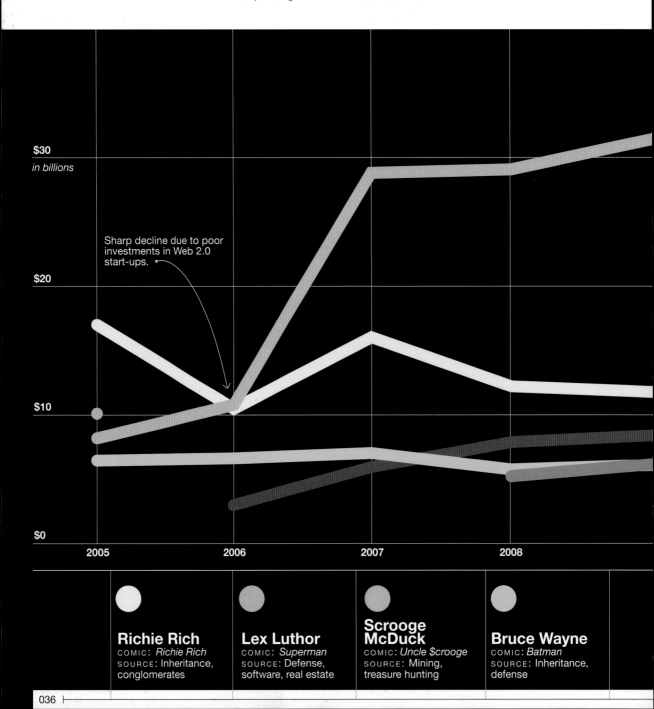

$30

in billings

Sharp decline due to poor investments in Web 2.0 start-ups.

$20

$10

$0

2005   2006   2007   2008

Richie Rich
COMIC: *Richie Rich*
SOURCE: Inheritance, conglomerates

Lex Luthor
COMIC: *Superman*
SOURCE: Defense, software, real estate

Scrooge McDuck
COMIC: *Uncle $crooge*
SOURCE: Mining, treasure hunting

Bruce Wayne
COMIC: *Batman*
SOURCE: Inheritance, defense

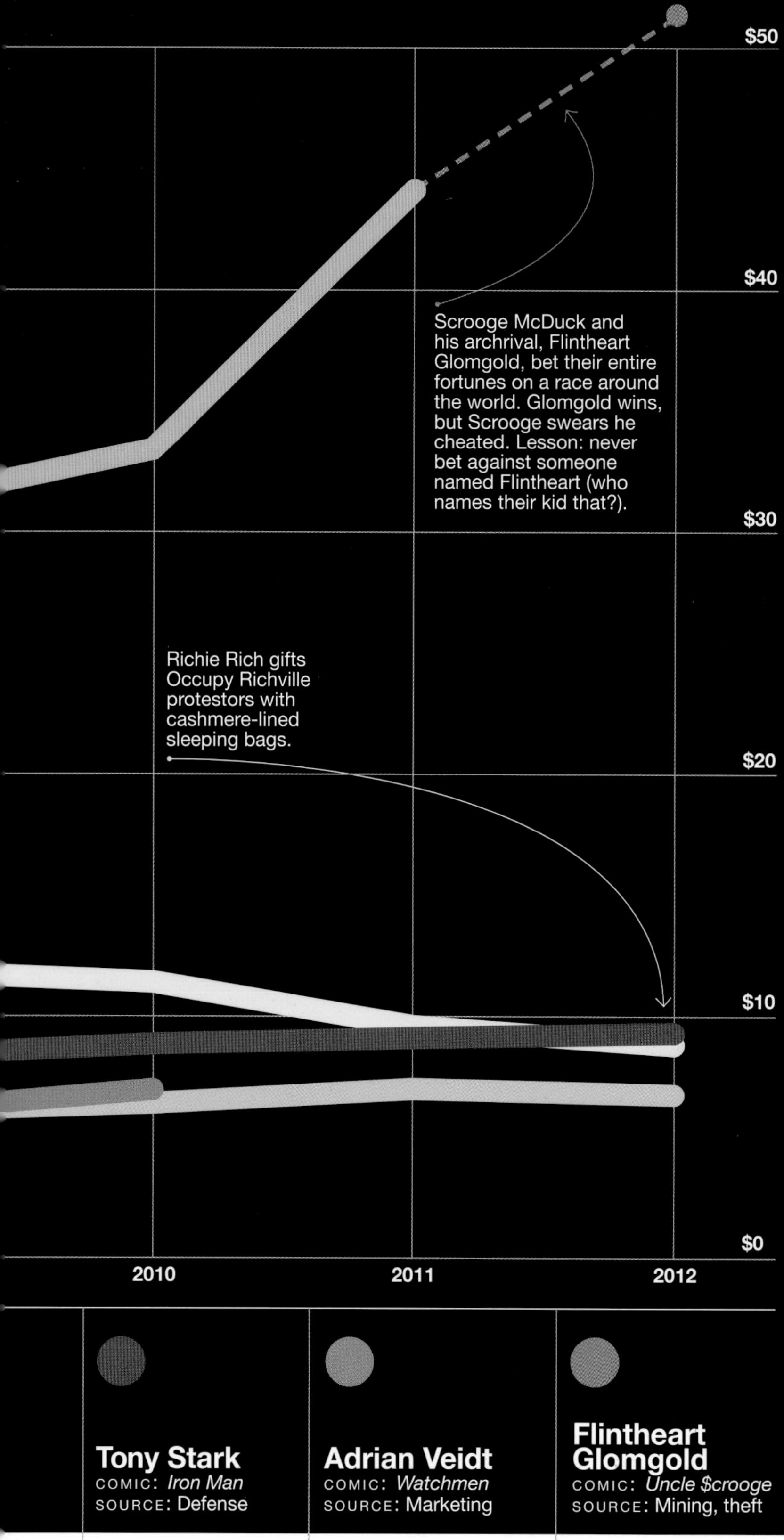
$50
$40
$30
$20
$10
$0
2010
2011
2012
Scrooge McDuck and his archrival, Flintheart Glomgold, bet their entire fortunes on a race around the world. Glomgold wins, but Scrooge swears he cheated. Lesson: never bet against someone named Flintheart (who names their kid that?).
Richie Rich gifts Occupy Richville protestors with cashmere-lined sleeping bags.
Tony Stark
COMIC: Iron Man
SOURCE: Defense
Adrian Veidt
COMIC: Watchmen
SOURCE: Marketing
Flintheart Glomgold
COMIC: Uncle $crooge
SOURCE: Mining, theft

Highest grossing companies

In 2007, *Forbes* also rated the net worth of fictional corporations.

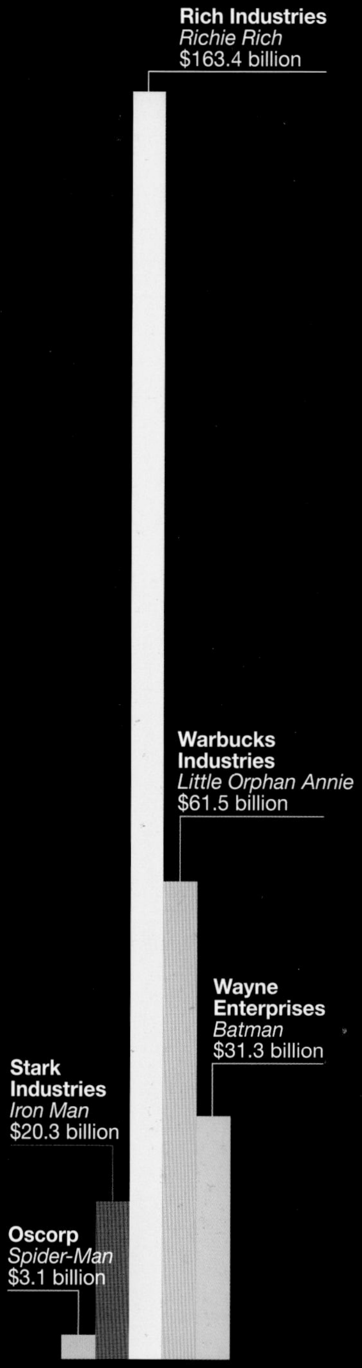
Rich Industries
Richie Rich
$163.4 billion
Warbucks Industries
Little Orphan Annie
$61.5 billion
Wayne Enterprises
Batman
$31.3 billion
Stark Industries
Iron Man
$20.3 billion
Oscorp
Spider-Man
$3.1 billion

Team Colors

Teenage Mutant Ninja Turtles

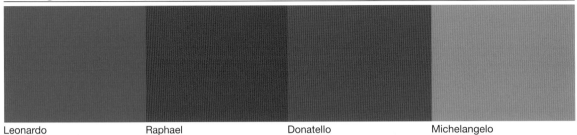

Leonardo   Raphael   Donatello   Michelangelo

Mighty Morphin Power Rangers

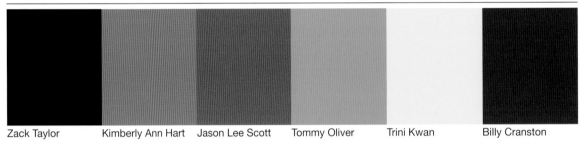

Zack Taylor   Kimberly Ann Hart   Jason Lee Scott   Tommy Oliver   Trini Kwan   Billy Cranston

Lantern Power Rings

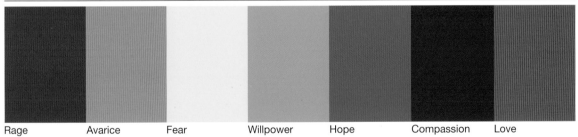

Rage   Avarice   Fear   Willpower   Hope   Compassion   Love

Voltron

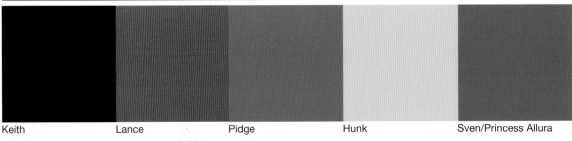

Keith   Lance   Pidge   Hunk   Sven/Princess Allura

The Metal Men

Copper	Gold	Lead	Iron	Platinum	Mercury	Tin

The Beagle Boys

Baggy	Babyface	Bankjob	Bigtime	Bouncer	Bugle	Burger

The Fantastic Four

Mister Fantastic	Invisible Woman	The Thing	Human Torch

The Avengers

Black Widow	Captain America	Hawkeye	Hulk	Iron Man	Thor

Richie Rich vs. Royal Roy

Harvey Comics first published *Richie Rich*, a comic about an extremely wealthy and kind boy, in 1953. Marvel Comics decided to enter the rich-and-nice-boy market in 1985. As you can see, *Royal Roy* was a totally original take on the theme.

Richie Rich: The Poor Little Rich Boy

Royal Roy: A Prince of a Boy

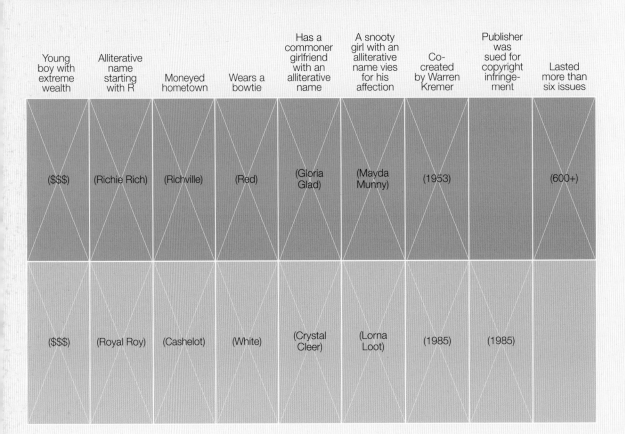

	Young boy with extreme wealth	Alliterative name starting with R	Moneyed hometown	Wears a bowtie	Has a commoner girlfriend with an alliterative name	A snooty girl with an alliterative name vies for his affection	Co-created by Warren Kremer	Publisher was sued for copyright infringe-ment	Lasted more than six issues
Richie Rich: The Poor Little Rich Boy	($$$)	(Richie Rich)	(Richville)	(Red)	(Gloria Glad)	(Mayda Munny)	(1953)		(600+)
Royal Roy: A Prince of a Boy	($$$)	(Royal Roy)	(Cashelot)	(White)	(Crystal Cleer)	(Lorna Loot)	(1985)	(1985)	

The Definitive R. Crumb Butt Matrix

R. Crumb was responsible for sparking the underground comix (with an x) revolution of the '60s and '70s that brought satirical and adult-themed titles into the mainstream. He was one of the most important figures in comic history. Also: he really liked big butts.

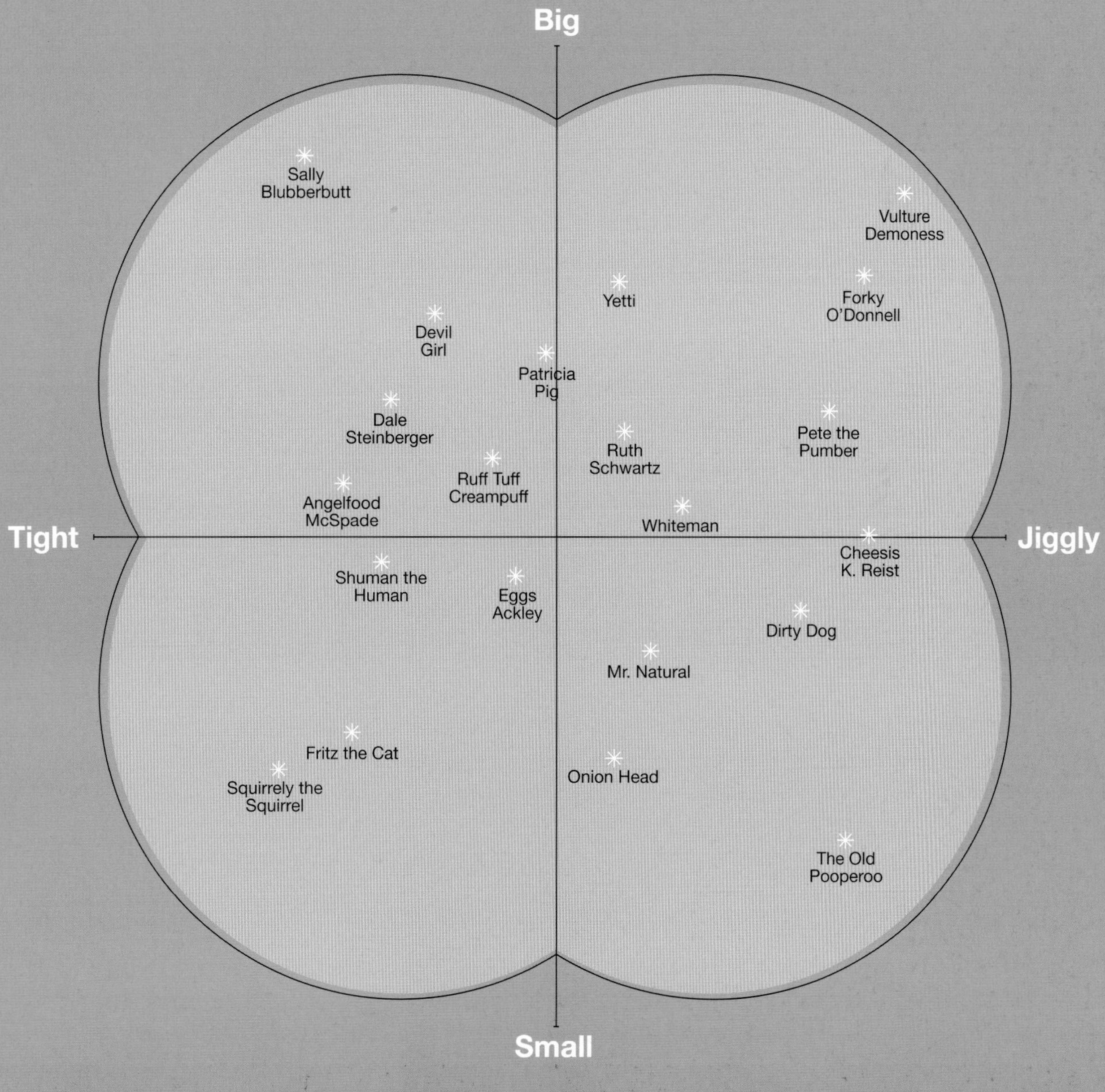
Big
Tight
Jiggly
Small
Sally Blubberbutt
Vulture Demoness
Yetti
Forky O'Donnell
Devil Girl
Patricia Pig
Dale Steinberger
Pete the Pumber
Ruth Schwartz
Ruff Tuff Creampuff
Angelfood McSpade
Whiteman
Cheesis K. Reist
Shuman the Human
Eggs Ackley
Dirty Dog
Mr. Natural
Fritz the Cat
Squirrely the Squirrel
Onion Head
The Old Pooperoo

SECOND CITY

The Real Metropolis

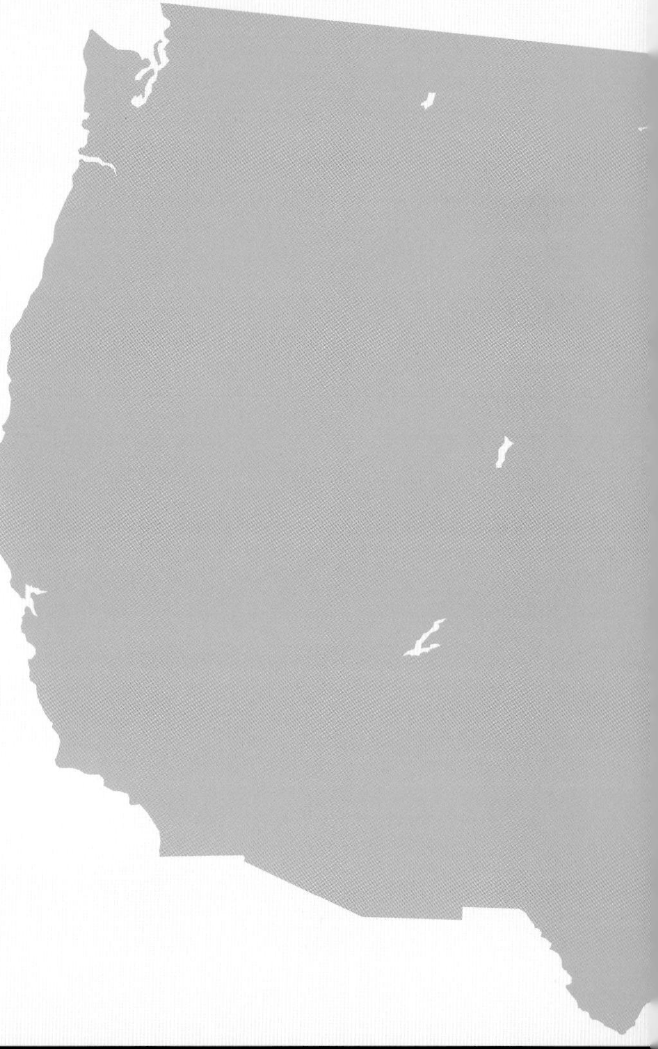

THE ILLINOIS HOUSE OF REPRESENTATIVES DECLARED METROPOLIS, ILLINOIS, THE OFFICIAL HOMETOWN OF SUPERMAN ON JUNE 9, 1972.

The Amazing World of Superman, a theme park planned in Metropolis, Illinois, should have opened in 1973. A simulated rocket ride to Krypton, an interplanetary zoo, and a Bizarro playground were to be attractions. A 200-foot Superman statue and a giant key to the Fortress of Solitude were supposed to stand beside boating and skating rinks, a movie theatre, and a supermarket on the grounds. But the oil crisis, compounded by an interstate construction delay, effectively shuttered the park to be. The town had already made a significant investment when the project collapsed, and it took years to recover. A Superman museum did open in 1973, but it only lasted a year. In 1993, across the street from the city's (substantially smaller than planned) 15-foot Superman statue, the town gave the Man of Steel museum idea another shot. Today the Super Museum is home to more than 20,000 Superman-related items, including kryptonite from the Christopher Reeve films and the device that allowed actor George Reeves to "fly" in the 1950s television show. The museum currently attracts around 200 visitors a day.

Population

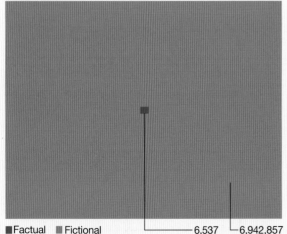

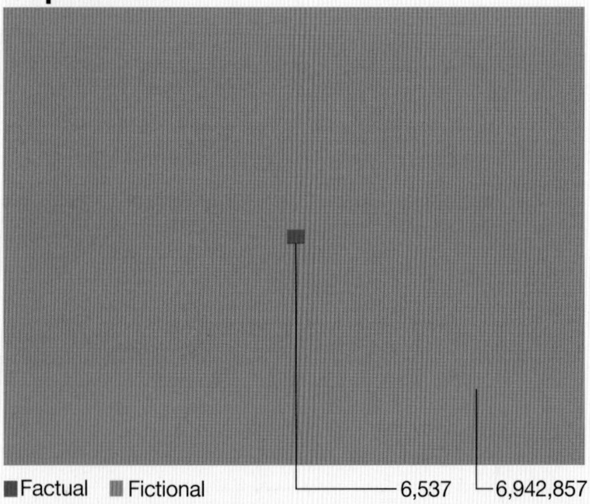
Factual
Fictional
6,537
6,942,857

Geographical size in square miles

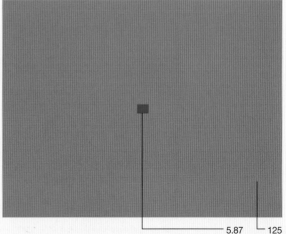

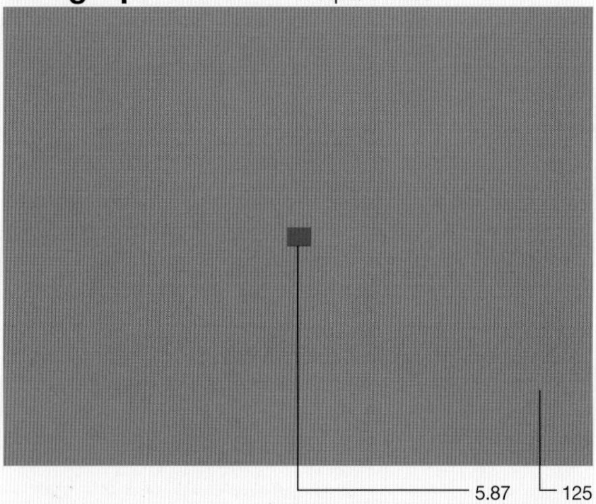
5.87
125

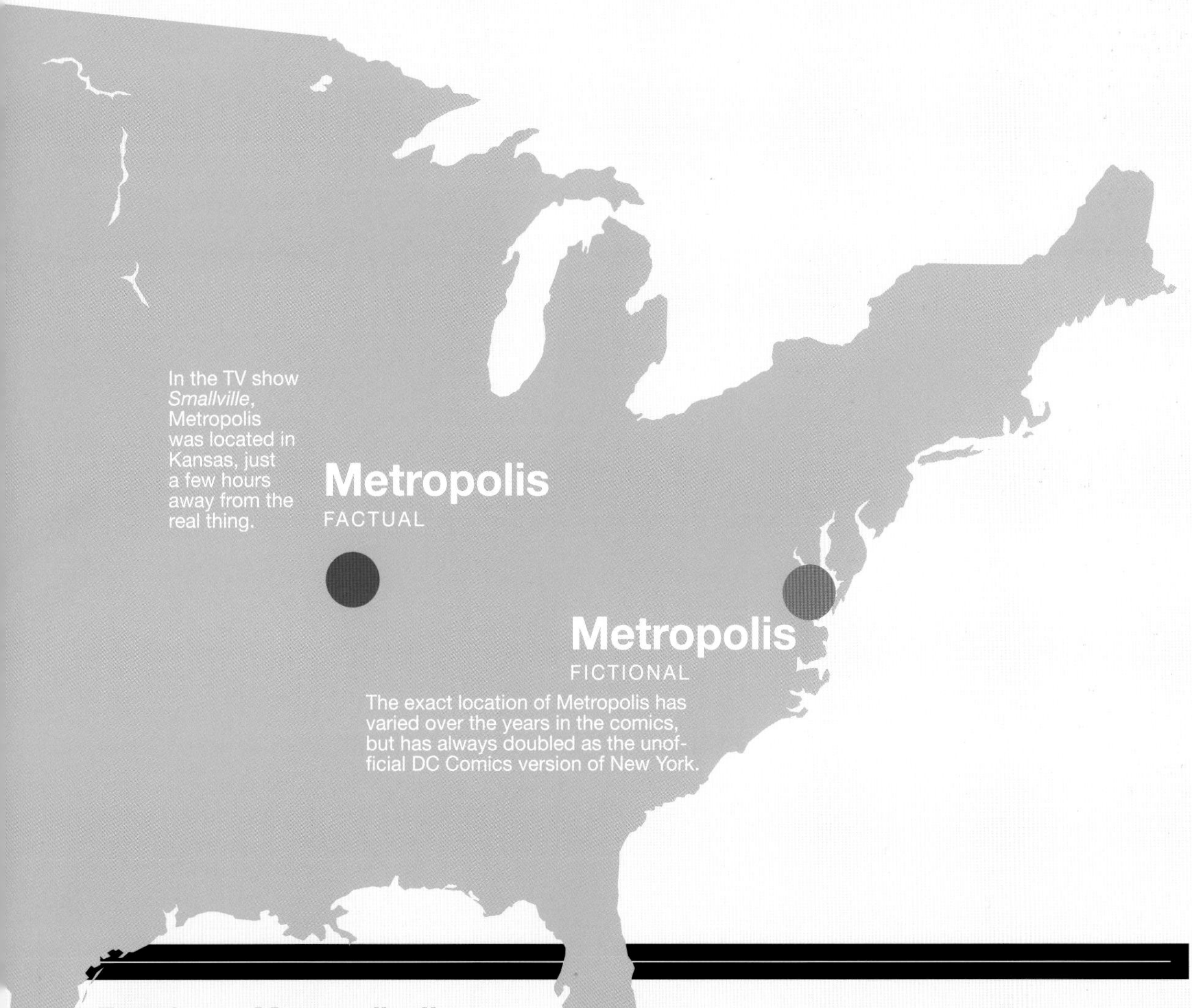
In the TV show *Smallville*, Metropolis was located in Kansas, just a few hours away from the real thing.
Metropolis
FACTUAL
Metropolis
FICTIONAL
The exact location of Metropolis has varied over the years in the comics, but has always doubled as the unofficial DC Comics version of New York.

Fast facts: Metropolis, IL

GENDER BREAKDOWN

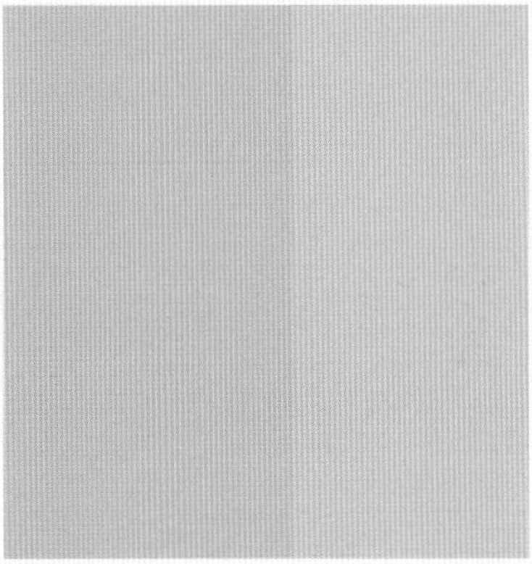
Female
Male

RACE BREAKDOWN

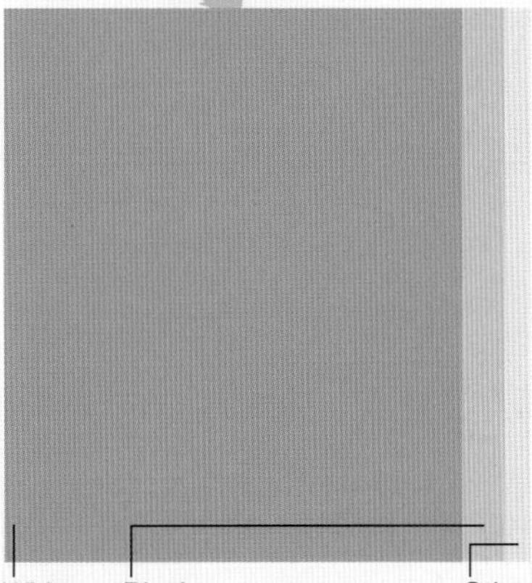
White
Black
Other

AGE BREAKDOWN

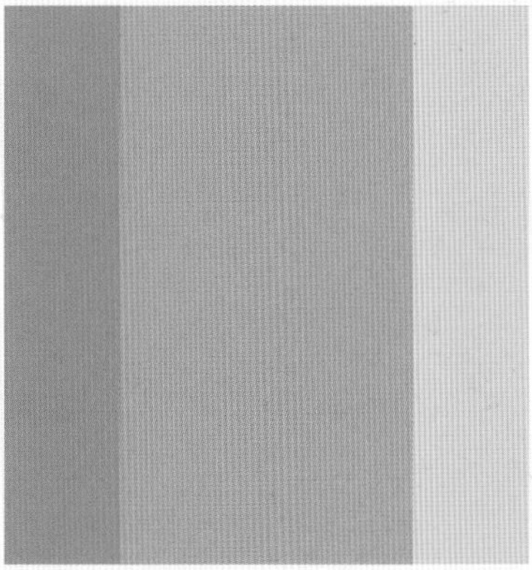
<18
18–65
>65

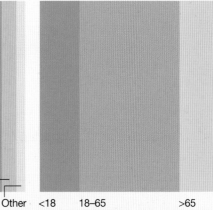

NUFF SAID

Stan Lee Has Issues

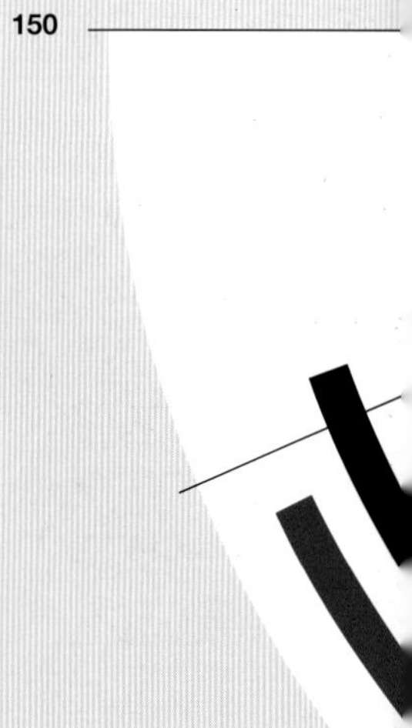
150
125

Stan Lee was Marvel Comics' top editor for nearly 30 years (ending in 1972). During that time he co-created some of the most iconic characters of all time, including Spider-Man, the Fantastic Four, and the Hulk. But, as it turns out, his longest-running author credits occurred on comics you've probably never heard of. (He had quite a fling with *Millie the Model*!) Here's a look at the man and (most of) his issues.

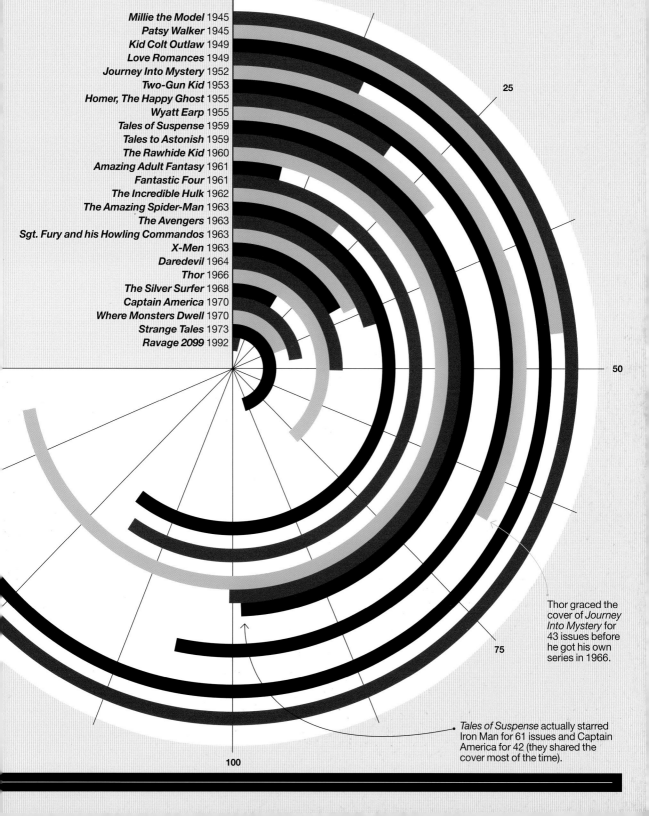

0 issues

Millie the Model 1945
Patsy Walker 1945
Kid Colt Outlaw 1949
Love Romances 1949
Journey Into Mystery 1952
Two-Gun Kid 1953
Homer, The Happy Ghost 1955
Wyatt Earp 1955
Tales of Suspense 1959
Tales to Astonish 1959
The Rawhide Kid 1960
Amazing Adult Fantasy 1961
Fantastic Four 1961
The Incredible Hulk 1962
The Amazing Spider-Man 1963
The Avengers 1963
Sgt. Fury and his Howling Commandos 1963
X-Men 1963
Daredevil 1964
Thor 1966
The Silver Surfer 1968
Captain America 1970
Where Monsters Dwell 1970
Strange Tales 1973
Ravage 2099 1992

25

50

75

100

Thor graced the cover of *Journey Into Mystery* for 43 issues before he got his own series in 1966.

Tales of Suspense actually starred Iron Man for 61 issues and Captain America for 42 (they shared the cover most of the time).

A Fantastic Four Primer

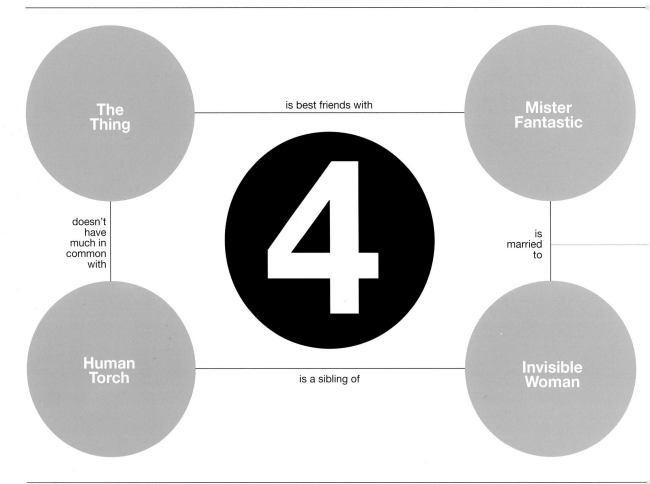

The Thing — is best friends with — Mister Fantastic

The Thing — doesn't have much in common with — Human Torch

Mister Fantastic — is married to — Invisible Woman

Human Torch — is a sibling of — Invisible Woman

Official Marvel Rankings

DURABILITY

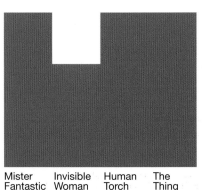

Mister Fantastic | Invisible Woman | Human Torch | The Thing

ENERGY PROJECTION

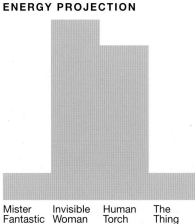

Mister Fantastic | Invisible Woman | Human Torch | The Thing

FIGHTING SKILLS

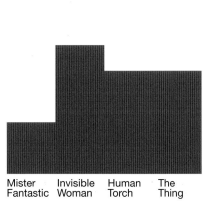

Mister Fantastic | Invisible Woman | Human Torch | The Thing

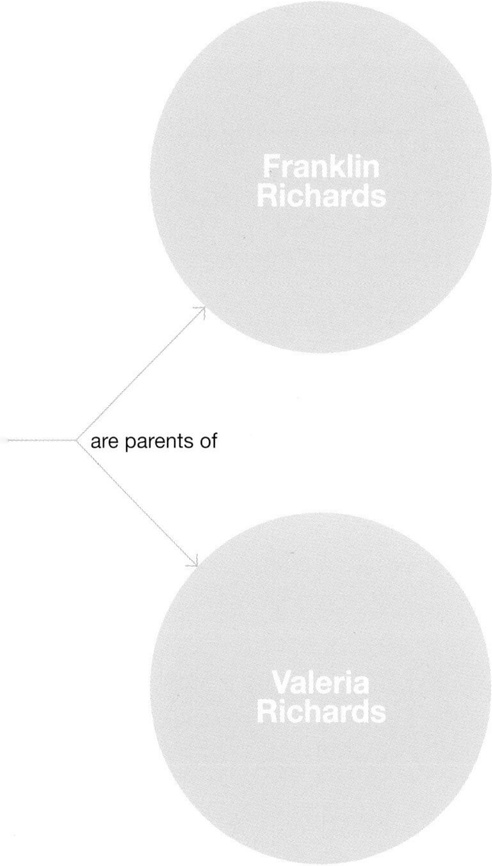
Franklin Richards
are parents of
Valeria Richards

WEIGHT

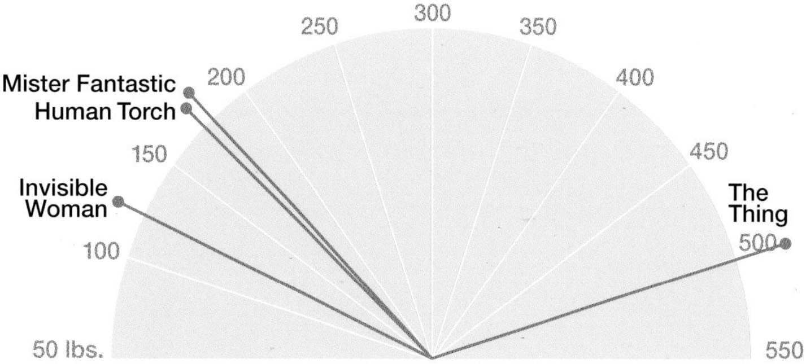
50 lbs.
100
150
200
250
300
350
400
450
500
550
Mister Fantastic
Human Torch
Invisible Woman
The Thing

HEIGHT

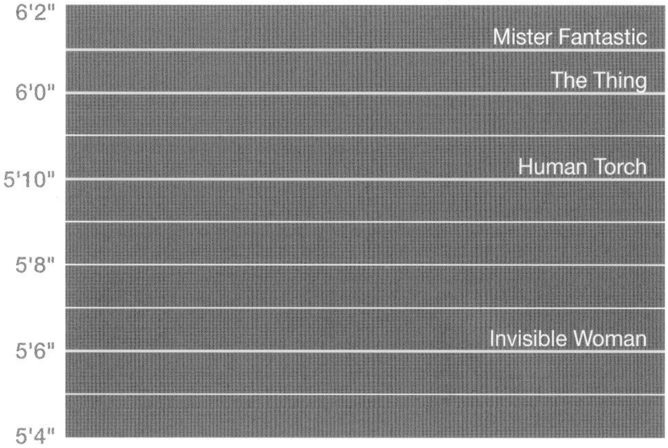
6'2"
6'0"
5'10"
5'8"
5'6"
5'4"
Mister Fantastic
The Thing
Human Torch
Invisible Woman

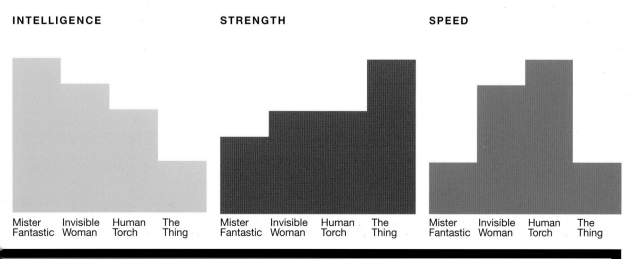

INTELLIGENCE

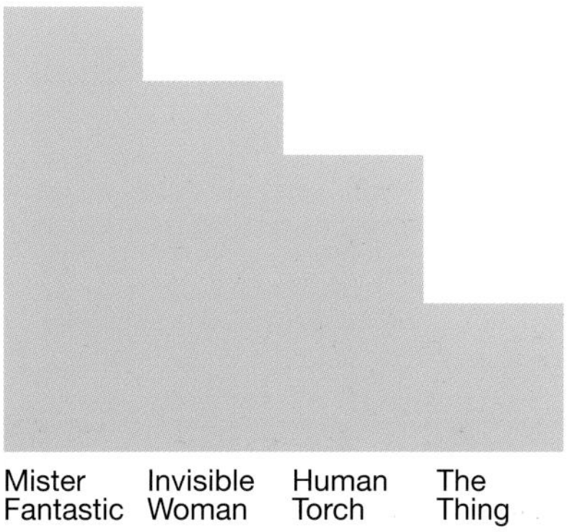
Mister Fantastic
Invisible Woman
Human Torch
The Thing

STRENGTH

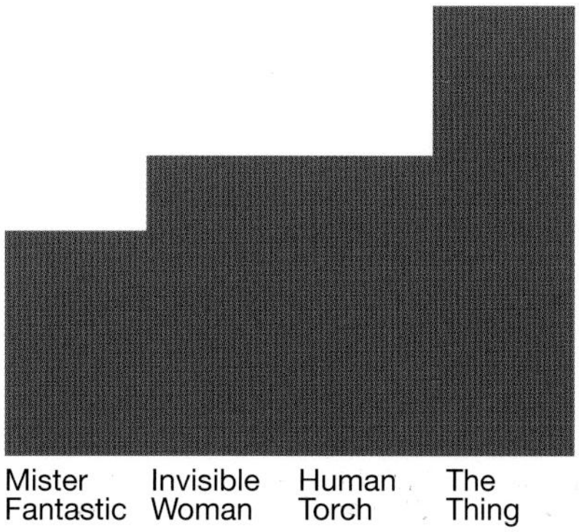
Mister Fantastic
Invisible Woman
Human Torch
The Thing

SPEED

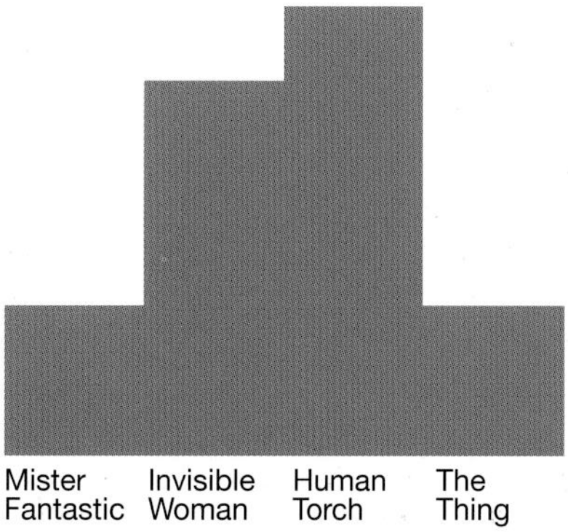
Mister Fantastic
Invisible Woman
Human Torch
The Thing

Super-Rollercoasters

Because Six Flags and DC Comics were once owned by the same company (with licensing agreements afterwards), it kicked off a numb

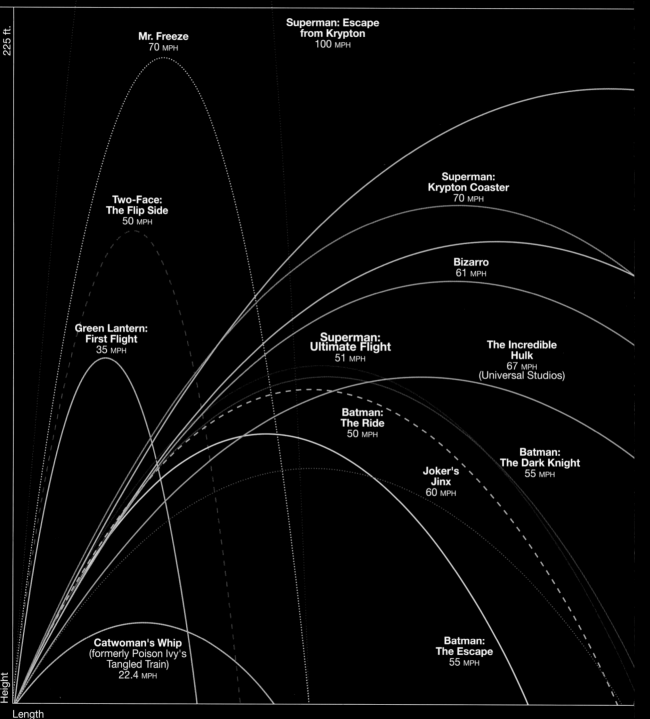

225 ft.

Mr. Freeze
70 MPH

Superman: Escape
from Krypton
100 MPH

Superman:
Krypton Coaster
70 MPH

Two-Face:
The Flip Side
50 MPH

Bizarro
61 MPH

Green Lantern:
First Flight
35 MPH

Superman:
Ultimate Flight
51 MPH

The Incredible
Hulk
67 MPH
(Universal Studios)

Batman:
The Ride
50 MPH

Batman:
The Dark Knight
55 MPH

Joker's
Jinx
60 MPH

Catwoman's Whip
(formerly Poison Ivy's
Tangled Train)
22.4 MPH

Batman:
The Escape
55 MPH

Height

Length

superhero- and supervillain-themed rides around the country. Here's how their power measures up.

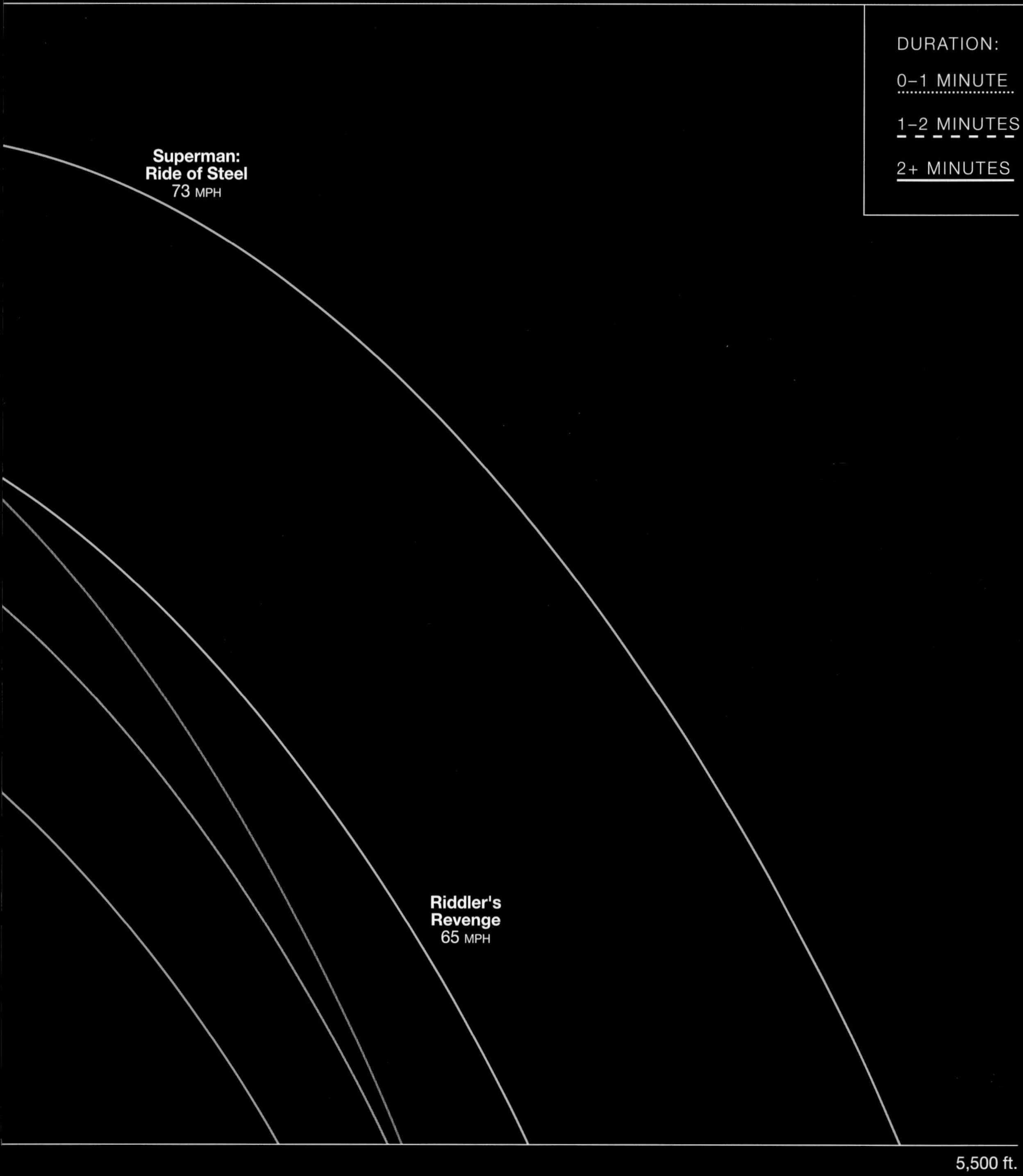
DURATION:
0–1 MINUTE
1–2 MINUTES
2+ MINUTES
Superman: Ride of Steel
73 MPH
Riddler's Revenge
65 MPH
5,500 ft.

The Politics of Good vs. Evil

When your business is either saving the world or destroying it, it's only natural that characters would ideologically identify themselves.

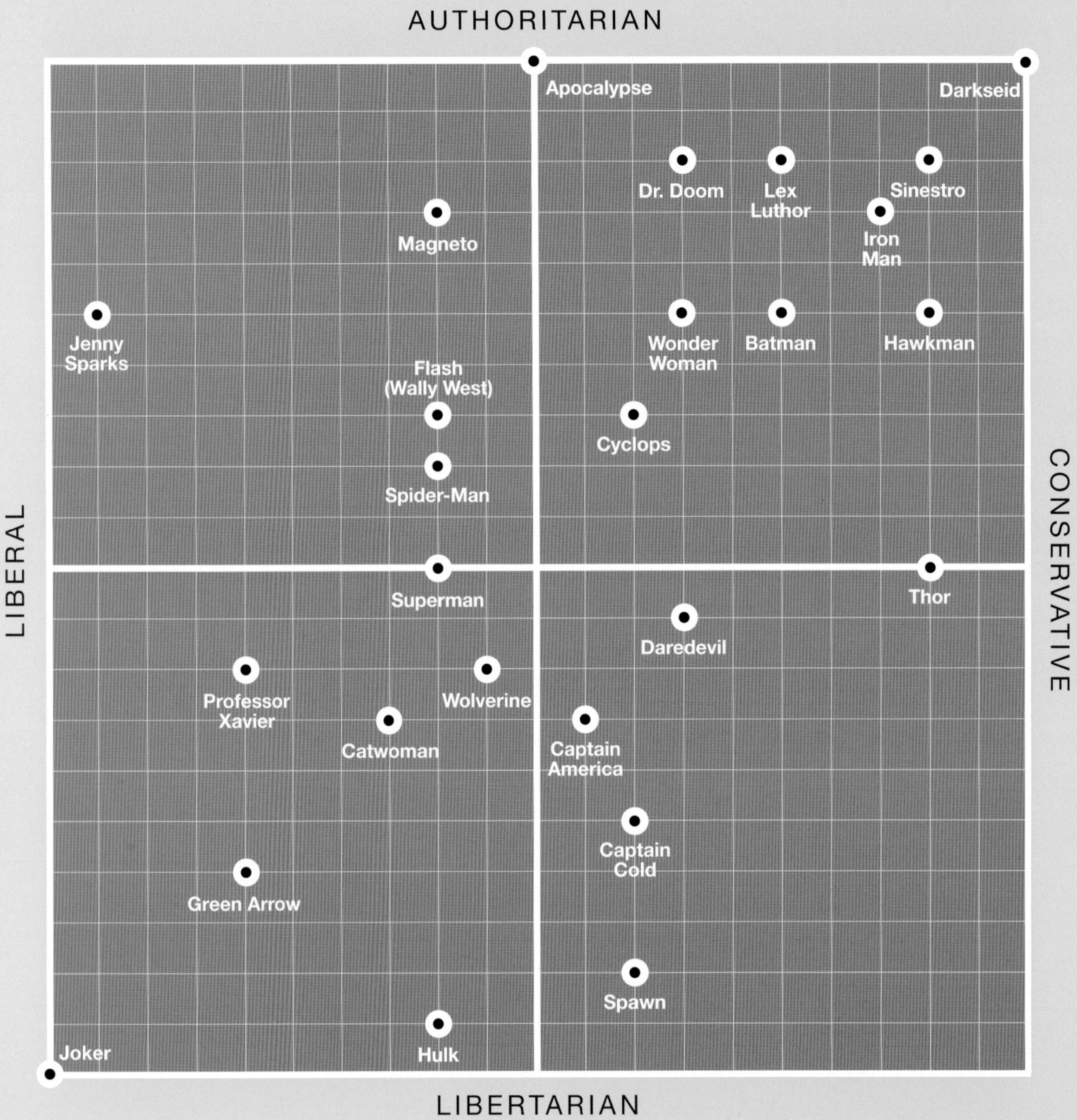

AUTHORITARIAN
LIBERTARIAN
LIBERAL
CONSERVATIVE
Apocalypse
Darkseid
Dr. Doom
Lex Luthor
Sinestro
Iron Man
Magneto
Jenny Sparks
Wonder Woman
Batman
Hawkman
Flash (Wally West)
Cyclops
Spider-Man
Superman
Thor
Daredevil
Professor Xavier
Wolverine
Catwoman
Captain America
Captain Cold
Green Arrow
Spawn
Joker
Hulk

A Calvin and Hobbes Trajectory

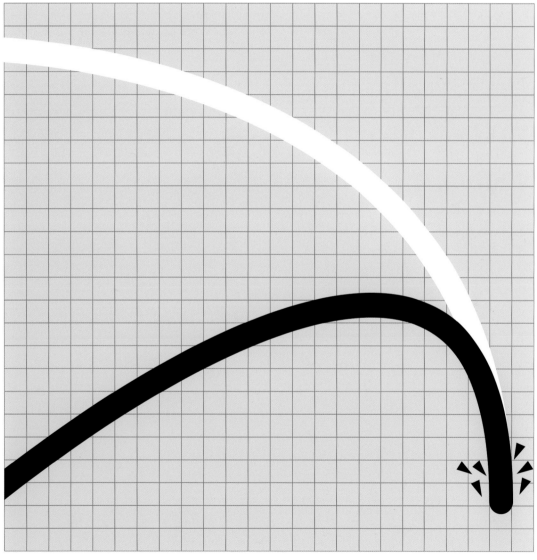

■ Urine trajectory on "Calvin peeing" decals   □ My faith in humanity every time I see one of those decals

Fast-Ball Special

THE MARVEL COMICS EDITORIAL BASEBALL TEAM

For years, Marvel Comics has had a company softball team. Here's how Marvel's Bullpen Bombers fared against the Warren Warriors on August 3, 1982.

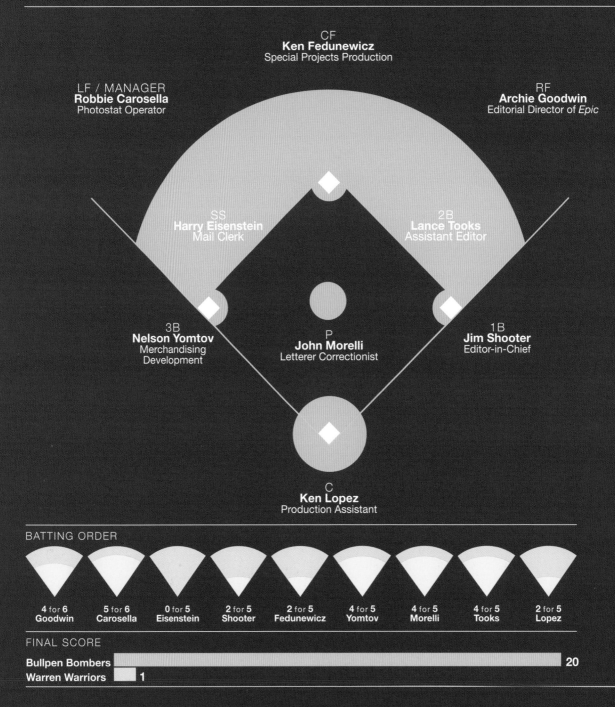

CF
Ken Fedunewicz
Special Projects Production

LF / MANAGER
Robbie Carosella
Photostat Operator

RF
Archie Goodwin
Editorial Director of *Epic*

SS
Harry Eisenstein
Mail Clerk

2B
Lance Tooks
Assistant Editor

3B
Nelson Yomtov
Merchandising
Development

P
John Morelli
Letterer Correctionist

1B
Jim Shooter
Editor-in-Chief

C
Ken Lopez
Production Assistant

BATTING ORDER

| **4** for **6** Goodwin | **5** for **6** Carosella | **0** for **5** Eisenstein | **2** for **5** Shooter | **2** for **5** Fedunewicz | **4** for **5** Yomtov | **4** for **5** Morelli | **4** for **5** Tooks | **2** for **5** Lopez |

FINAL SCORE

| Bullpen Bombers | 20 |
| Warren Warriors | 1 |

CHARLIE BROWN'S BASEBALL TEAM

Save for Snoopy, Charlie Brown's team was notoriously terrible. Good grief.

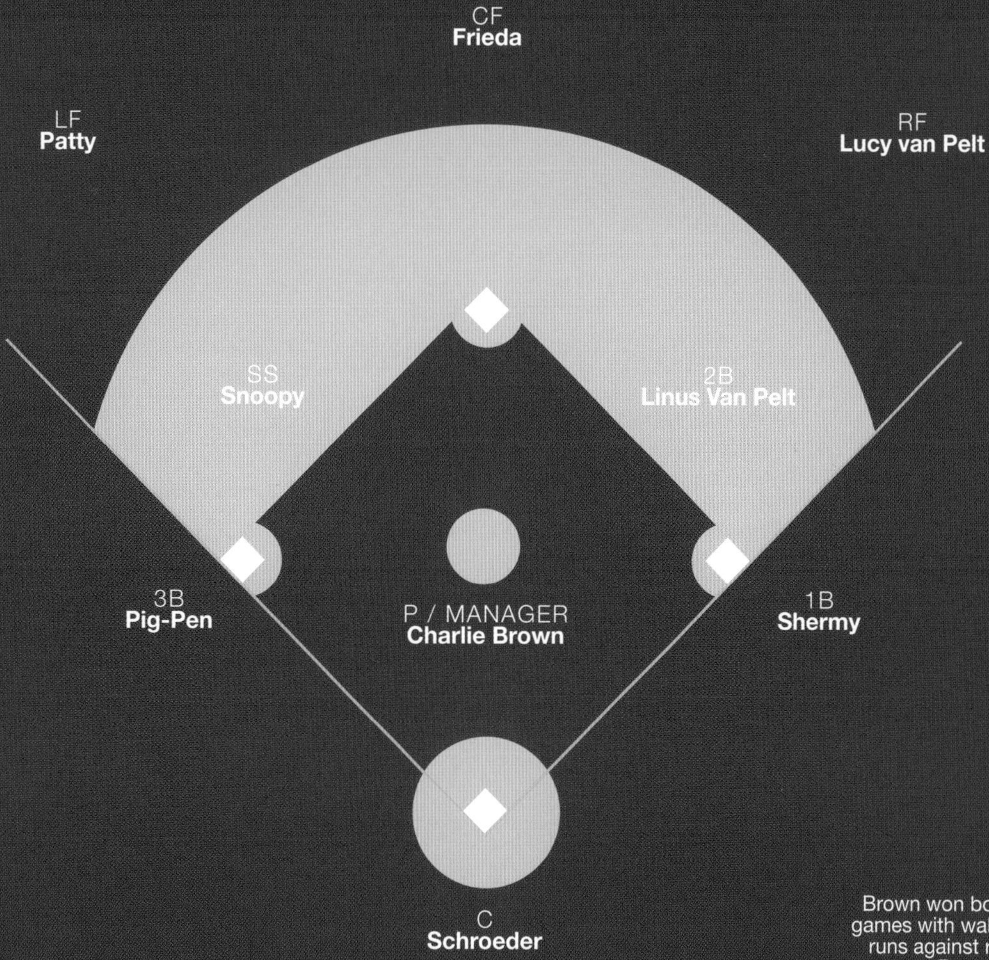
CF
Frieda
LF
Patty
RF
Lucy van Pelt
SS
Snoopy
2B
Linus Van Pelt
3B
Pig-Pen
P / MANAGER
Charlie Brown
1B
Shermy
C
Schroeder

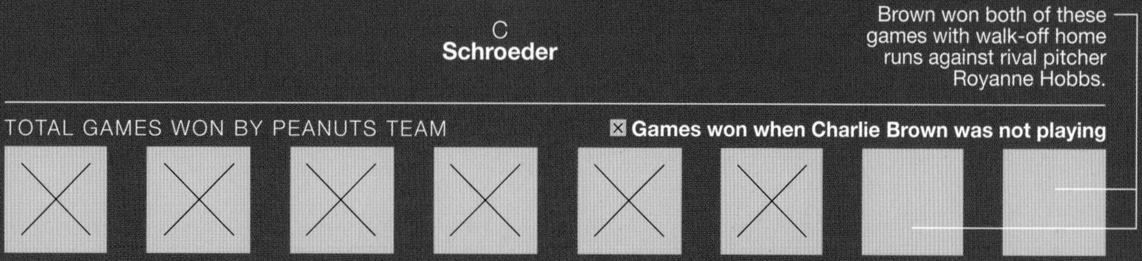
Brown won both of these games with walk-off home runs against rival pitcher Royanne Hobbs.
TOTAL GAMES WON BY PEANUTS TEAM
Games won when Charlie Brown was not playing

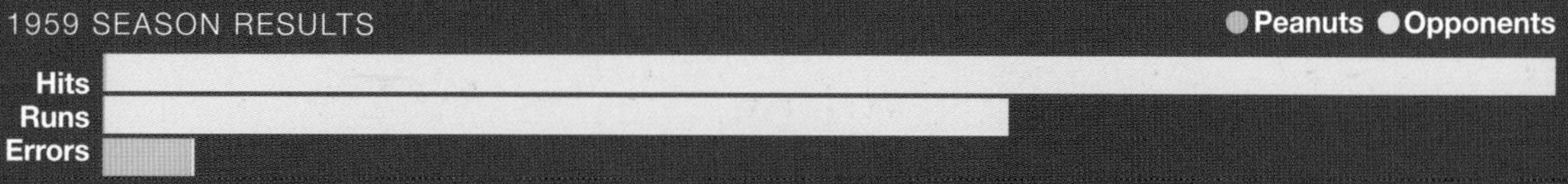
1959 SEASON RESULTS
Peanuts
Opponents
Hits
Runs
Errors

Changes in Costume Color

● Original color

∨ New color

CATWOMAN

MR. FREEZE Originally called
Mr. Zero. He changed costumes
when he changed names.

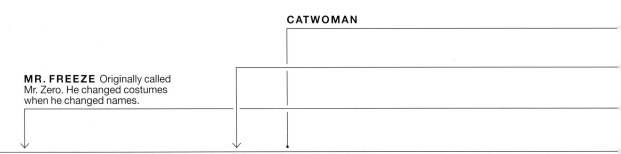

BLUE BEETLE

DONATELLO In fact, all the Teenage Mutant
Ninja Turtles started off with red masks—they were
only identifiable by their weapons. Raphael was the
only one who kept the red mask.

Costumes are important elements in comics. They help identify not only who the character is, but what they're about as well. That's why costume redesigns are so significant. Everyone's style changes a bit over time—especially when characters have been around for 70 years; the makeovers below mark some of the most drastic and longest-lasting in comics.

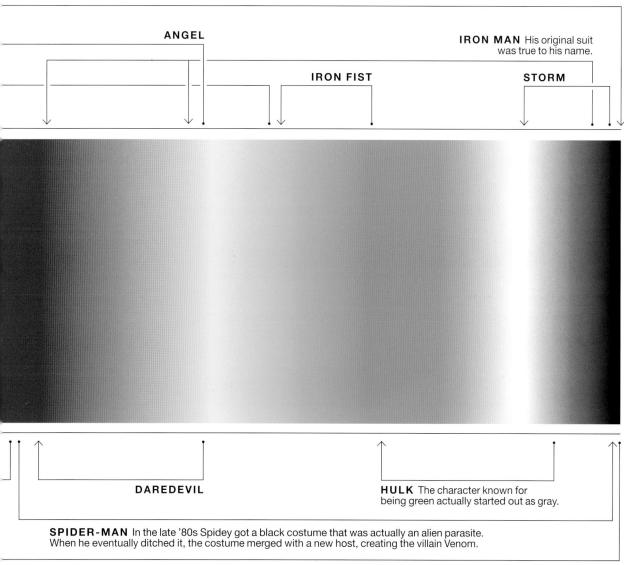

ANGEL

IRON FIST

IRON MAN His original suit was true to his name.

STORM

DAREDEVIL

HULK The character known for being green actually started out as gray.

SPIDER-MAN In the late '80s Spidey got a black costume that was actually an alien parasite. When he eventually ditched it, the costume merged with a new host, creating the villain Venom.

HAVOK

Cerebus: Judging a Comic By Its Covers

Over the course of 27 years starting in 1977, the writer and artist Dave Sim (with additional art by Gerhard) produced 300 issues—a whopping 6,000 pages—of his independent comic *Cerebus the Aardvark*. Below is a representation of the dominant colors in each issue's cover. Although the interior panels were printed in black and white, the comic's covers were a kind of color compass for what was to come.

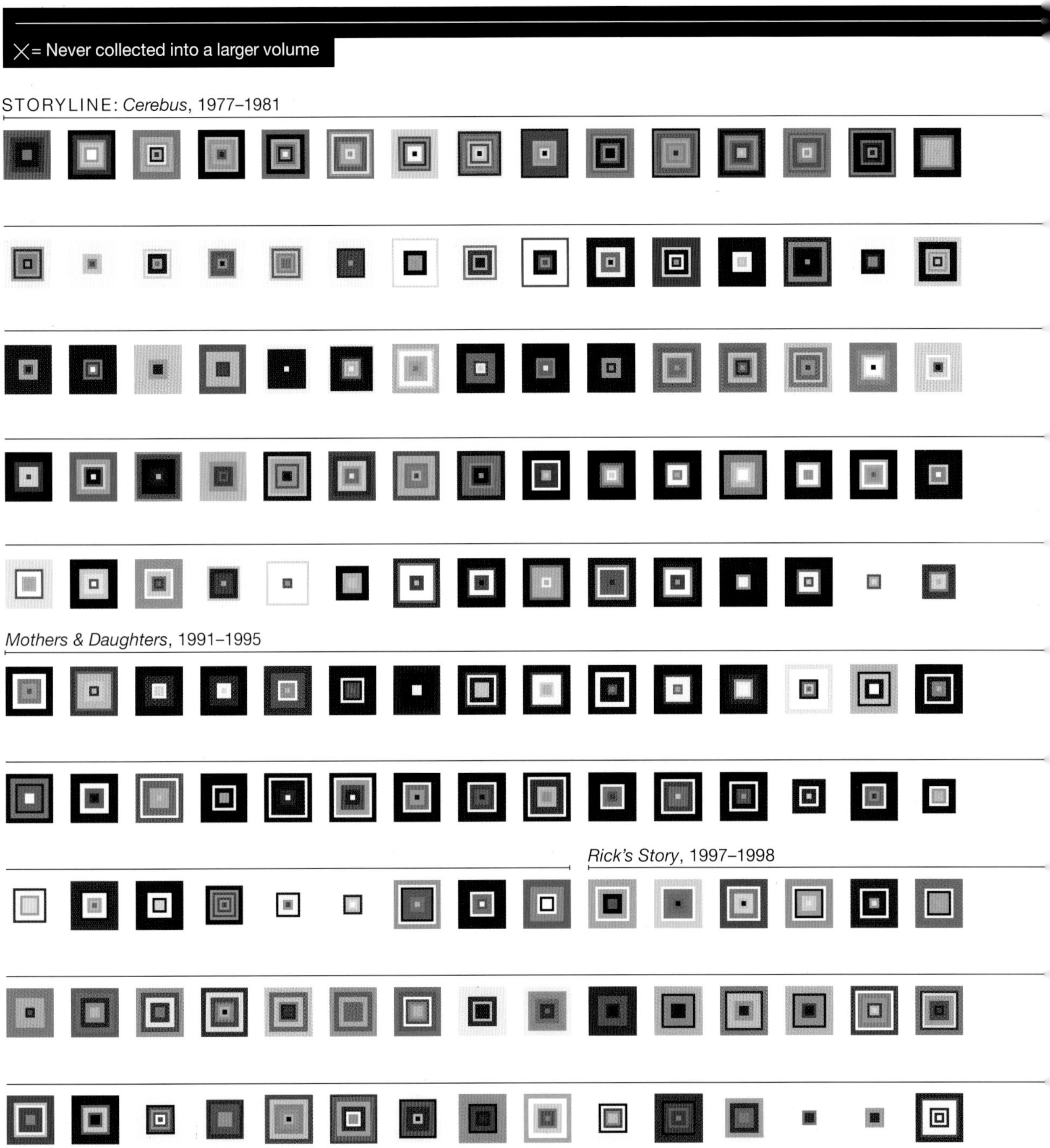

X= Never collected into a larger volume
STORYLINE: *Cerebus*, 1977–1981
Mothers & Daughters, 1991–1995
Rick's Story, 1997–1998

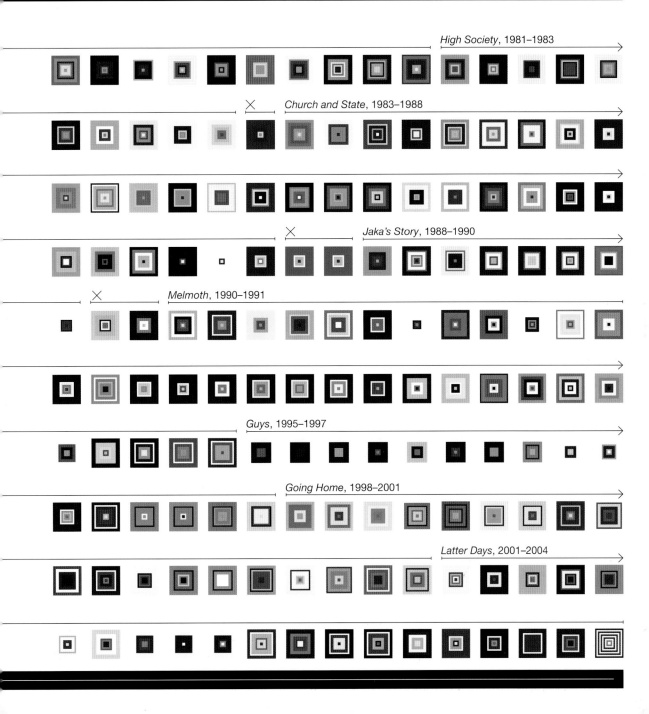

High Society, 1981–1983

Church and State, 1983–1988

Jaka's Story, 1988–1990

Melmoth, 1990–1991

Guys, 1995–1997

Going Home, 1998–2001

Latter Days, 2001–2004

Archer Appeal

GREEN ARROW: The DC Comics archer has a vast array of arrows that's always changing. Here are a few classics.

First used in 1947, the boxing glove arrowhead was originally the size of a baseball. Later in his career it increases in size (and hilarity) to a full-scale glove.

When chasing a criminal in a car, Green Arrow fires this arrow. It attaches to the bumper, inking the path to the criminal hideout with a pen that drags on the ground.

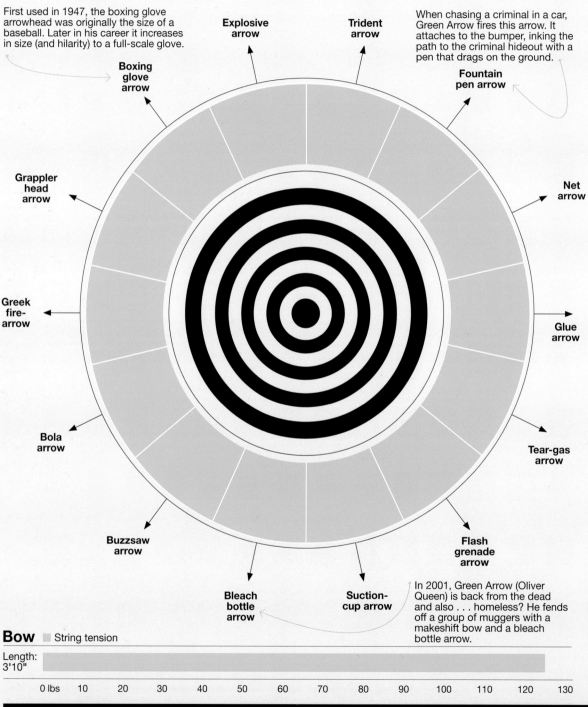

Boxing glove arrow

Explosive arrow

Trident arrow

Fountain pen arrow

Grappler head arrow

Net arrow

Greek fire-arrow

Glue arrow

Bola arrow

Tear-gas arrow

Buzzsaw arrow

Flash grenade arrow

Bleach bottle arrow

Suction-cup arrow

In 2001, Green Arrow (Oliver Queen) is back from the dead and also . . . homeless? He fends off a group of muggers with a makeshift bow and a bleach bottle arrow.

Bow   ▪ String tension

Length: 3'10"

0 lbs	10	20	30	40	50	60	70	80	90	100	110	120	130

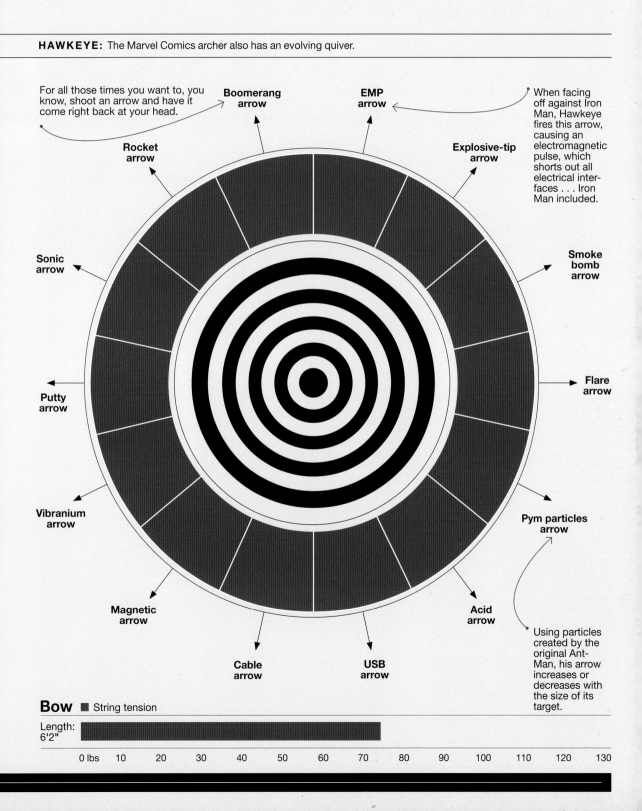

For all those times you want to, you know, shoot an arrow and have it come right back at your head.

Boomerang arrow

EMP arrow

When facing off against Iron Man, Hawkeye fires this arrow, causing an electromagnetic pulse, which shorts out all electrical inter-faces . . . Iron Man included.

Rocket arrow

Explosive-tip arrow

Sonic arrow

Smoke bomb arrow

Putty arrow

Flare arrow

Vibranium arrow

Pym particles arrow

Magnetic arrow

Acid arrow

Using particles created by the original Ant-Man, his arrow increases or decreases with the size of its target.

Cable arrow

USB arrow

Bow ■ String tension

Length: 6'2"

| 0 lbs | 10 | 20 | 30 | 40 | 50 | 60 | 70 | 80 | 90 | 100 | 110 | 120 | 130 |

The Flash

Ranking the Scarlet Speedsters by likability.

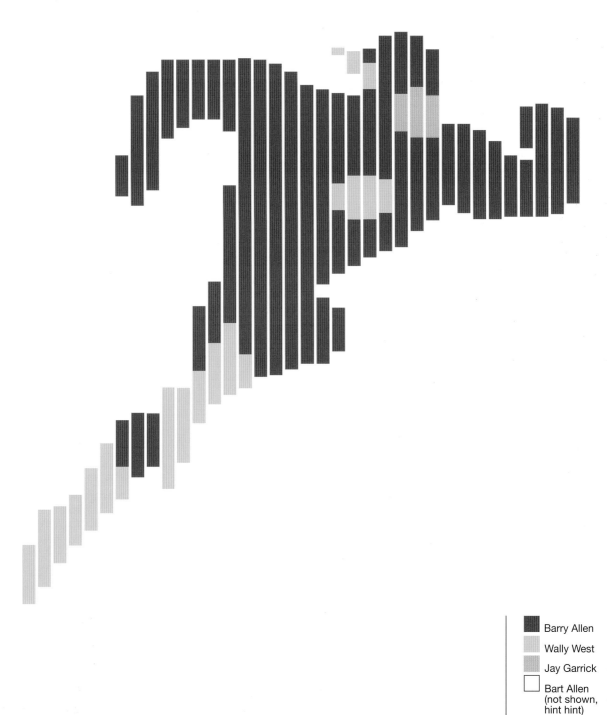

Barry Allen

Wally West

Jay Garrick

Bart Allen
(not shown,
hint hint)

Superman's Movies

Ranking the Man of Steel's films by enjoyment.

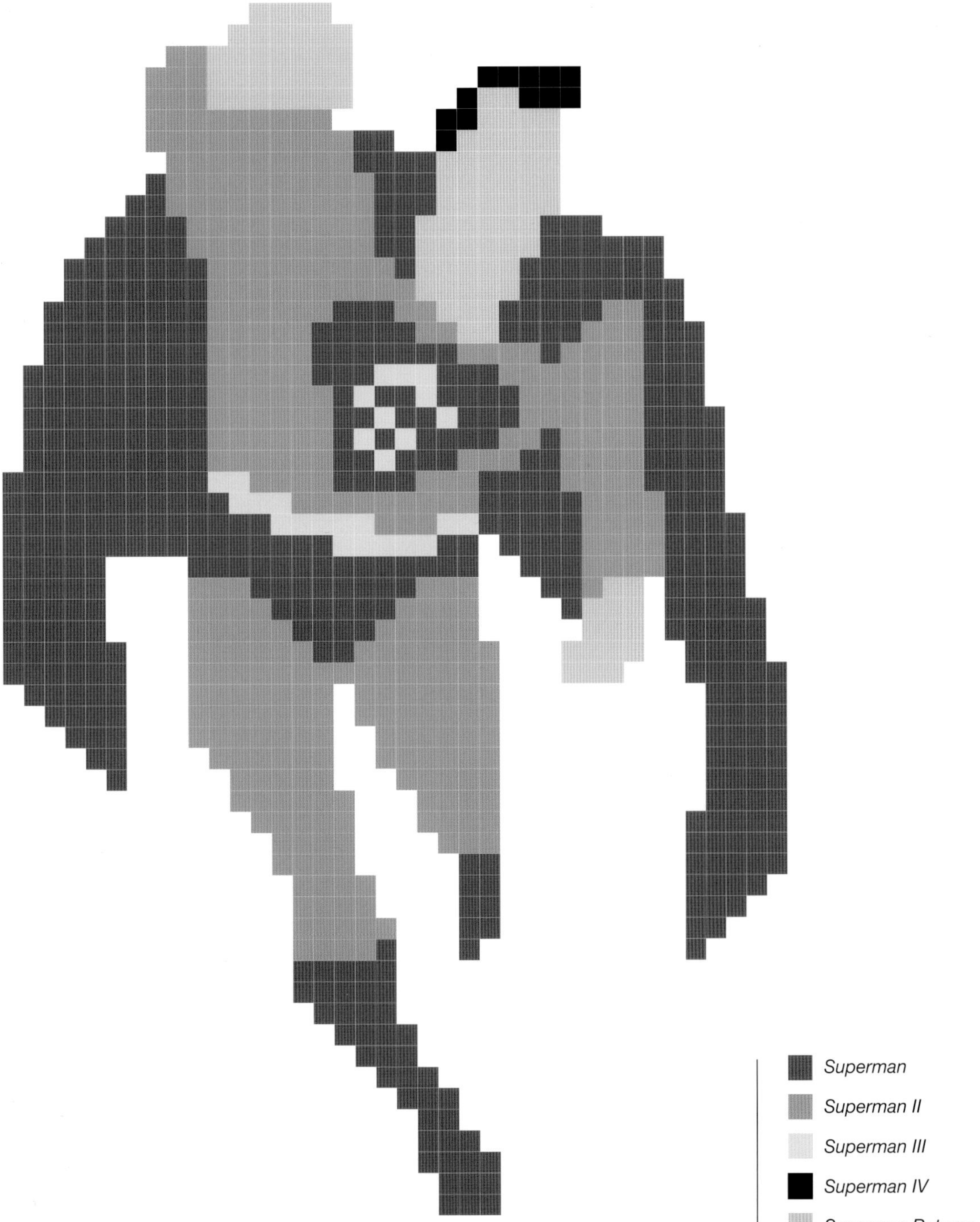

Superman
Superman II
Superman III
Superman IV
Superman Returns

Who Is the Fastest Man Alive?

Clocking the races between Flash and Superman.

1967 The United Nations organizes a race between the two speedy superheroes for charity. Rival gangs place heavy bets and try to rig the outcome. Flash and Superman decide to tie to prevent either gang from profiting.

Flash

Superman

1967 Frustrated with the outcome of the first race, two gambling aliens (yup, it's exactly what it sounds like) force Flash and Superman to a rematch—with their home cities at stake. The race to the edge of the Milky Way and back turns out just to be a ploy to kill Flash. The two heroes outsmart the aliens and tie a second time.

1970 Flash and Superman try to hunt down robots traveling at the speed of light—and decide to race in the process. In pursuit, they beam to an alien planet, injure their legs, and end up scooting to the finish on their elbows. Superman admits defeat. The Flash is the fastest man alive . . . on this particular alien planet.

1978 During a time-traveling mission to stop a war between two alien nations, Flash and Superman square off.

1990 After Barry Allen dies, Wally West takes over as The Flash and he too races Superman. The race determines if the villain Mr. Mxyzptlk will have to leave Earth. The triumph sends the evil imp abroad for 90 days.

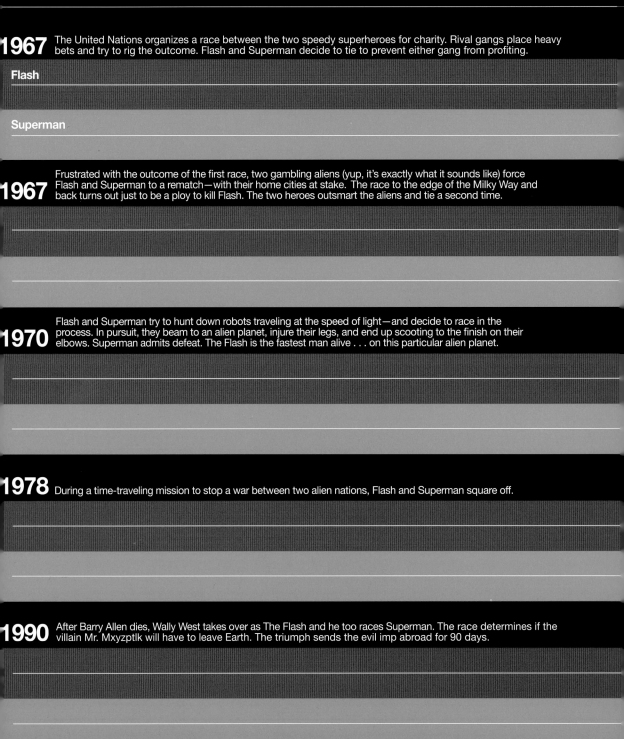

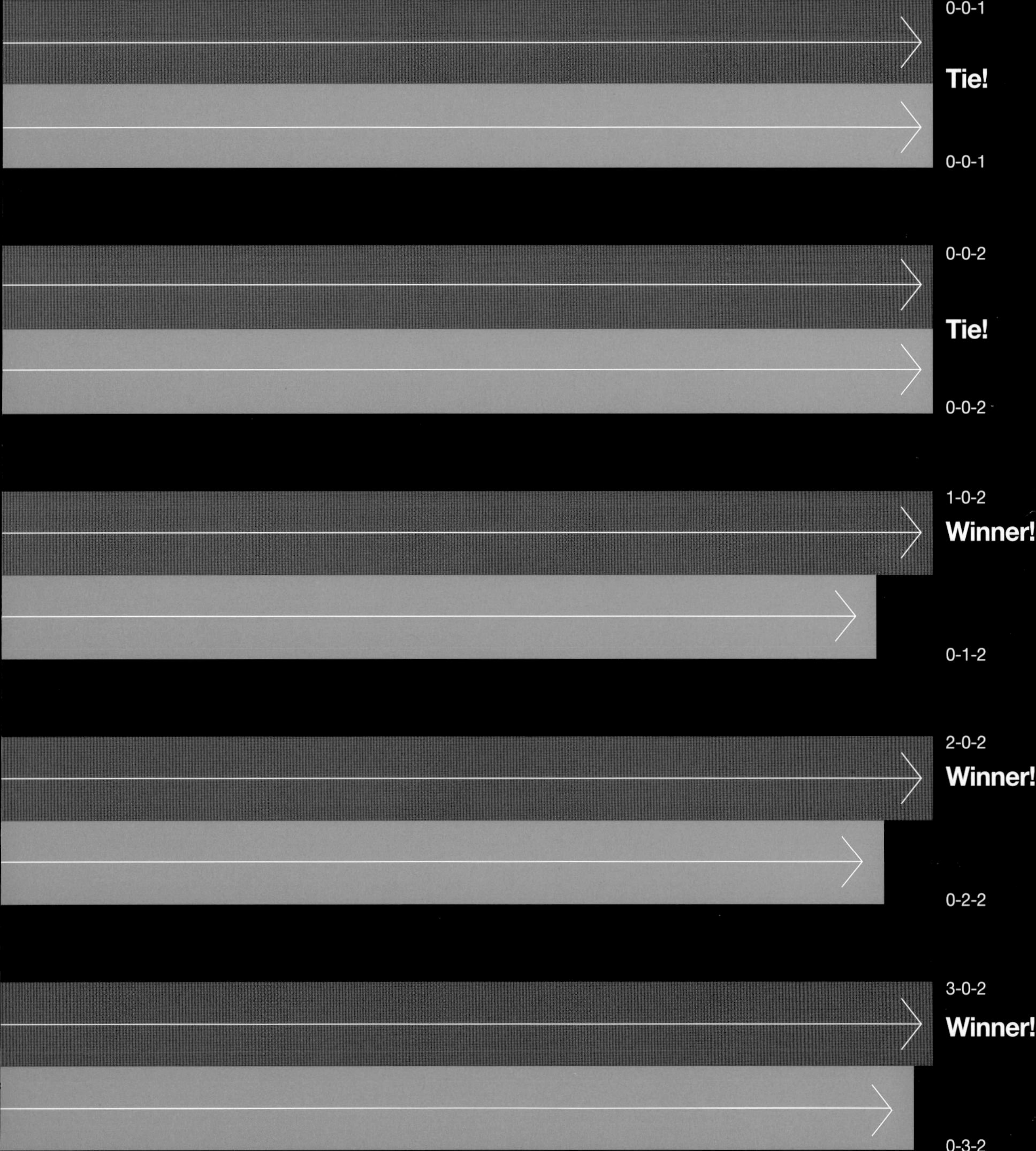
0-0-1
Tie!
0-0-1
0-0-2
Tie!
0-0-2
1-0-2
Winner!
0-1-2
2-0-2
Winner!
0-2-2
3-0-2
Winner!
0-3-2

SMALL WONDER

How Big Is the Miniature City of Kandor?

Kandor, the capital city of Krypton, was stolen and shrunk by the alien android Brainiac. Superman keeps the city and its inhabitants in his Fortress of Solitude.

● **= 10,000 people**

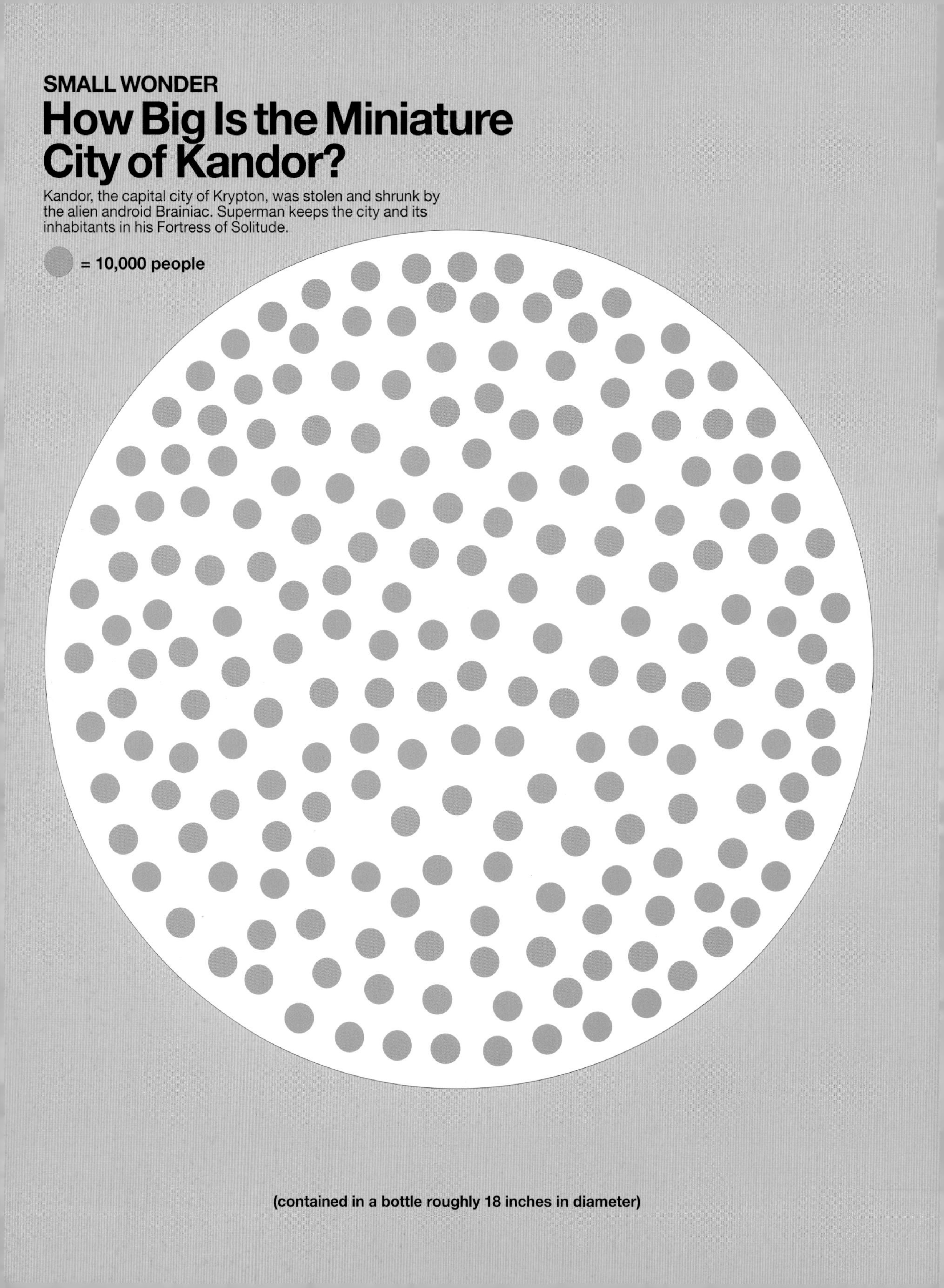

(contained in a bottle roughly 18 inches in diameter)

PUT A RING ON IT
A History of Concentric Circles

A common graphic device, the concentric circle comes back around over time.

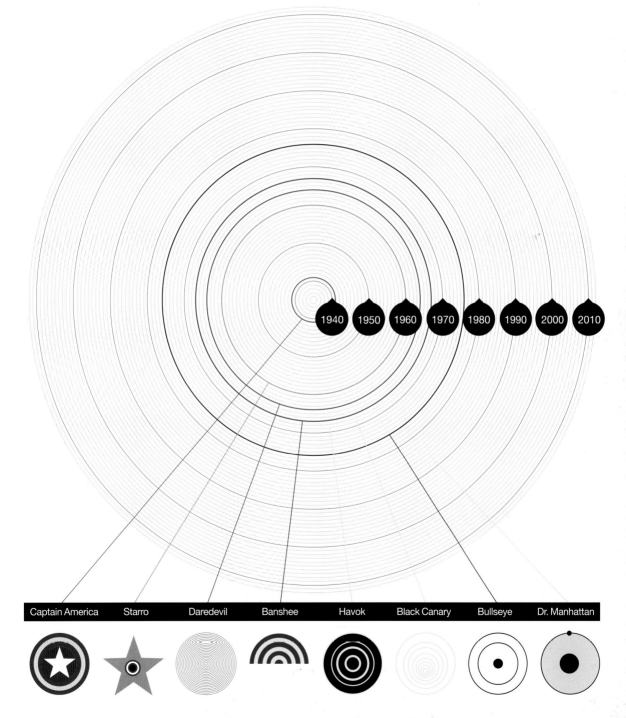

1940 1950 1960 1970 1980 1990 2000 2010

Captain America | Starro | Daredevil | Banshee | Havok | Black Canary | Bullseye | Dr. Manhattan

Who's Who in *Sin City*

In Frank Miller's dark classic, everyone knows your name—and has your number. Here's how they're all connected.

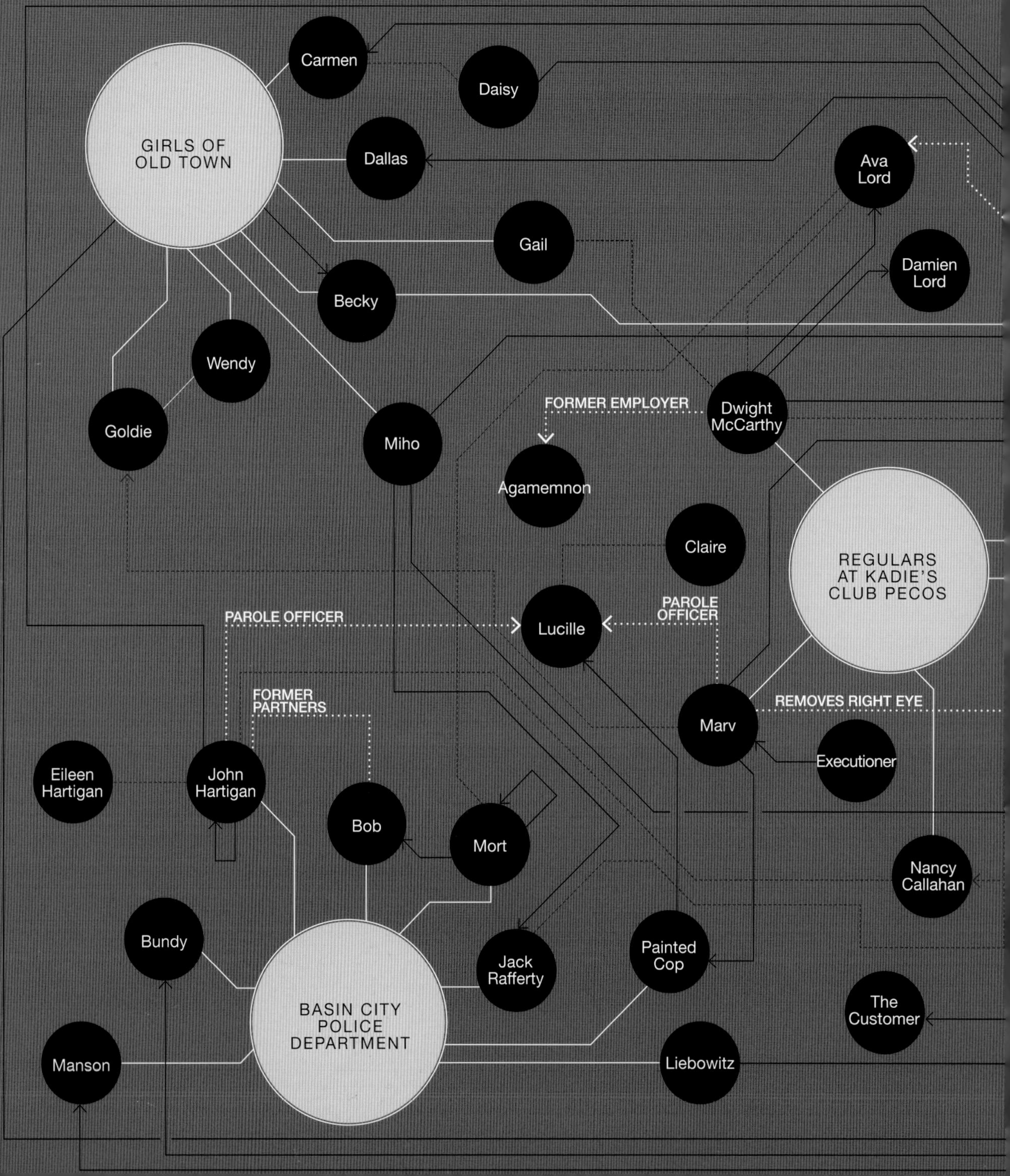

GIRLS OF OLD TOWN
Carmen
Daisy
Dallas
Ava Lord
Gail
Damien Lord
Becky
Wendy
Goldie
Miho
FORMER EMPLOYER
Dwight McCarthy
Agamemnon
Claire
REGULARS AT KADIE'S CLUB PECOS
PAROLE OFFICER
Lucille
PAROLE OFFICER
FORMER PARTNERS
Marv
REMOVES RIGHT EYE
Executioner
Eileen Hartigan
John Hartigan
Bob
Mort
Nancy Callahan
Bundy
Jack Rafferty
Painted Cop
BASIN CITY POLICE DEPARTMENT
The Customer
Manson
Liebowitz

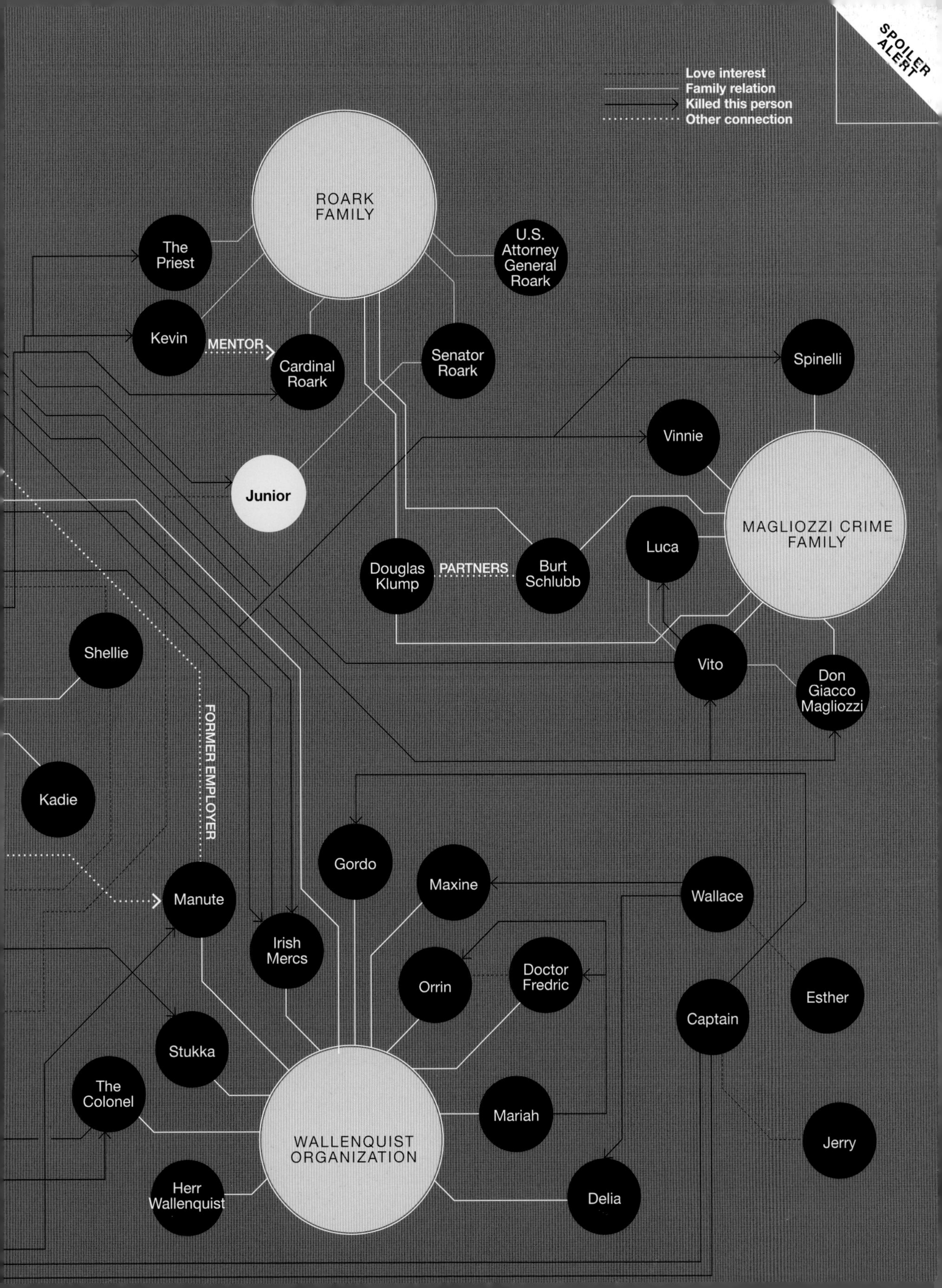
SPOILER ALERT
Love interest
Family relation
Killed this person
Other connection
ROARK FAMILY
The Priest
U.S. Attorney General Roark
Kevin
MENTOR
Cardinal Roark
Senator Roark
Spinelli
Vinnie
Junior
MAGLIOZZI CRIME FAMILY
Luca
Douglas Klump
PARTNERS
Burt Schlubb
Shellie
Vito
Don Giacco Magliozzi
FORMER EMPLOYER
Kadie
Gordo
Maxine
Wallace
Manute
Irish Mercs
Orrin
Doctor Fredric
Esther
Captain
Stukka
The Colonel
Mariah
Jerry
WALLENQUIST ORGANIZATION
Herr Wallenquist
Delia

SECRET IDENTITIES

Stan Lee's Nicknames for the Marvel Bullpen

While Stan Lee was Marvel's editor-in-chief, he wrote a column called "Stan's Soapbox," which ran in each of Marvel's titles that month. In the Soapbox, Lee opined on reader mail, talked up the fan club, and gave shout outs to Marvel staff members—but always with a nickname. The tradition of calling employees like Flo Steinberg "Fabulous" and Todd McFarlane "Tumultuous" lasted for decades. Here's a collection of the best nicknames, categorized by type.

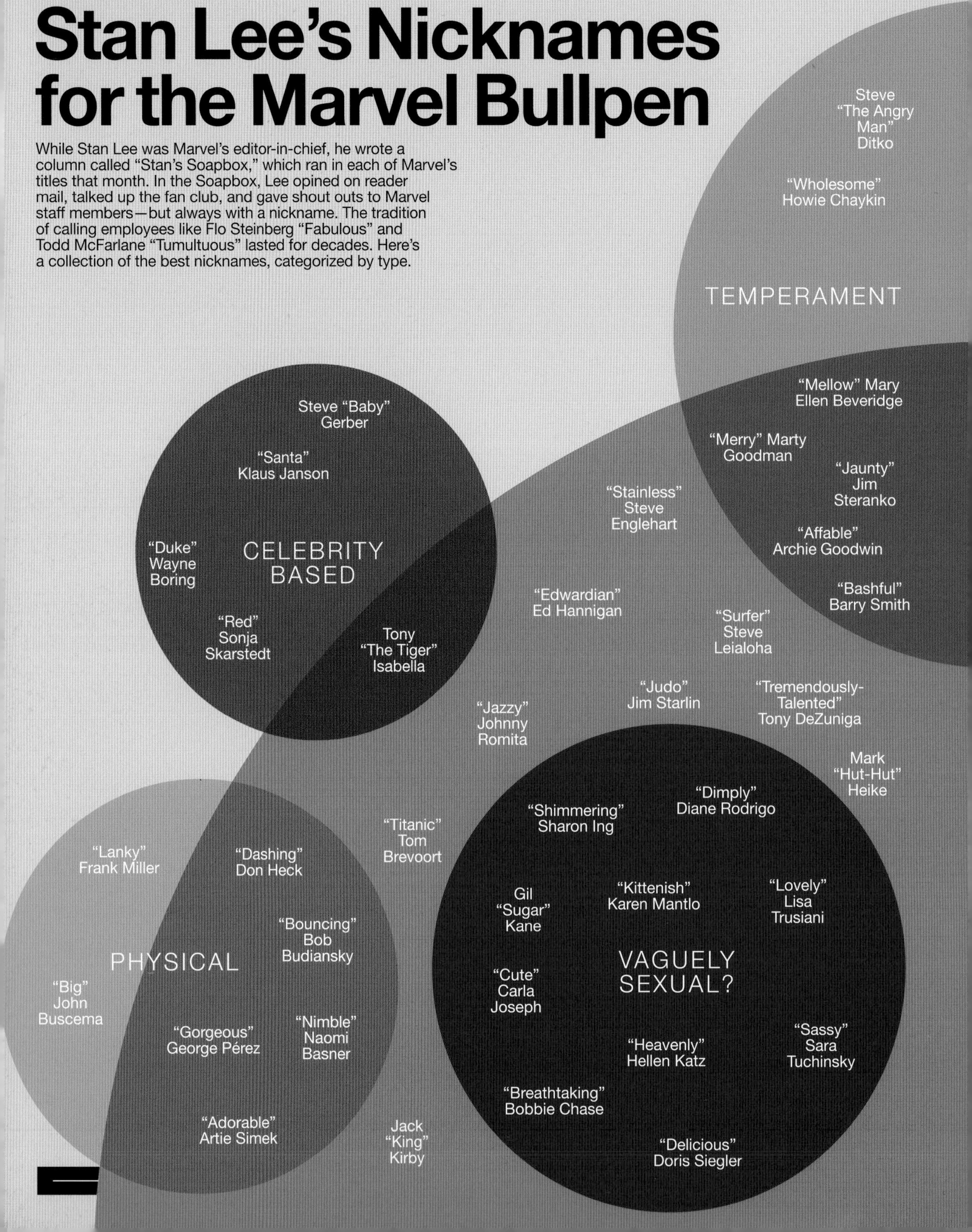

TEMPERAMENT
Steve "The Angry Man" Ditko
"Wholesome" Howie Chaykin
"Mellow" Mary Ellen Beveridge
"Merry" Marty Goodman
"Jaunty" Jim Steranko
"Affable" Archie Goodwin
"Bashful" Barry Smith
CELEBRITY BASED
Steve "Baby" Gerber
"Santa" Klaus Janson
"Duke" Wayne Boring
"Red" Sonja Skarstedt
Tony "The Tiger" Isabella
"Stainless" Steve Englehart
"Edwardian" Ed Hannigan
"Surfer" Steve Leialoha
"Judo" Jim Starlin
"Tremendously-Talented" Tony DeZuniga
"Jazzy" Johnny Romita
Mark "Hut-Hut" Heike
"Titanic" Tom Brevoort
Jack "King" Kirby
PHYSICAL
"Lanky" Frank Miller
"Dashing" Don Heck
"Bouncing" Bob Budiansky
"Big" John Buscema
"Gorgeous" George Pérez
"Nimble" Naomi Basner
"Adorable" Artie Simek
VAGUELY SEXUAL?
"Shimmering" Sharon Ing
"Dimply" Diane Rodrigo
Gil "Sugar" Kane
"Kittenish" Karen Mantlo
"Lovely" Lisa Trusiani
"Cute" Carla Joseph
"Heavenly" Hellen Katz
"Sassy" Sara Tuchinsky
"Breathtaking" Bobbie Chase
"Delicious" Doris Siegler

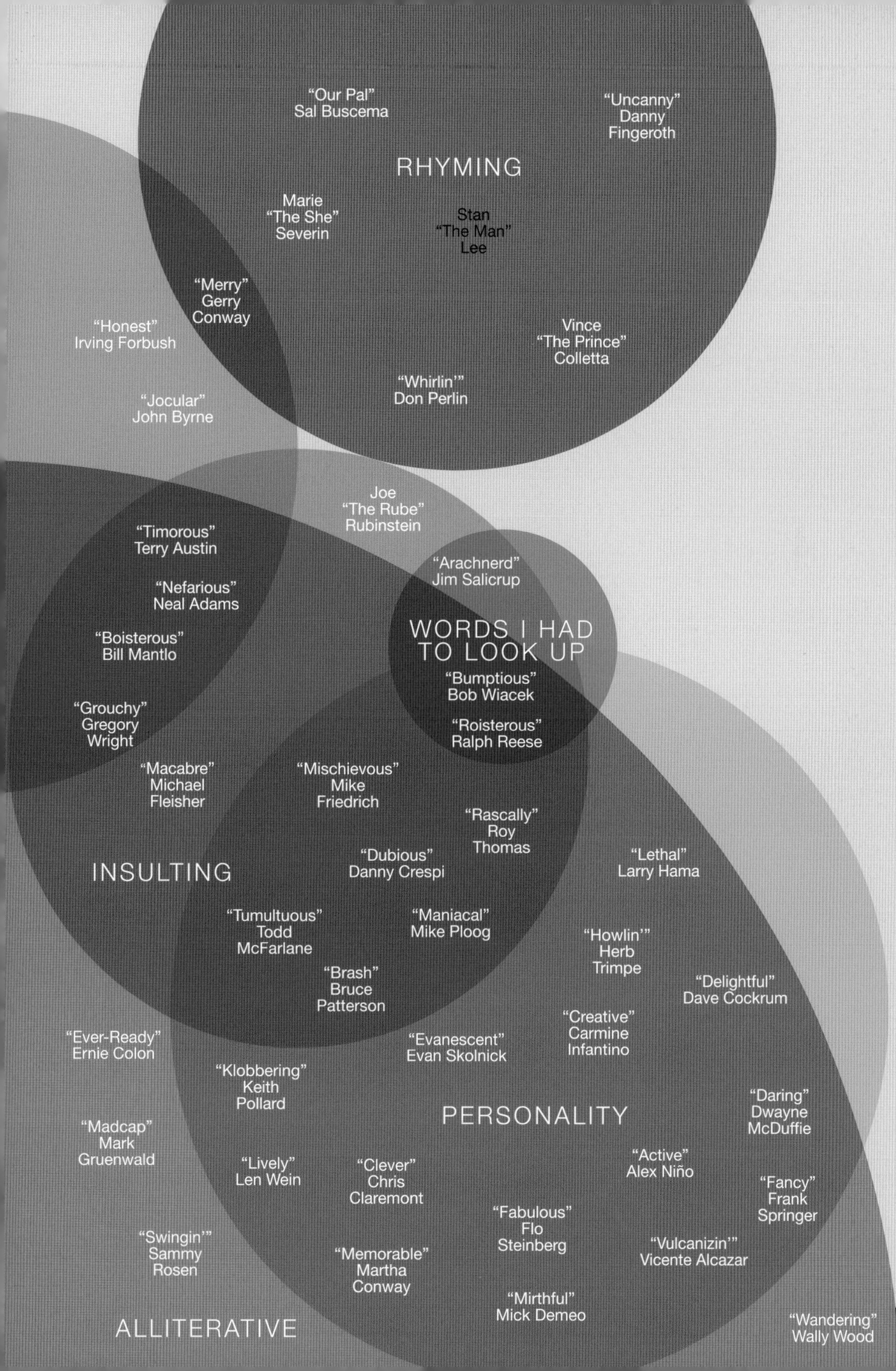
RHYMING
"Our Pal" Sal Buscema
"Uncanny" Danny Fingeroth
Marie "The She" Severin
Stan "The Man" Lee
"Merry" Gerry Conway
"Honest" Irving Forbush
Vince "The Prince" Colletta
"Whirlin'" Don Perlin
"Jocular" John Byrne
Joe "The Rube" Rubinstein
"Timorous" Terry Austin
"Arachnerd" Jim Salicrup
"Nefarious" Neal Adams
WORDS I HAD TO LOOK UP
"Boisterous" Bill Mantlo
"Bumptious" Bob Wiacek
"Grouchy" Gregory Wright
"Roisterous" Ralph Reese
"Macabre" Michael Fleisher
"Mischievous" Mike Friedrich
"Rascally" Roy Thomas
"Dubious" Danny Crespi
"Lethal" Larry Hama
INSULTING
"Tumultuous" Todd McFarlane
"Maniacal" Mike Ploog
"Howlin'" Herb Trimpe
"Brash" Bruce Patterson
"Delightful" Dave Cockrum
"Creative" Carmine Infantino
"Ever-Ready" Ernie Colon
"Evanescent" Evan Skolnick
"Klobbering" Keith Pollard
"Daring" Dwayne McDuffie
PERSONALITY
"Madcap" Mark Gruenwald
"Active" Alex Niño
"Lively" Len Wein
"Clever" Chris Claremont
"Fancy" Frank Springer
"Fabulous" Flo Steinberg
"Swingin'" Sammy Rosen
"Vulcanizin'" Vicente Alcazar
"Memorable" Martha Conway
"Mirthful" Mick Demeo
ALLITERATIVE
"Wandering" Wally Wood

The Periodic Table of The Metal Men

The Metal Men are a team of robots who pull their names and abilities from—yup, you guessed it—different metals. The members of the original team, created in 1962, were Gold, Iron, Lead, Mercury, Platinum, and Tin. But over time, more were created—spin-off teams and enemies—all springing from the Periodic Table.

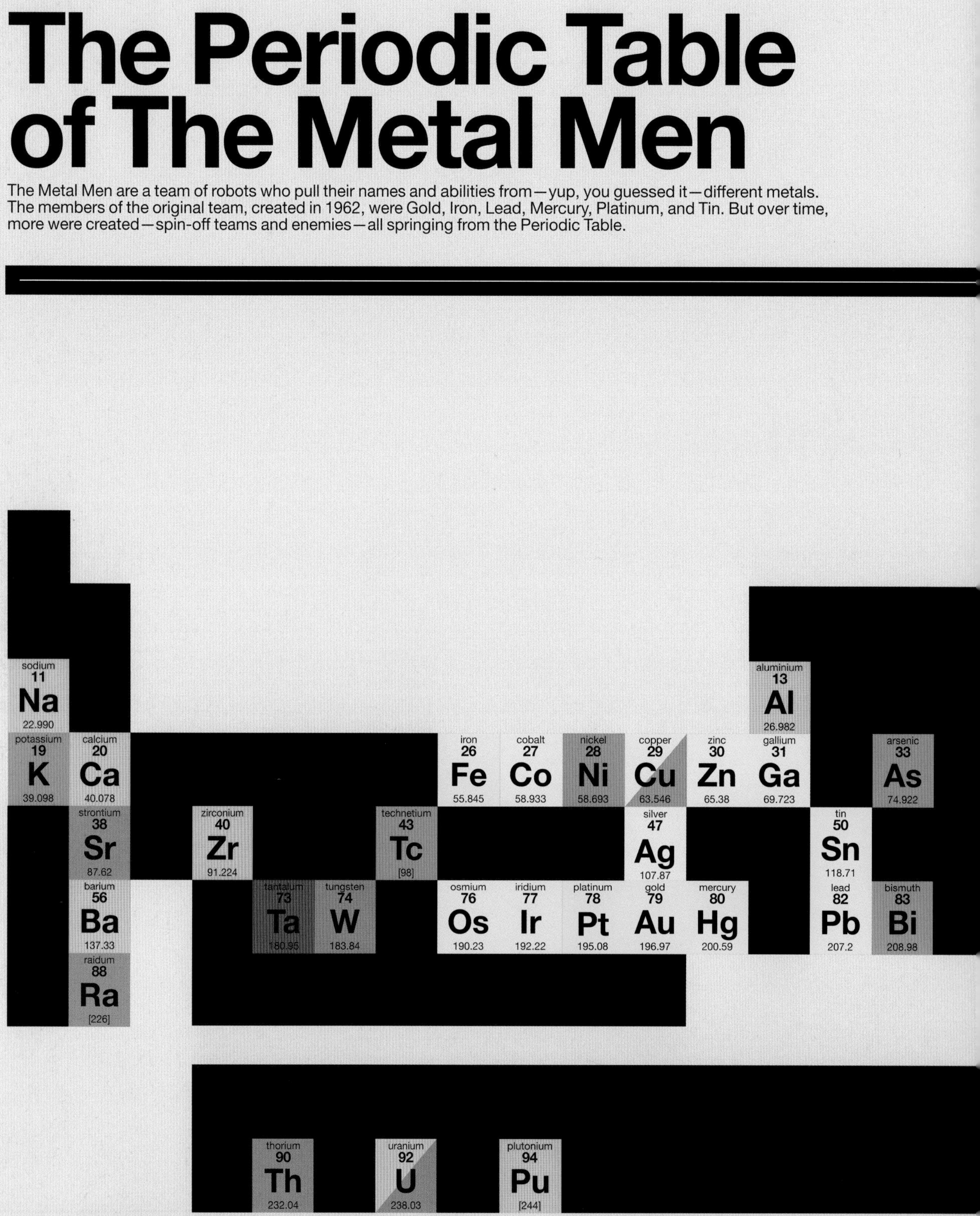
sodium 11 Na 22.990
aluminium 13 Al 26.982
potassium 19 K 39.098
calcium 20 Ca 40.078
iron 26 Fe 55.845
cobalt 27 Co 58.933
nickel 28 Ni 58.693
copper 29 Cu 63.546
zinc 30 Zn 65.38
gallium 31 Ga 69.723
arsenic 33 As 74.922
strontium 38 Sr 87.62
zirconium 40 Zr 91.224
technetium 43 Tc [98]
silver 47 Ag 107.87
tin 50 Sn 118.71
barium 56 Ba 137.33
tantalum 73 Ta 180.95
tungsten 74 W 183.84
osmium 76 Os 190.23
iridium 77 Ir 192.22
platinum 78 Pt 195.08
gold 79 Au 196.97
mercury 80 Hg 200.59
lead 82 Pb 207.2
bismuth 83 Bi 208.98
raidum 88 Ra [226]
thorium 90 Th 232.04
uranium 92 U 238.03
plutonium 94 Pu [244]

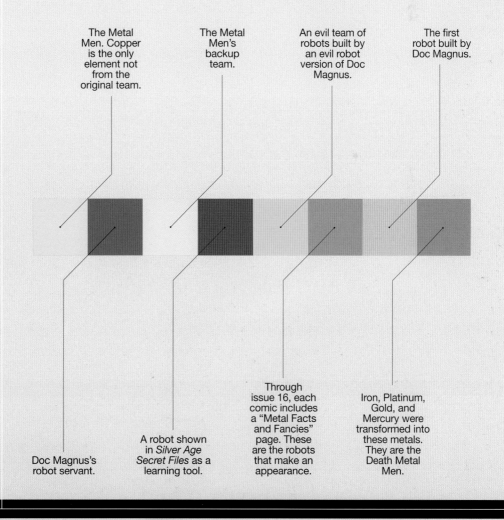

The Metal Men. Copper is the only element not from the original team.
Doc Magnus's robot servant.
The Metal Men's backup team.
A robot shown in *Silver Age Secret Files* as a learning tool.
An evil team of robots built by an evil robot version of Doc Magnus.
Through issue 16, each comic includes a "Metal Facts and Fancies" page. These are the robots that make an appearance.
The first robot built by Doc Magnus.
Iron, Platinum, Gold, and Mercury were transformed into these metals. They are the Death Metal Men.

Who Reads DC Comics?

In 2011, right after a massive relaunch of all their characters, DC Comics polled readers to find out whom their so-called *New 52* line was reaching. Here are the results.

Data collection

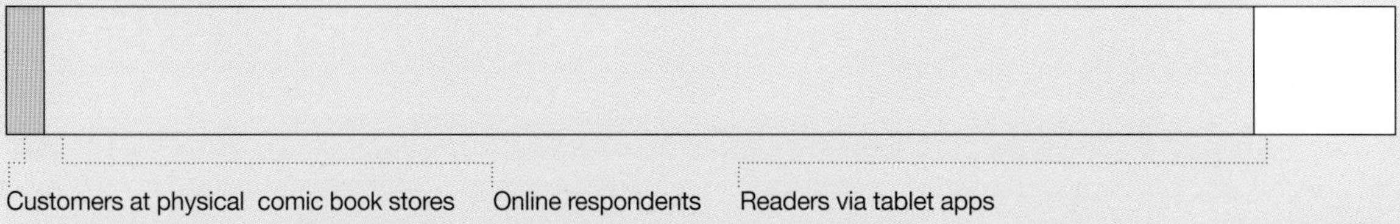
Customers at physical comic book stores
Online respondents
Readers via tablet apps

Distribution of total readership by age

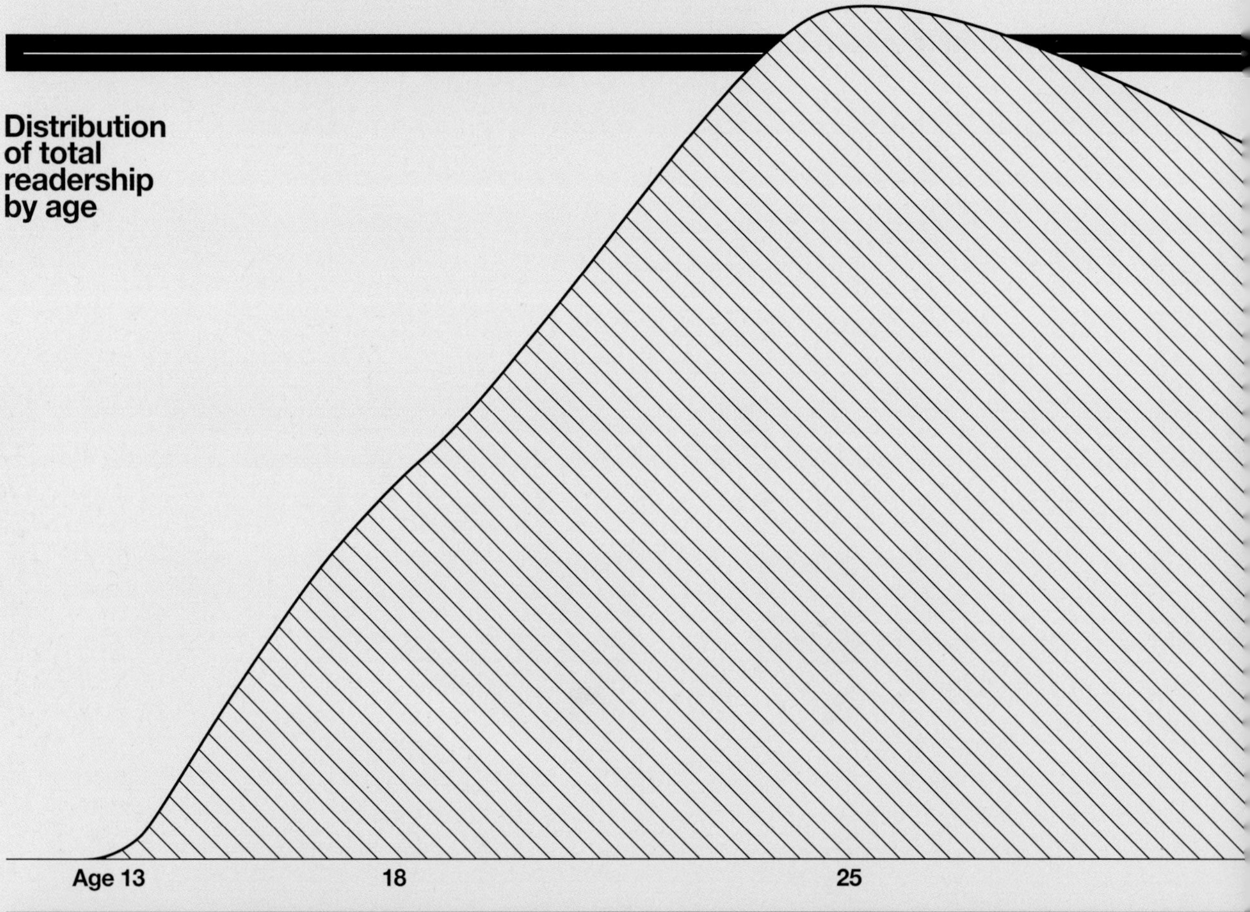
Age 13
18
25

Gender

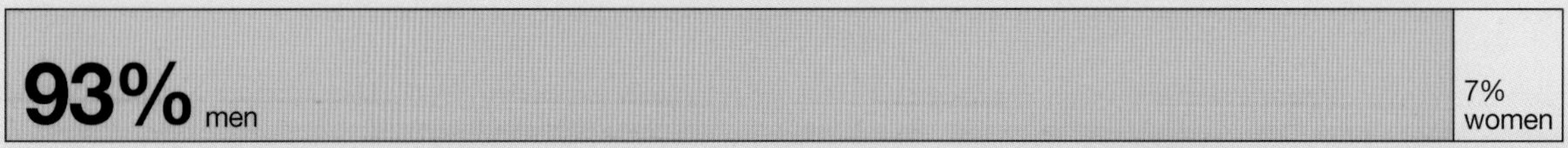
93% men
7% women

Income

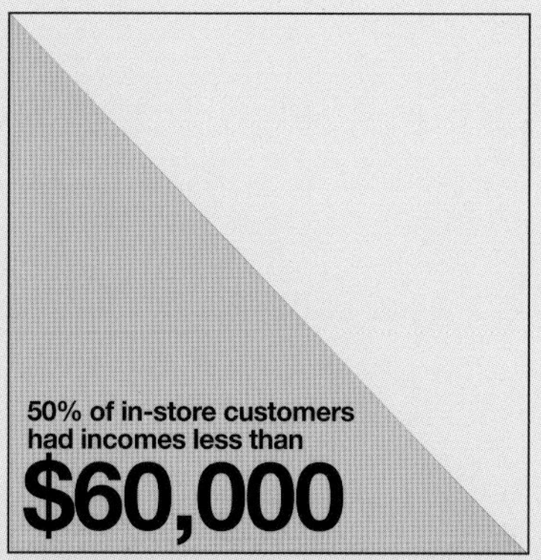
50% of in-store customers had incomes less than
$60,000

Types of readers

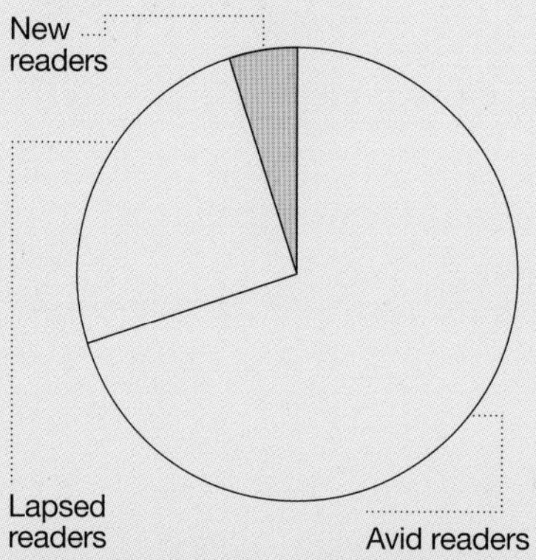
New readers
Lapsed readers
Avid readers

Digital readers polled who also read print comics

Print readers polled who also read digital comics

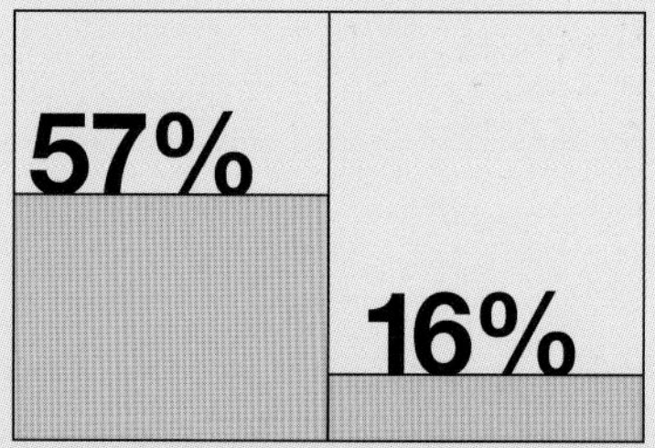
57%
16%

Readers over 35

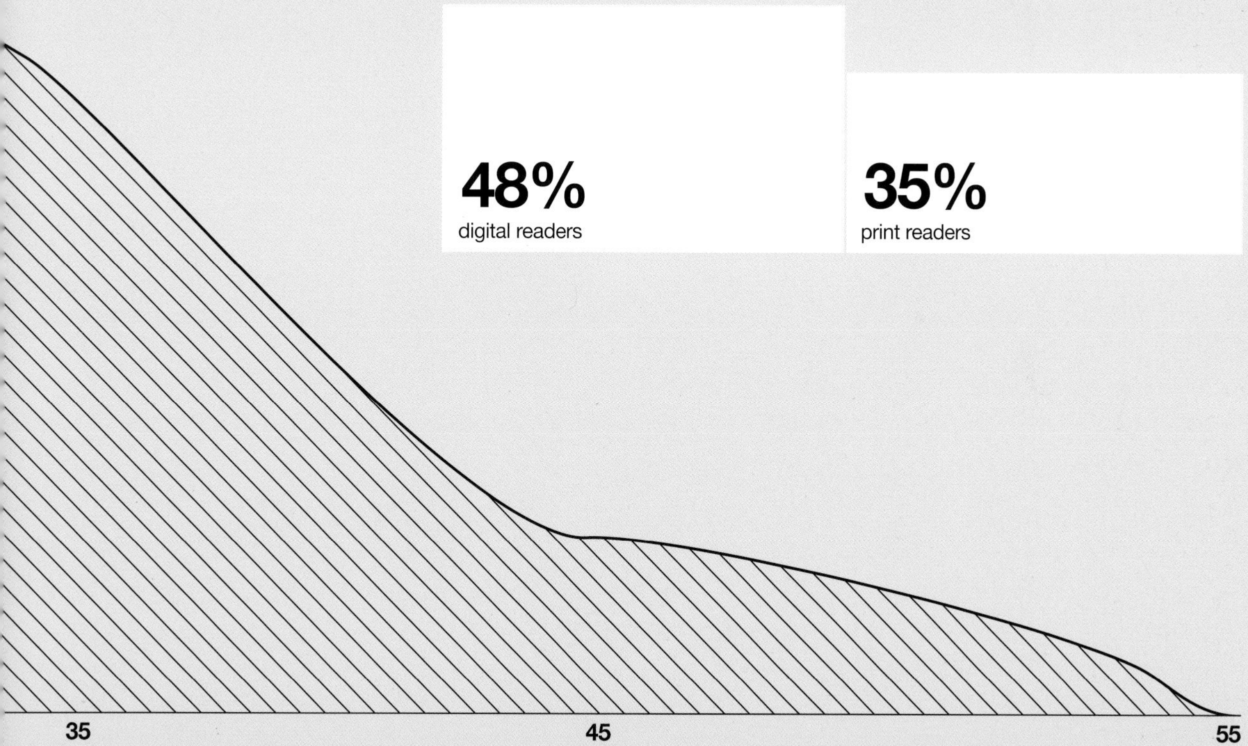
48%
digital readers
35%
print readers
35
45
55

Purchasing

Four in ten respondents said a *New 52* title they wanted was out of stock at their store.

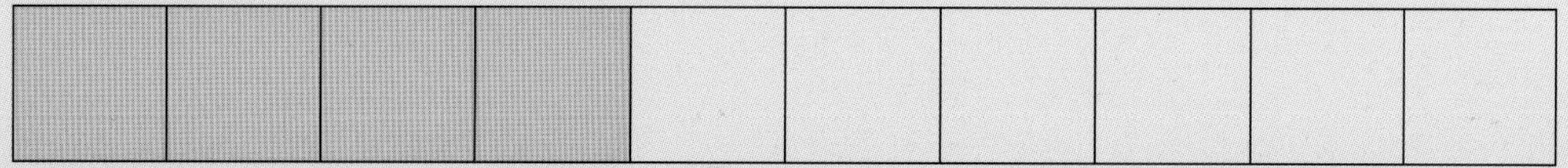

Two-thirds made an impulse buy.

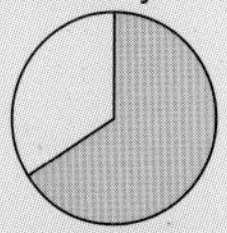

PLAYING FOR THE OTHER TEAM

The Many Affiliations of the Marvel Universe

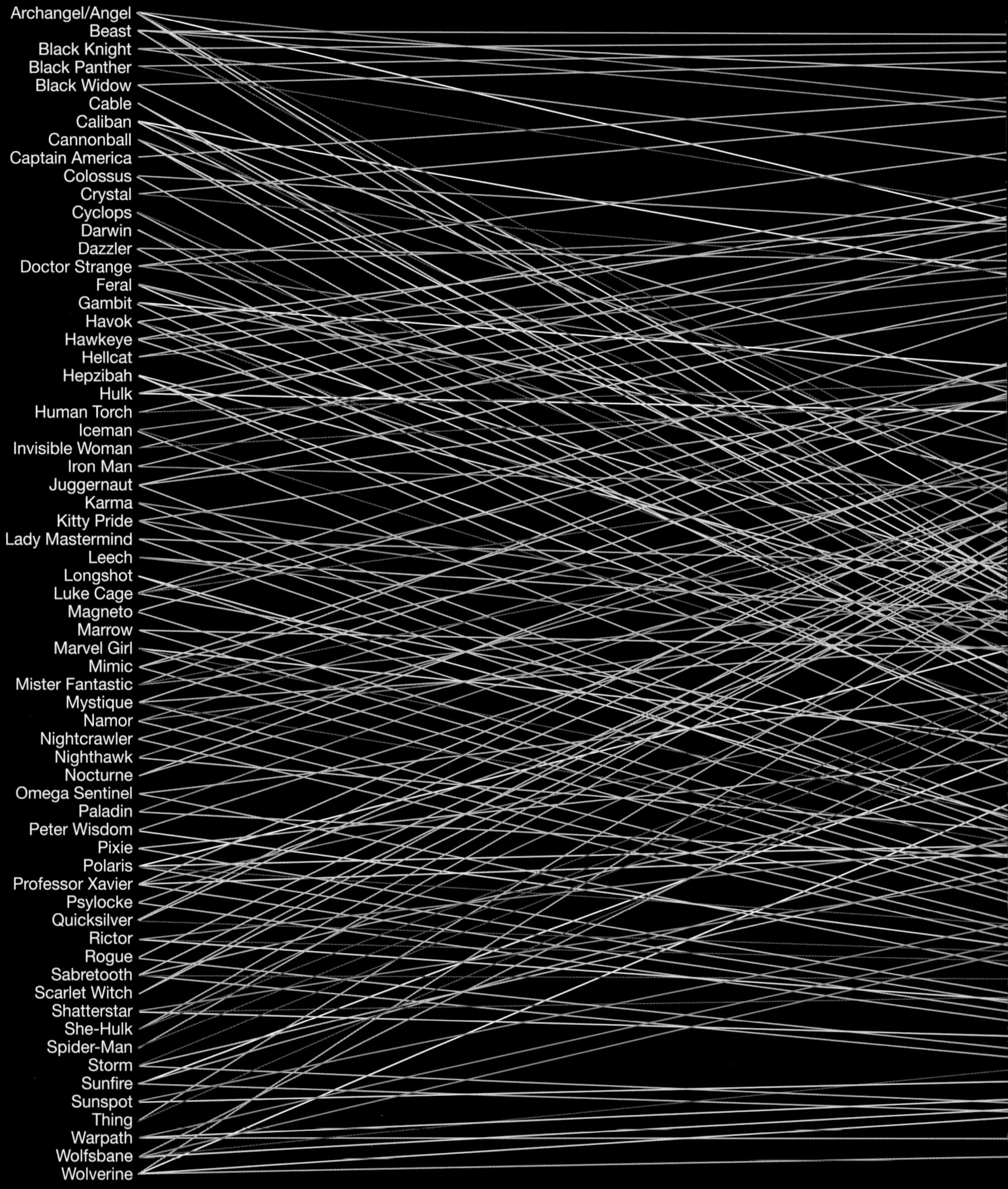
Archangel/Angel
Beast
Black Knight
Black Panther
Black Widow
Cable
Caliban
Cannonball
Captain America
Colossus
Crystal
Cyclops
Darwin
Dazzler
Doctor Strange
Feral
Gambit
Havok
Hawkeye
Hellcat
Hepzibah
Hulk
Human Torch
Iceman
Invisible Woman
Iron Man
Juggernaut
Karma
Kitty Pride
Lady Mastermind
Leech
Longshot
Luke Cage
Magneto
Marrow
Marvel Girl
Mimic
Mister Fantastic
Mystique
Namor
Nightcrawler
Nighthawk
Nocturne
Omega Sentinel
Paladin
Peter Wisdom
Pixie
Polaris
Professor Xavier
Psylocke
Quicksilver
Rictor
Rogue
Sabretooth
Scarlet Witch
Shatterstar
She-Hulk
Spider-Man
Storm
Sunfire
Sunspot
Thing
Warpath
Wolfsbane
Wolverine

If you're a superhero or a mutant, you're almost
required to spread your powers around.

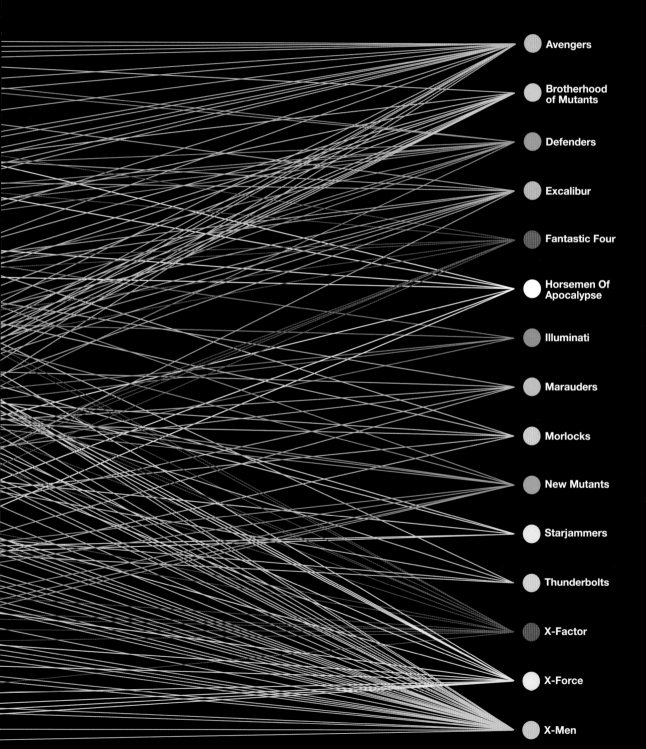

Avengers

Brotherhood
of Mutants

Defenders

Excalibur

Fantastic Four

Horsemen Of
Apocalypse

Illuminati

Marauders

Morlocks

New Mutants

Starjammers

Thunderbolts

X-Factor

X-Force

X-Men

Batman's Utility Belt, 1952

The Dark Knight is constantly updating the contents of his trusty belt with better gadgets; a lot changes in crime-fighting tech over the years.

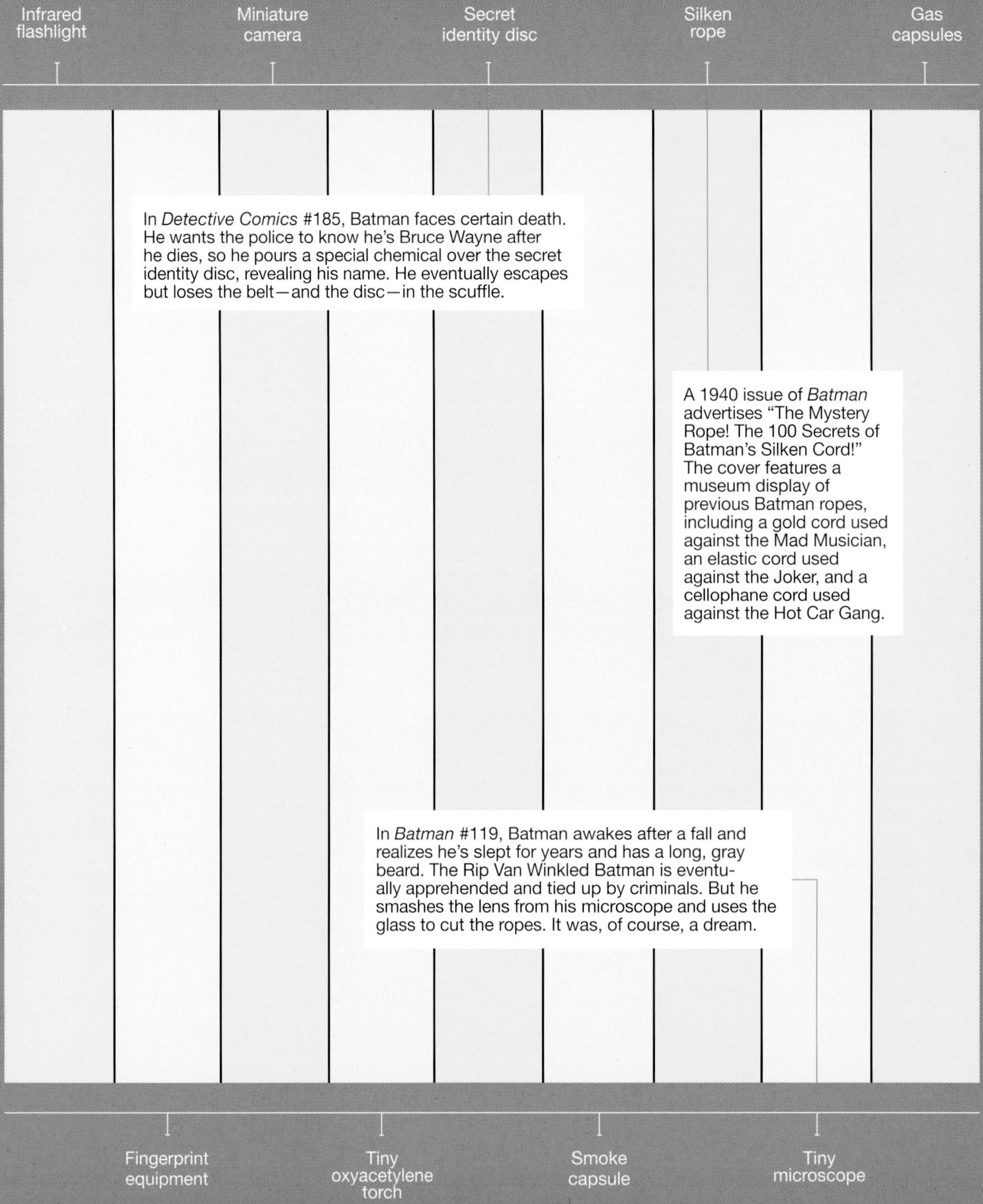

Infrared flashlight
Miniature camera
Secret identity disc
Silken rope
Gas capsules
Fingerprint equipment
Tiny oxyacetylene torch
Smoke capsule
Tiny microscope

In *Detective Comics* #185, Batman faces certain death. He wants the police to know he's Bruce Wayne after he dies, so he pours a special chemical over the secret identity disc, revealing his name. He eventually escapes but loses the belt—and the disc—in the scuffle.

A 1940 issue of *Batman* advertises "The Mystery Rope! The 100 Secrets of Batman's Silken Cord!" The cover features a museum display of previous Batman ropes, including a gold cord used against the Mad Musician, an elastic cord used against the Joker, and a cellophane cord used against the Hot Car Gang.

In *Batman* #119, Batman awakes after a fall and realizes he's slept for years and has a long, gray beard. The Rip Van Winkled Batman is eventually apprehended and tied up by criminals. But he smashes the lens from his microscope and uses the glass to cut the ropes. It was, of course, a dream.

Batman's Utility Belt, 1968

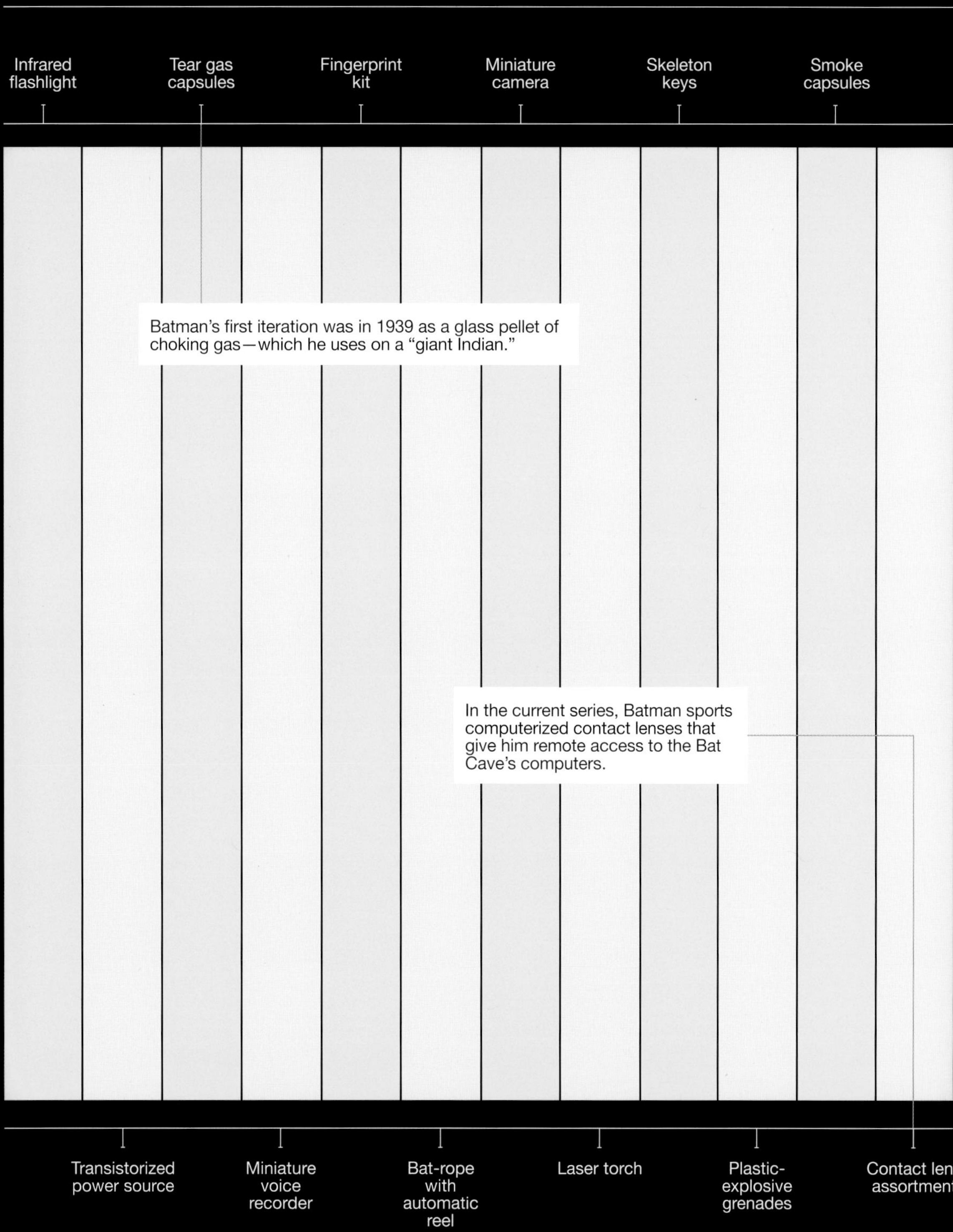
Infrared flashlight
Tear gas capsules
Fingerprint kit
Miniature camera
Skeleton keys
Smoke capsules
Batman's first iteration was in 1939 as a glass pellet of choking gas—which he uses on a "giant Indian."
In the current series, Batman sports computerized contact lenses that give him remote access to the Bat Cave's computers.
Transistorized power source
Miniature voice recorder
Bat-rope with automatic reel
Laser torch
Plastic-explosive grenades
Contact len assortment

Joker's Utility Belt, 1952

After being bested by Batman in *Batman* #73, the Joker decides he wants his own utility belt. It's a short-lived conceit.

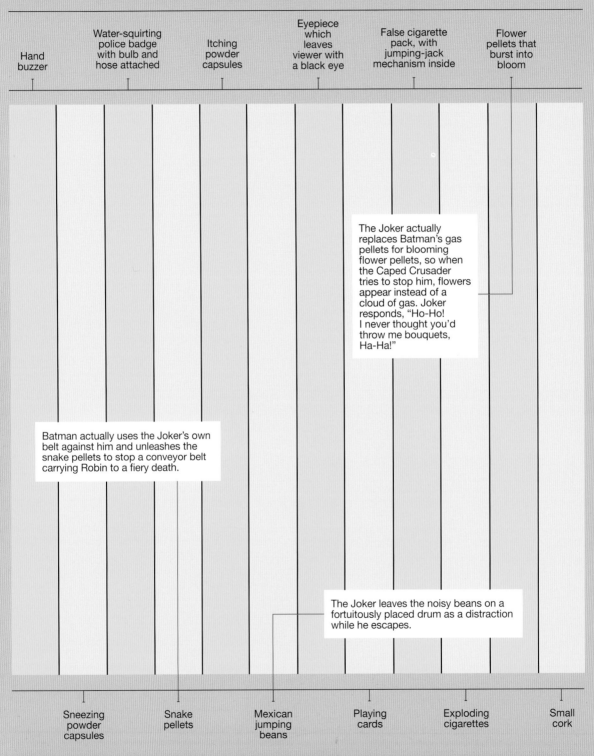

Hand buzzer

Water-squirting police badge with bulb and hose attached

Itching powder capsules

Eyepiece which leaves viewer with a black eye

False cigarette pack, with jumping-jack mechanism inside

Flower pellets that burst into bloom

The Joker actually replaces Batman's gas pellets for blooming flower pellets, so when the Caped Crusader tries to stop him, flowers appear instead of a cloud of gas. Joker responds, "Ho-Ho! I never thought you'd throw me bouquets, Ha-Ha!"

Batman actually uses the Joker's own belt against him and unleashes the snake pellets to stop a conveyor belt carrying Robin to a fiery death.

The Joker leaves the noisy beans on a fortuitously placed drum as a distraction while he escapes.

Sneezing powder capsules

Snake pellets

Mexican jumping beans

Playing cards

Exploding cigarettes

Small cork

Robin's Utility Belt, 1994

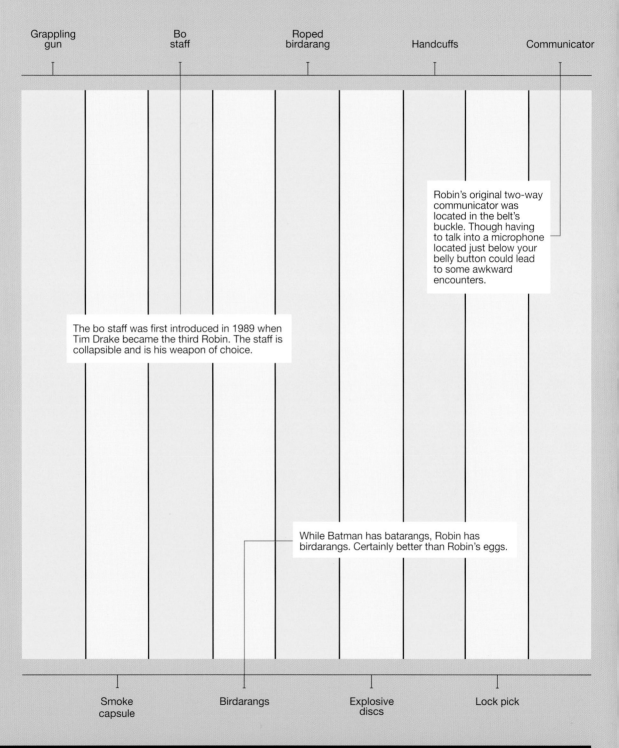

Grappling gun

Bo staff

Roped birdarang

Handcuffs

Communicator

Robin's original two-way communicator was located in the belt's buckle. Though having to talk into a microphone located just below your belly button could lead to some awkward encounters.

The bo staff was first introduced in 1989 when Tim Drake became the third Robin. The staff is collapsible and is his weapon of choice.

While Batman has batarangs, Robin has birdarangs. Certainly better than Robin's eggs.

Smoke capsule

Birdarangs

Explosive discs

Lock pick

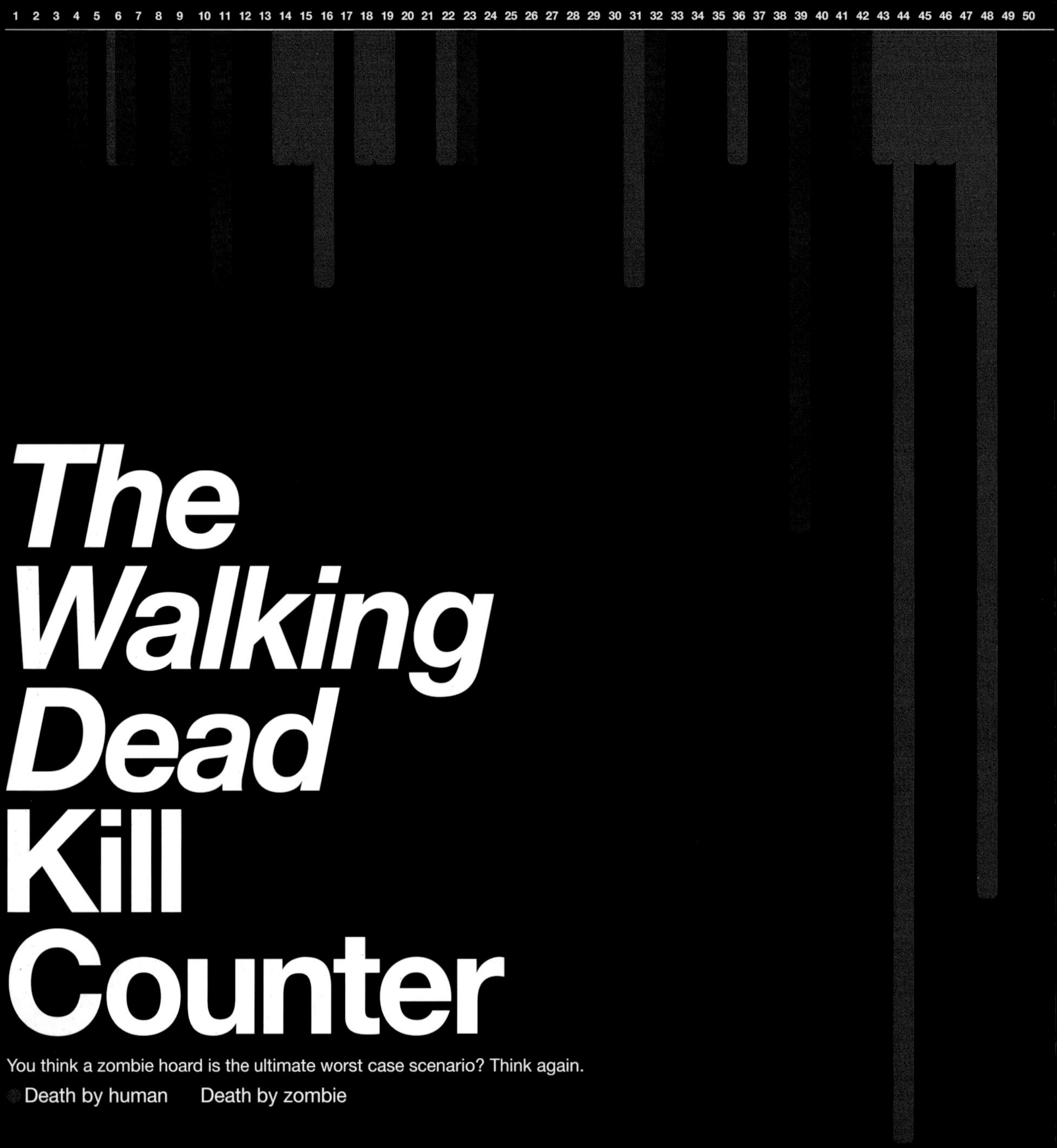
1 2 3 4 5 6 7 8 9 10 11 12 13 14 15 16 17 18 19 20 21 22 23 24 25 26 27 28 29 30 31 32 33 34 35 36 37 38 39 40 41 42 43 44 45 46 47 48 49 50

The Walking Dead Kill Counter

You think a zombie hoard is the ultimate worst case scenario? Think again.

Death by human   Death by zombie

OVERALL DEATHS BY HUMAN AND ZOMBIES

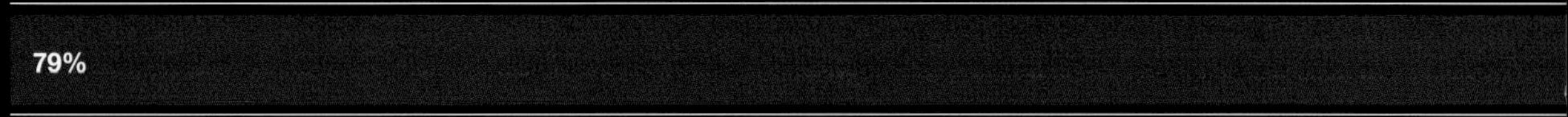
79%

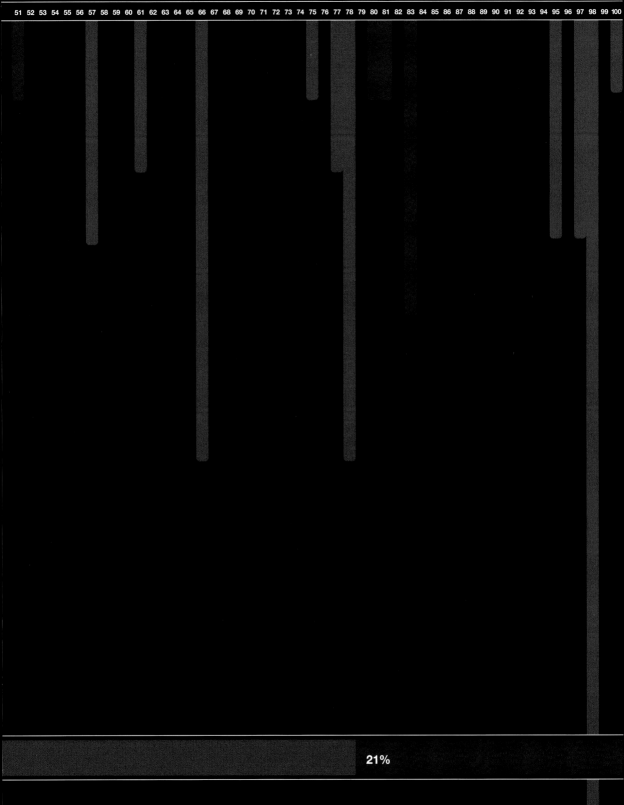

51 52 53 54 55 56 57 58 59 60 61 62 63 64 65 66 67 68 69 70 71 72 73 74 75 76 77 78 79 80 81 82 83 84 85 86 87 88 89 90 91 92 93 94 95 96 97 98 99 100

21%

Who is Left in *Y: The Last Man*

After a plague kills off every other man on the planet, Yorick Brown has to deal with being his gender's sole survivor. With most firefighters

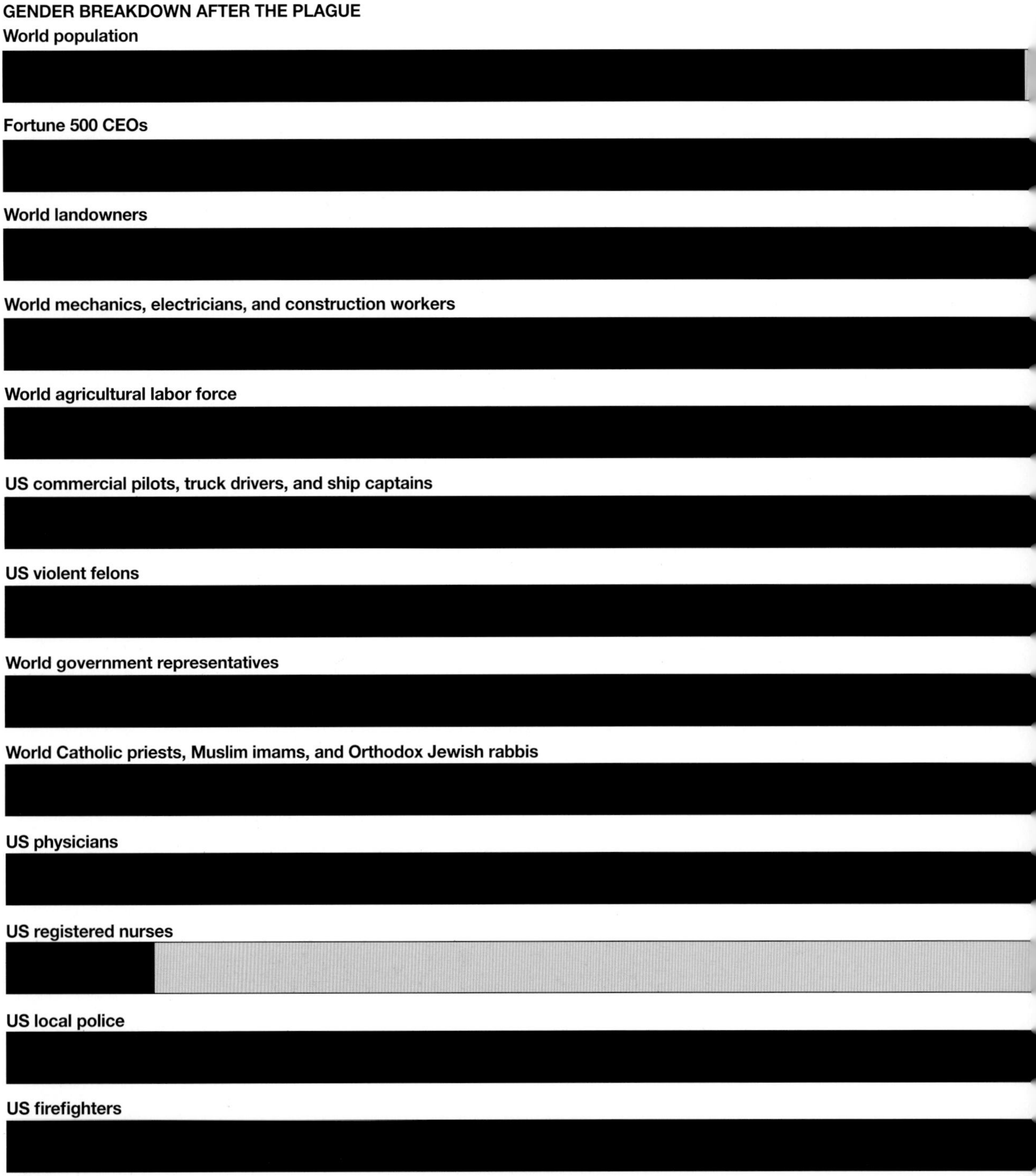
GENDER BREAKDOWN AFTER THE PLAGUE
World population
Fortune 500 CEOs
World landowners
World mechanics, electricians, and construction workers
World agricultural labor force
US commercial pilots, truck drivers, and ship captains
US violent felons
World government representatives
World Catholic priests, Muslim imams, and Orthodox Jewish rabbis
US physicians
US registered nurses
US local police
US firefighters

ons, and physicians now dead, this is what's left of the world.

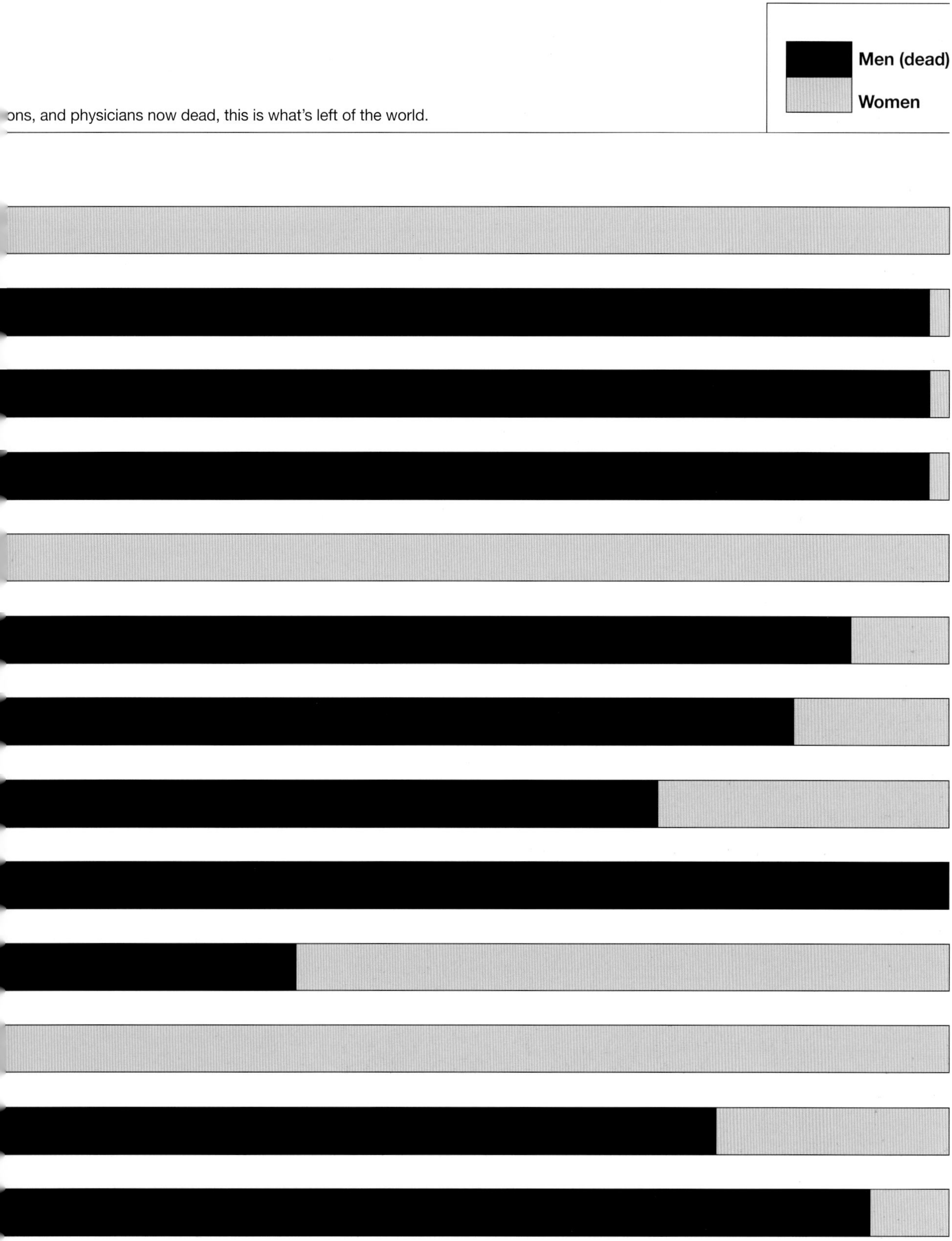

Men (dead)
Women

Why Guys Like Invisible Woman

☐ Her maiden name is Storm, which is just cool

☐ She makes force fields

☐ They're secretly hoping her clothes will turn invisible

Why Guys Relate to Spider-Man

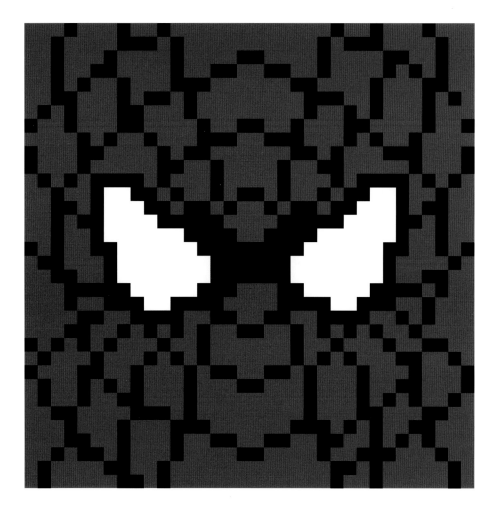

He's bullied in school

He has a crush on a girl out of his league

Constantly shoots sticky, white fluid from his body

Battle Breakdown

How Marvel characters stack up, according to the 1990 Marvel Universe Trading Cards Series.   Ⓥ = villain

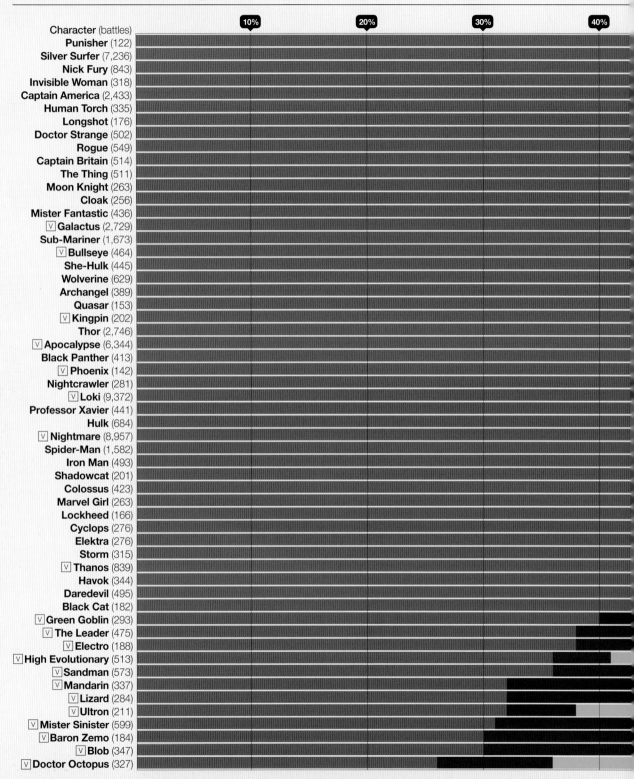

Character (battles)	10%	20%	30%	40%
Punisher (122)				
Silver Surfer (7,236)				
Nick Fury (843)				
Invisible Woman (318)				
Captain America (2,433)				
Human Torch (335)				
Longshot (176)				
Doctor Strange (502)				
Rogue (549)				
Captain Britain (514)				
The Thing (511)				
Moon Knight (263)				
Cloak (256)				
Mister Fantastic (436)				
Ⓥ Galactus (2,729)				
Sub-Mariner (1,673)				
Ⓥ Bullseye (464)				
She-Hulk (445)				
Wolverine (629)				
Archangel (389)				
Quasar (153)				
Ⓥ Kingpin (202)				
Thor (2,746)				
Ⓥ Apocalypse (6,344)				
Black Panther (413)				
Ⓥ Phoenix (142)				
Nightcrawler (281)				
Ⓥ Loki (9,372)				
Professor Xavier (441)				
Hulk (684)				
Ⓥ Nightmare (8,957)				
Spider-Man (1,582)				
Iron Man (493)				
Shadowcat (201)				
Colossus (423)				
Marvel Girl (263)				
Lockheed (166)				
Cyclops (276)				
Elektra (276)				
Storm (315)				
Ⓥ Thanos (839)				
Havok (344)				
Daredevil (495)				
Black Cat (182)				
Ⓥ Green Goblin (293)				
Ⓥ The Leader (475)				
Ⓥ Electro (188)				
Ⓥ High Evolutionary (513)				
Ⓥ Sandman (573)				
Ⓥ Mandarin (337)				
Ⓥ Lizard (284)				
Ⓥ Ultron (211)				
Ⓥ Mister Sinister (599)				
Ⓥ Baron Zemo (184)				
Ⓥ Blob (347)				
Ⓥ Doctor Octopus (327)				

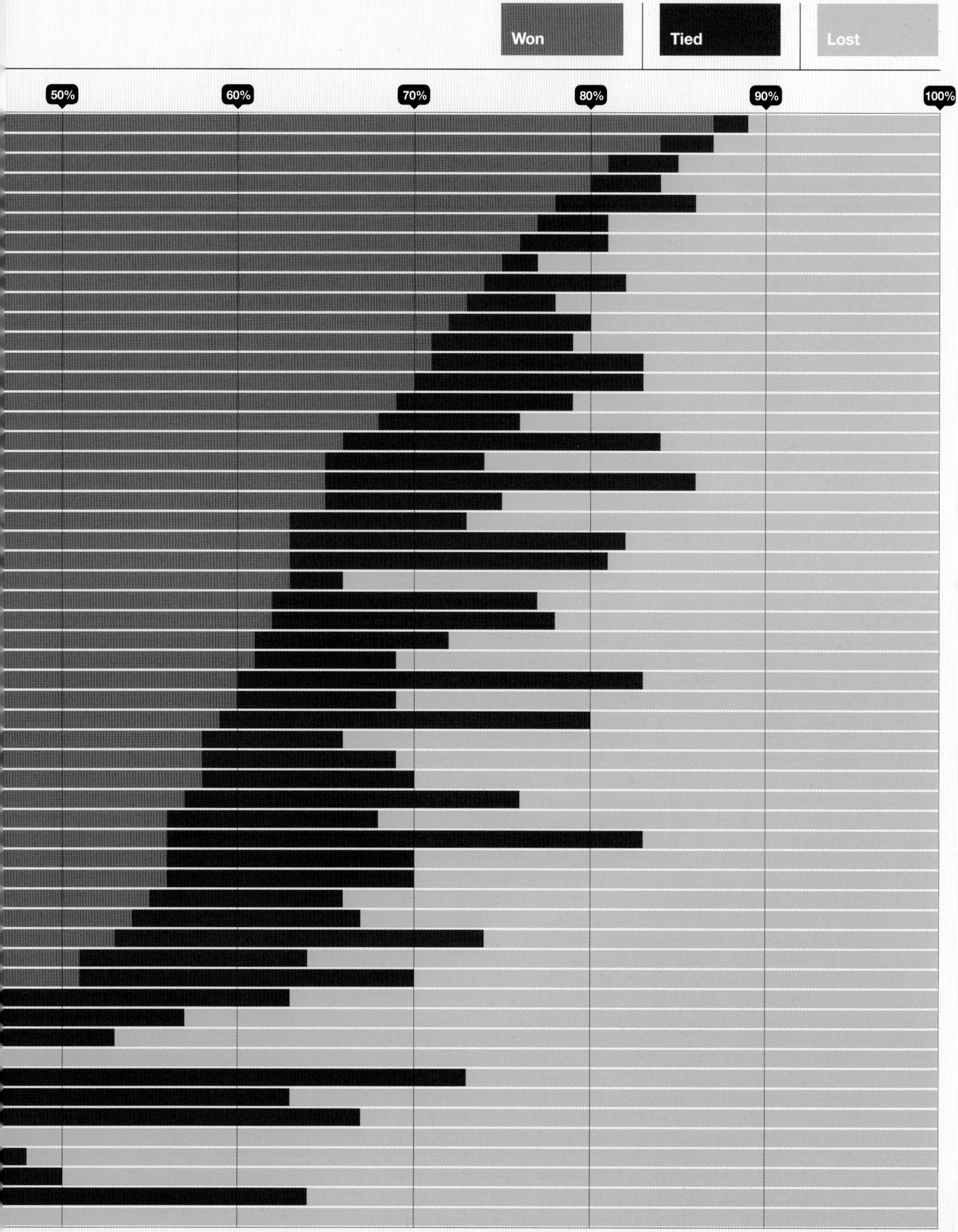
Won
Tied
Lost
50%
60%
70%
80%
90%
100%

The Five
Faces
of Robin

It's tough being Batman's sidekick. You get no thanks and crummy pay.
And some crazy guy in clown makeup is always trying to blow you up. It's
no wonder turnover for the position has been relatively high. Here's the
rundown of the five youths who have taken the mantle of the Boy Wonder
(and the characters they became afterwards).

⬤ Robin   ⬤ Nightwing   ⬤ Batman   ⬤ Red Hood   ⬤ Red Robin   ⬤ Batgirl

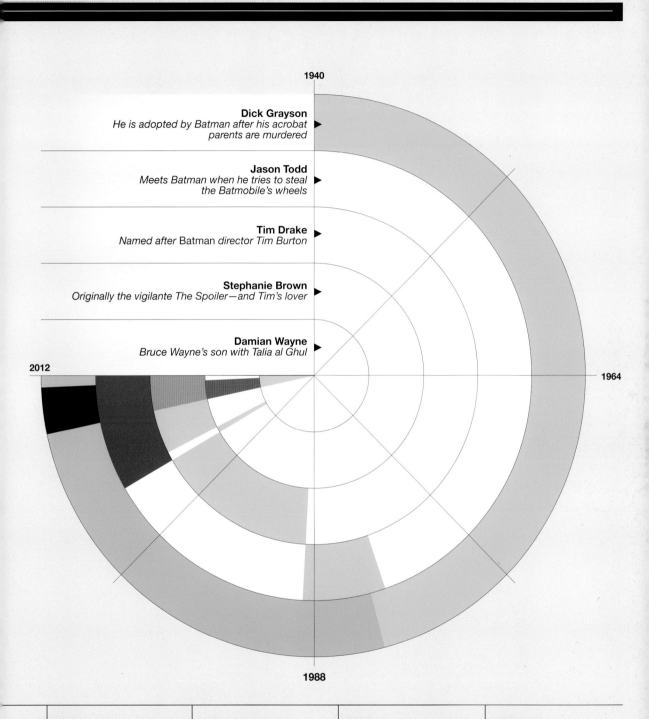

1940

1964

2012

1988

Dick Grayson
*He is adopted by Batman after his acrobat
parents are murdered* ▶

Jason Todd
*Meets Batman when he tries to steal
the Batmobile's wheels* ▶

Tim Drake
Named after Batman director Tim Burton ▶

Stephanie Brown
Originally the vigilante The Spoiler—and Tim's lover ▶

Damian Wayne
Bruce Wayne's son with Talia al Ghul ▶

1988
Fans kill the widely disliked Jason Todd by voting for his death in a phone-in campaign. He returns, miraculously, in 2005 as the anti-hero Red Hood.

2006
Batman meets his previously unknown ten-year-old son Damian, whom The League of Assassins grew in a lab and trained to be a killer.

2004
Stephanie gets the boot after refusing to follow orders. Oh, and then she fakes her death after inadvertently starting a Gotham gang war.

2009
Dick becomes Batman for a bit when Bruce Wayne is sent through time by Darkseid's Omega beams.

The Chris Ware Sadness Scale

Chris Ware's work blends succinct, emotional storytelling with high-end illustration and graphic design.
His work is beautiful, colorful . . . and really, really sad.

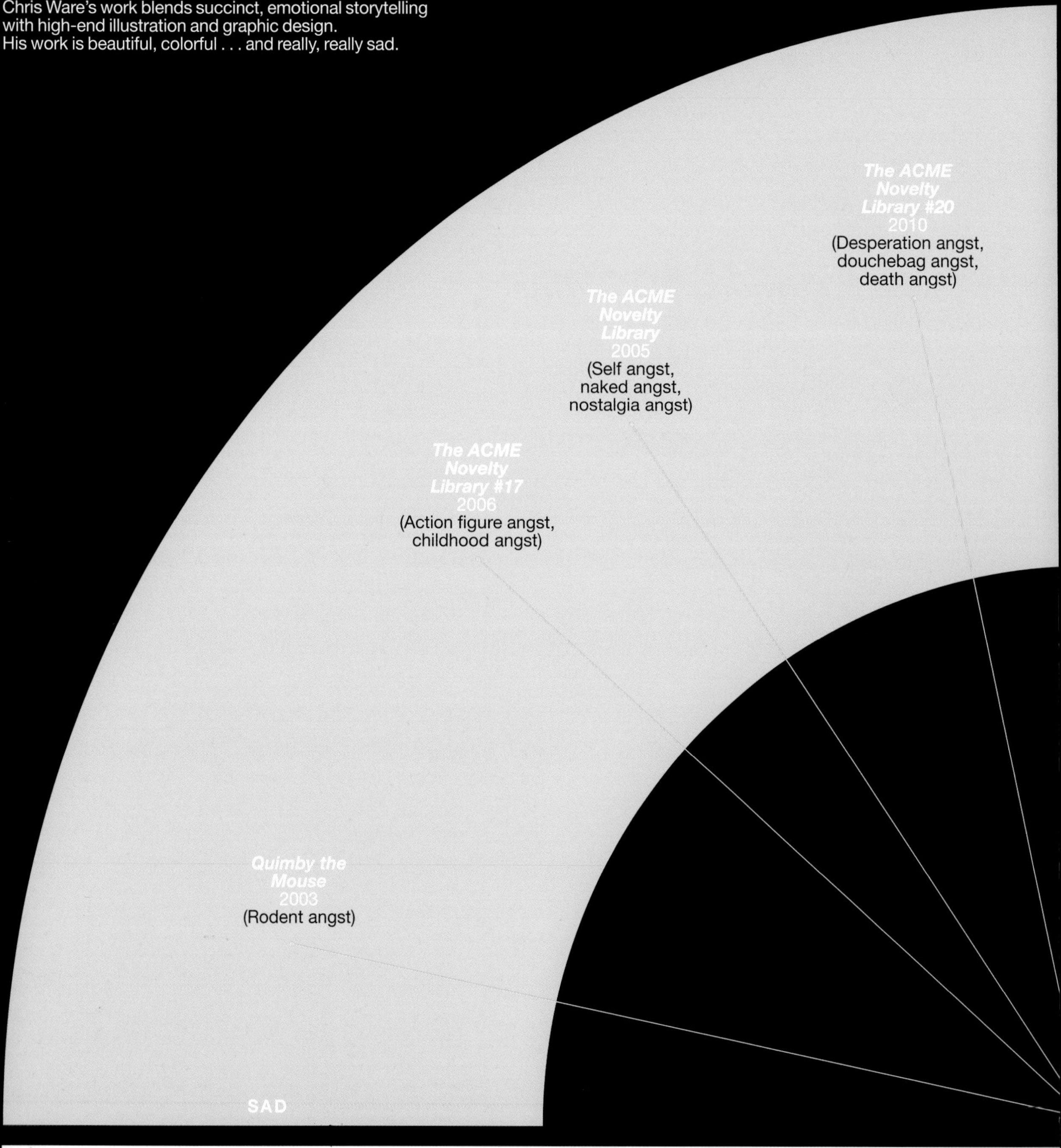

The ACME Novelty Library #20
2010
(Desperation angst, douchebag angst, death angst)
The ACME Novelty Library
2005
(Self angst, naked angst, nostalgia angst)
The ACME Novelty Library #17
2006
(Action figure angst, childhood angst)
Quimby the Mouse
2003
(Rodent angst)
SAD

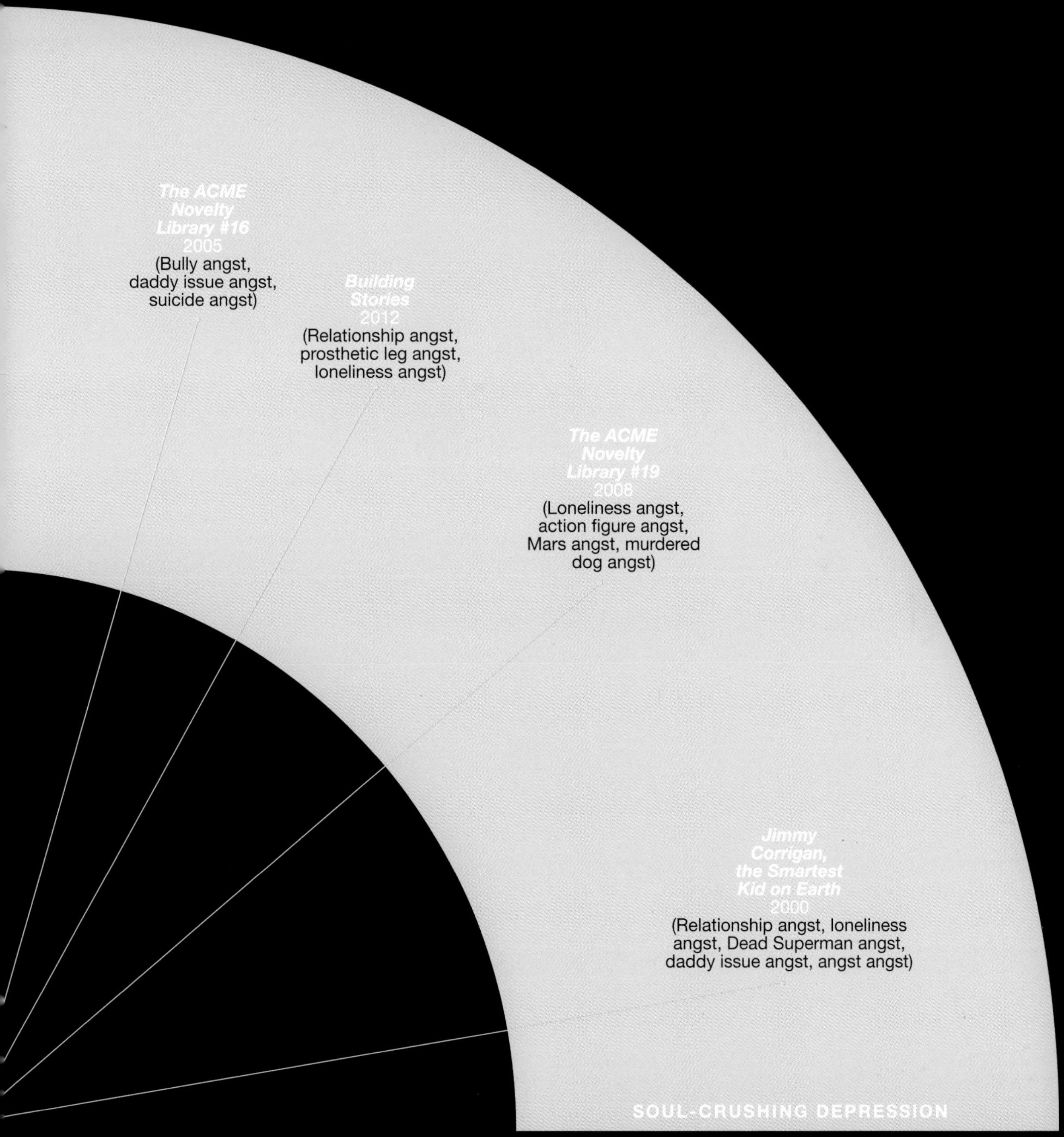
The ACME Novelty Library #16
2005
(Bully angst, daddy issue angst, suicide angst)
Building Stories
2012
(Relationship angst, prosthetic leg angst, loneliness angst)
The ACME Novelty Library #19
2008
(Loneliness angst, action figure angst, Mars angst, murdered dog angst)
Jimmy Corrigan, the Smartest Kid on Earth
2000
(Relationship angst, loneliness angst, Dead Superman angst, daddy issue angst, angst angst)
SOUL-CRUSHING DEPRESSION

META HUMAN

Pop Culture in *Scott Pilgrim*

Although Bryan Lee O'Malley's series may star a Canadian slacker, its set of cultural references are absolutely on point, from Scott Pilgrim's band's name (Sex Bob-Omb) to his ex-girlfriend's (The Clash at Demonhead).

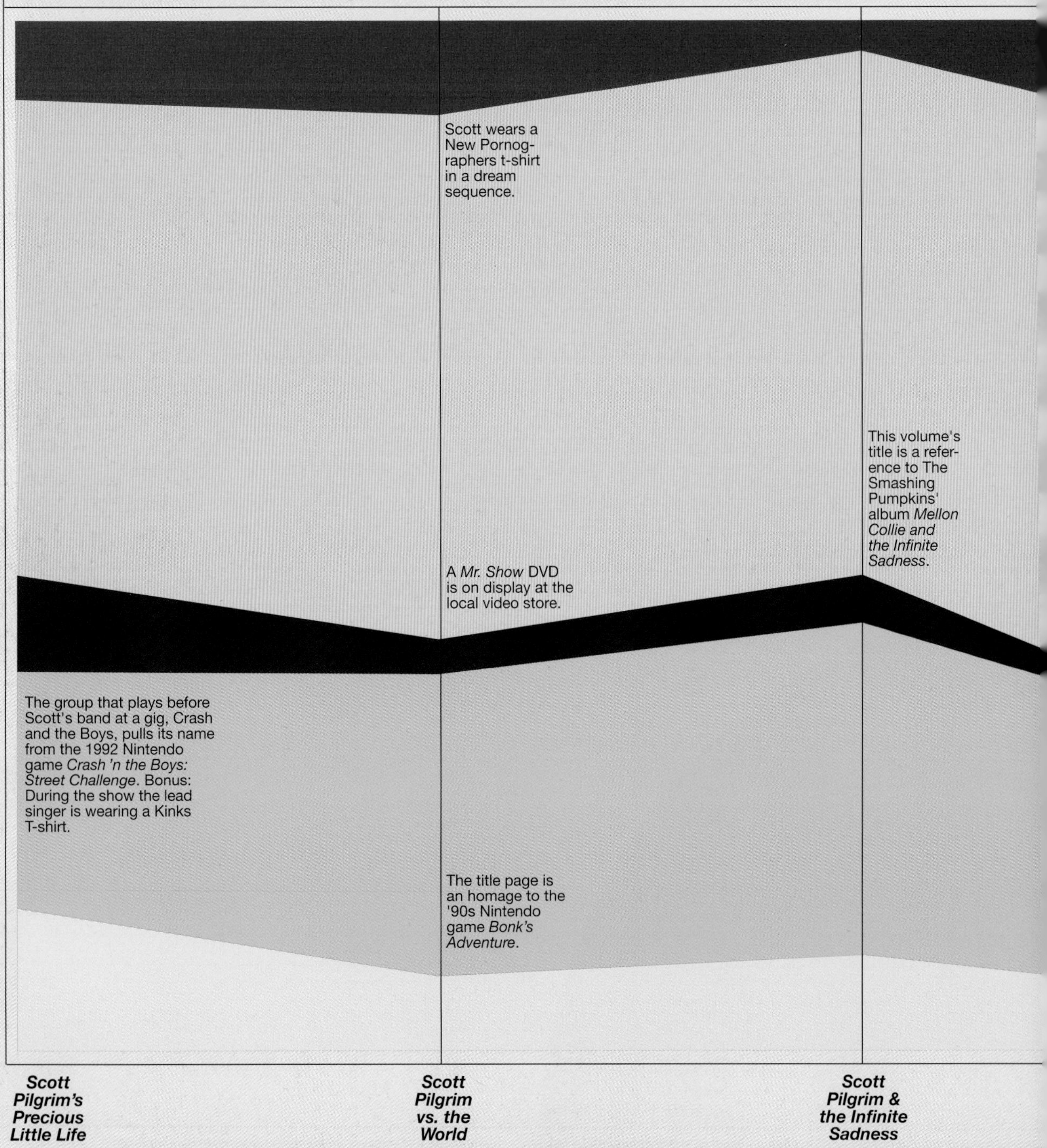

Scott wears a New Pornographers t-shirt in a dream sequence.
This volume's title is a reference to The Smashing Pumpkins' album *Mellon Collie and the Infinite Sadness*.
A *Mr. Show* DVD is on display at the local video store.
The group that plays before Scott's band at a gig, Crash and the Boys, pulls its name from the 1992 Nintendo game *Crash 'n the Boys: Street Challenge*. Bonus: During the show the lead singer is wearing a Kinks T-shirt.
The title page is an homage to the '90s Nintendo game *Bonk's Adventure*.
Scott Pilgrim's Precious Little Life
Scott Pilgrim vs. the World
Scott Pilgrim & the Infinite Sadness

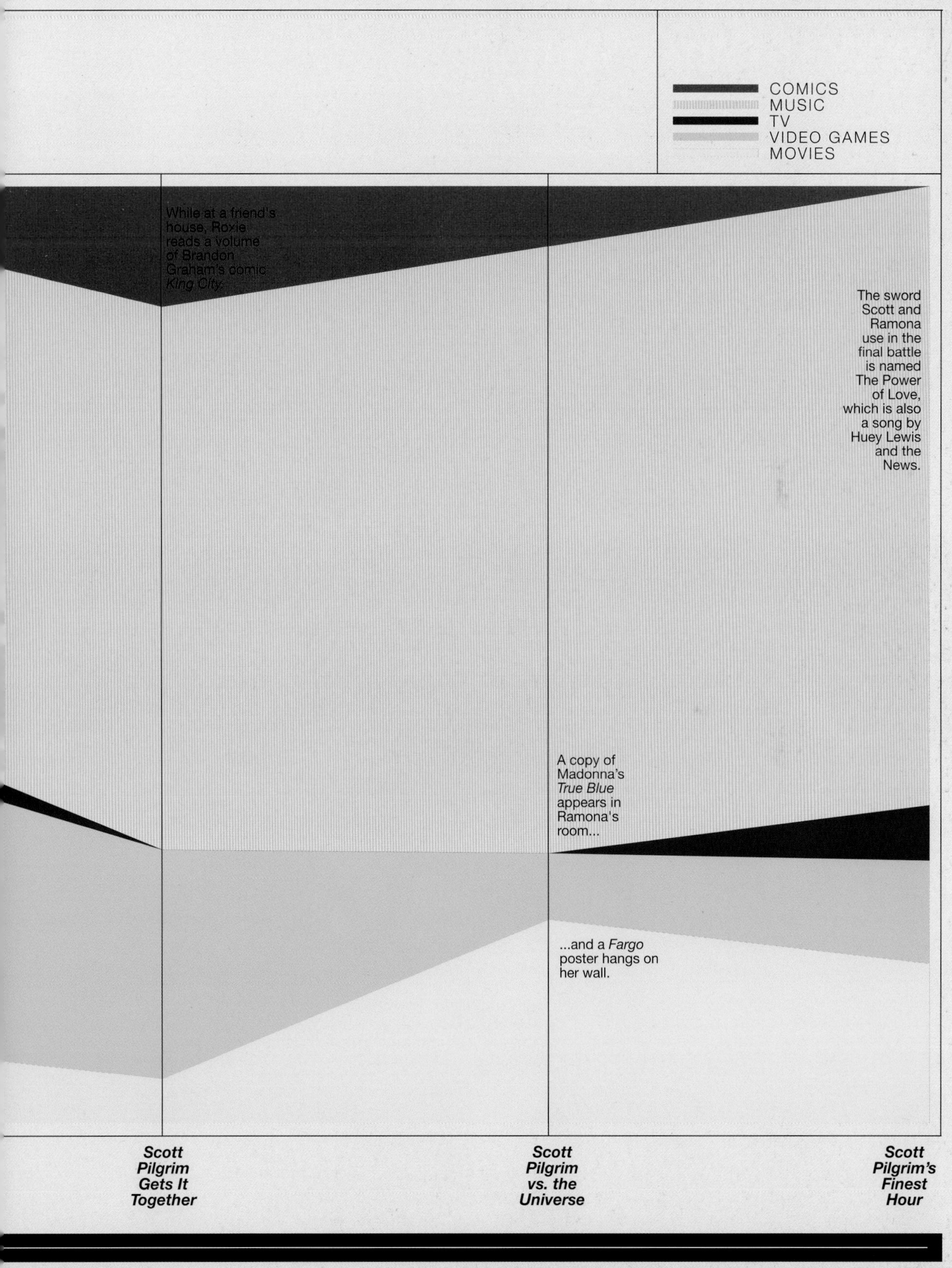
COMICS
MUSIC
TV
VIDEO GAMES
MOVIES
While at a friend's house, Roxie reads a volume of Brandon Graham's comic *King City.*
The sword Scott and Ramona use in the final battle is named The Power of Love, which is also a song by Huey Lewis and the News.
A copy of Madonna's *True Blue* appears in Ramona's room...
...and a *Fargo* poster hangs on her wall.
Scott Pilgrim Gets It Together
Scott Pilgrim vs. the Universe
Scott Pilgrim's Finest Hour

Venom's Family Web

When Spider-Man receives a new, black costume in 1984's *Secret Wars* storyline, it turns out the outfit is actually alive. It's a Symbiote, or a member of an alien race that gives powers to the host it bonds with. Spider-Man eventually rejects the Symbiote and the costume escapes, quickly finding a new host in the former *Daily Bugle* reporter Eddie Brock. Brock and the Symbiote bond, and together they become Venom, creating one of Spider-Man's arch rivals. The Symbiote, however, doesn't stop at Brock. It's history with hosts, transformations and offspring (yup, the costume has spawn) created a tangled...er, web of hosts.

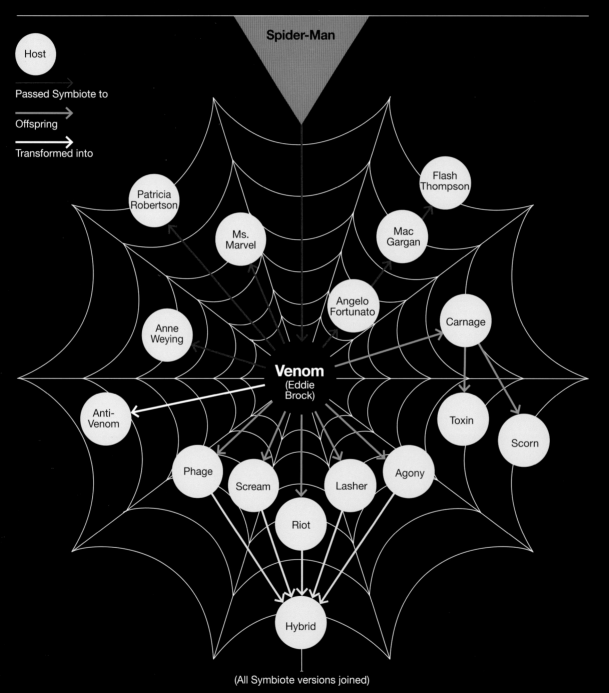

Host

Passed Symbiote to

Offspring

Transformed into

Spider-Man

Patricia Robertson

Ms. Marvel

Flash Thompson

Mac Gargan

Angelo Fortunato

Carnage

Anne Weying

Venom (Eddie Brock)

Anti-Venom

Toxin

Scorn

Phage

Scream

Lasher

Agony

Riot

Hybrid

(All Symbiote versions joined)

Explaining Cosplay and Crossplay

Want to dress up as your favorite character? Make sure you know what terms are in fashion.

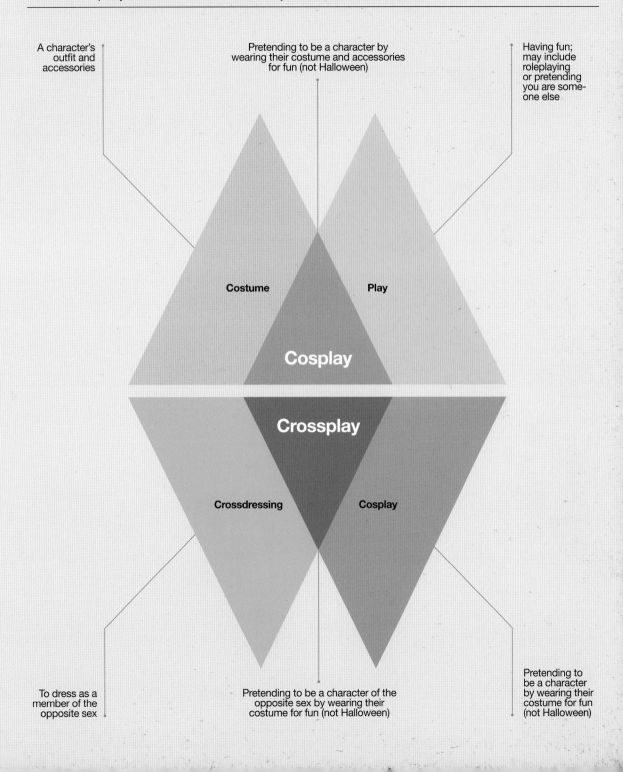

A character's outfit and accessories

Pretending to be a character by wearing their costume and accessories for fun (not Halloween)

Having fun; may include roleplaying or pretending you are someone else

Costume

Play

Cosplay

Crossplay

Crossdressing

Cosplay

To dress as a member of the opposite sex

Pretending to be a character of the opposite sex by wearing their costume for fun (not Halloween)

Pretending to be a character by wearing their costume for fun (not Halloween)

NERD PROM

Comic-Con Attendance

San Diego Comic-Con International has attracted more than 100,000 people every year since 2005. It's a beacon for comics, movies, and video games—a major pop-culture force. But it wasn't always the behemoth it is today; when it started more than 40 years ago as the Golden State Comic-Con, it was just a few hundred people talking about comics. Here's how the biggest event in comics has grown up.

March 1970
145 people turn up for a one-day miniature convention to raise money for a bigger show that August.

1972
The name changes to San Diego's West Coast Comic Convention.

1975
Guests include Milton Caniff, Frank Capra, Chuck Jones, Russ Manning, and Charles Schulz. It's the first year of the costume masquerade.

1984
The convention takes place in June—a month earlier than usual because of the summer Olympics in Los Angeles.

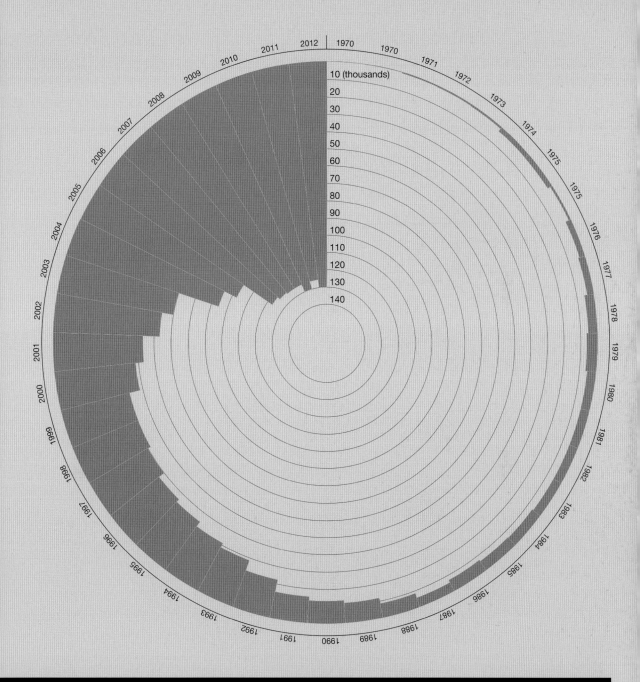

10 (thousands)
20
30
40
50
60
70
80
90
100
110
120
130
140

1970 1970 1971 1972 1973 1974 1975 1975 1976 1977 1978 1979 1980 1981 1982 1983 1984 1985 1986 1987 1988 1989 1990 1991 1992 1993 1994 1995 1996 1997 1998 1999 2000 2001 2002 2003 2004 2005 2006 2007 2008 2009 2010 2011 2012

1992
The convention hosts Jack Kirby's 75th birthday party. (The cake had vanilla icing).

1996
Due to the Republican National Convention in San Diego, Comic-Con is held a month earlier on July 4th.

2011
Between attendee spending, hotels, and taxes, Comic-Con brings in more than $162 million to San Diego.

2012
All passes sell out just 90 minutes after they become available online.

The Hulk

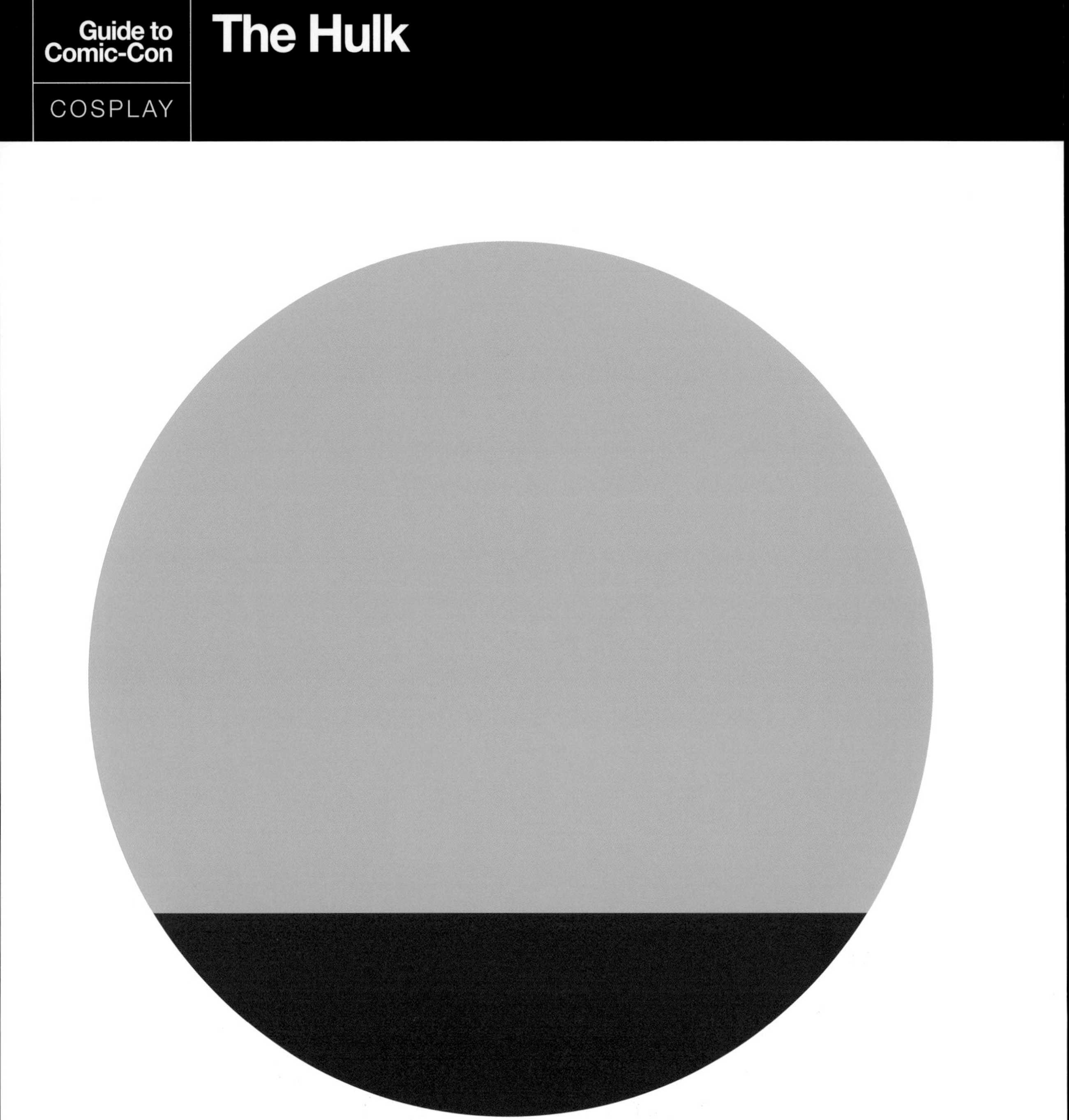

Bare skin Padded costume

X-Men Characters I Remembered Thanks to Cosplay

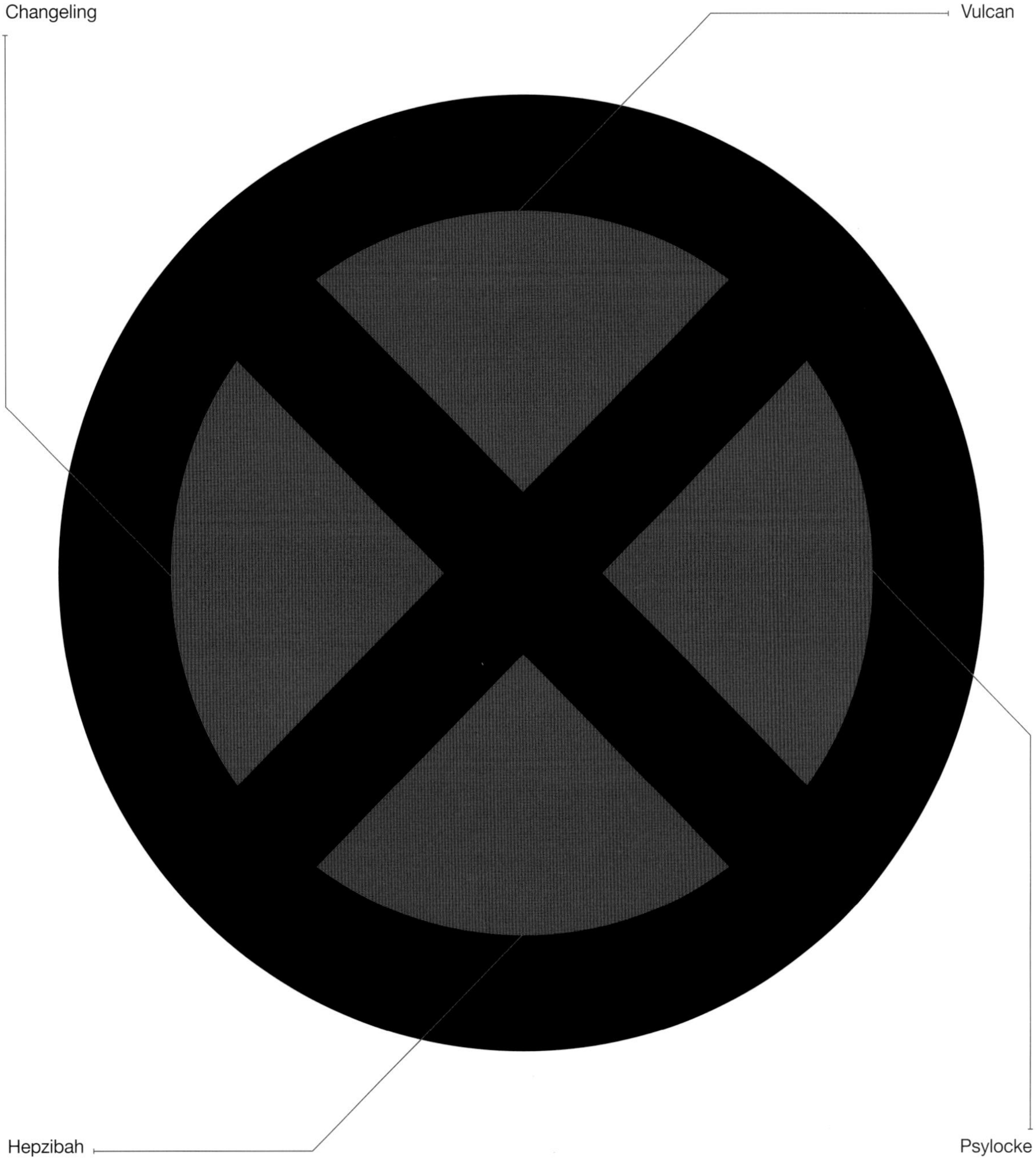
Changeling
Vulcan
Hepzibah
Psylocke

Spider-Man

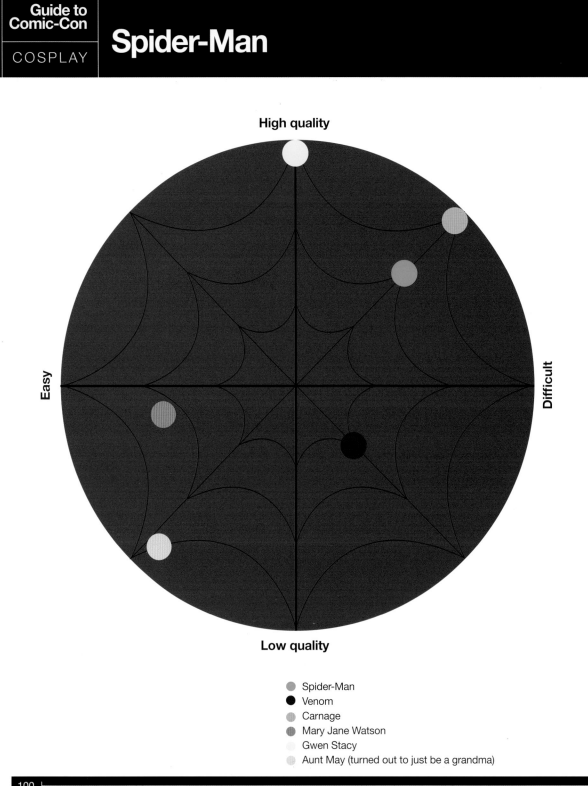

High quality

Easy

Difficult

Low quality

- Spider-Man
- Venom
- Carnage
- Mary Jane Watson
- Gwen Stacy
- Aunt May (turned out to just be a grandma)

Pac-Man

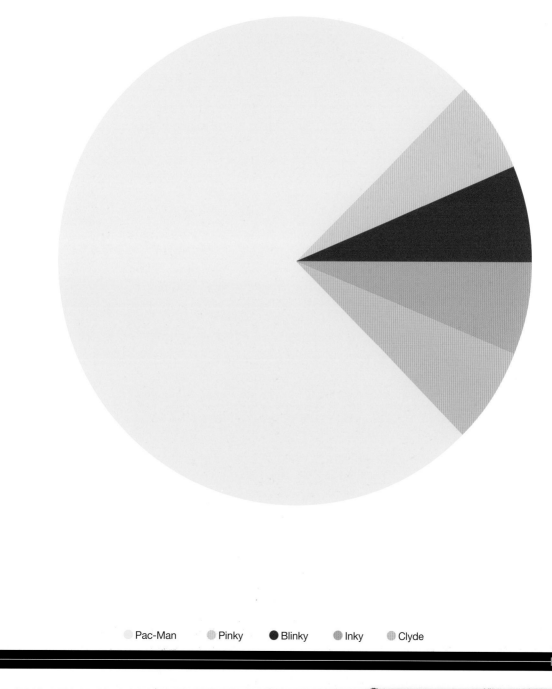

Pac-Man · Pinky · Blinky · Inky · Clyde

Wolverine

by prevalence of defining feature

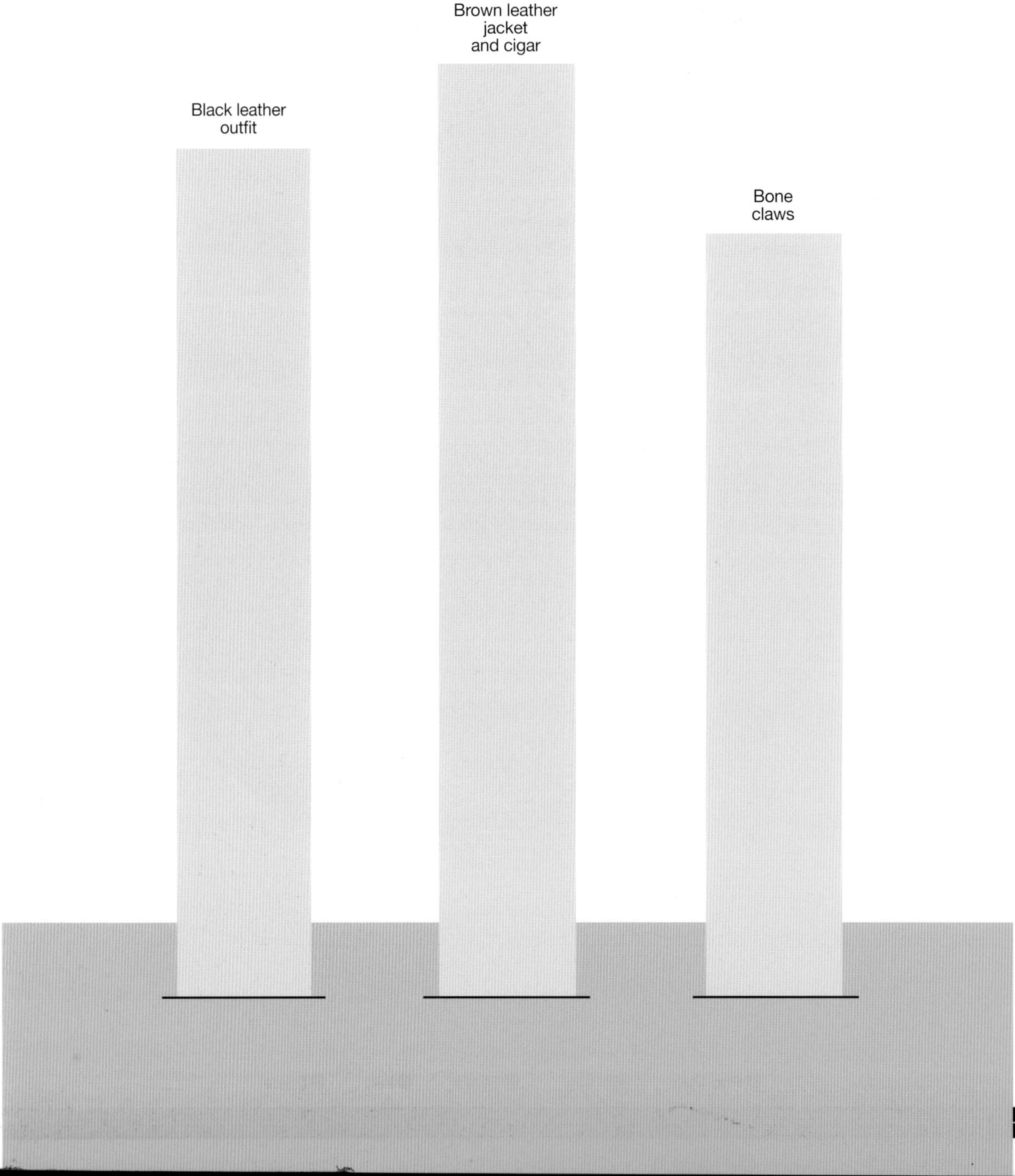
Black leather outfit
Brown leather jacket and cigar
Bone claws

Popular Costumes

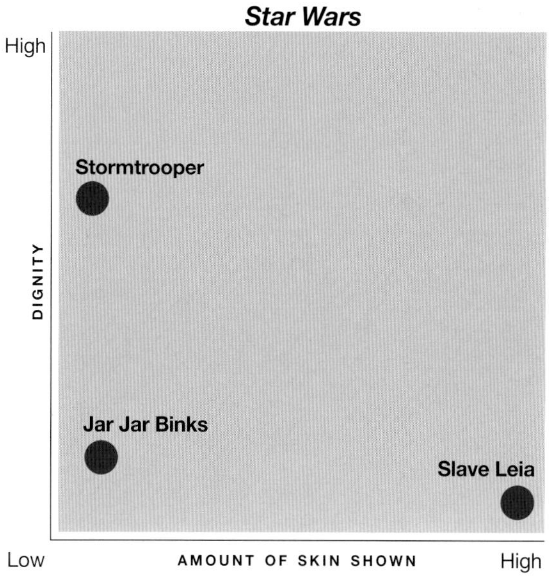
Star Wars
High
Stormtrooper
DIGNITY
Jar Jar Binks
Slave Leia
Low
AMOUNT OF SKIN SHOWN
High

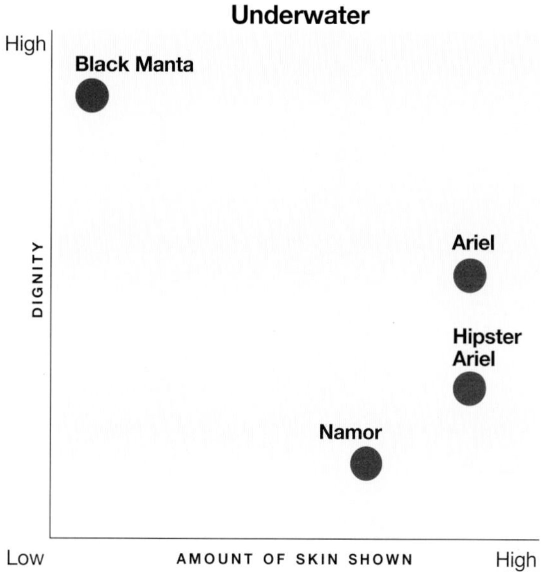
Underwater
High
Black Manta
DIGNITY
Ariel
Hipster Ariel
Namor
Low
AMOUNT OF SKIN SHOWN
High

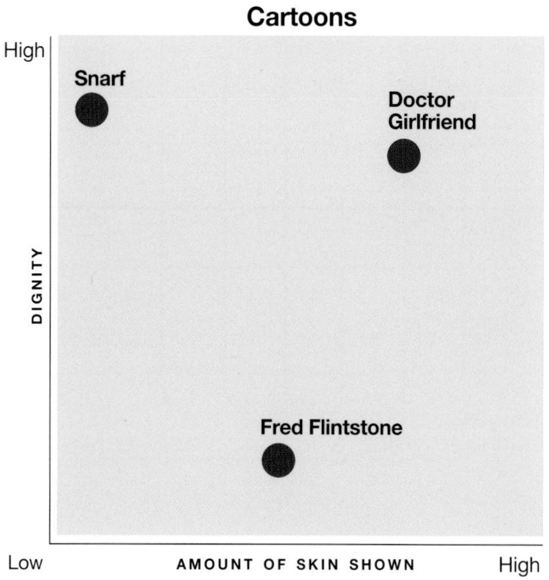
Cartoons
High
Snarf
Doctor Girlfriend
DIGNITY
Fred Flintstone
Low
AMOUNT OF SKIN SHOWN
High

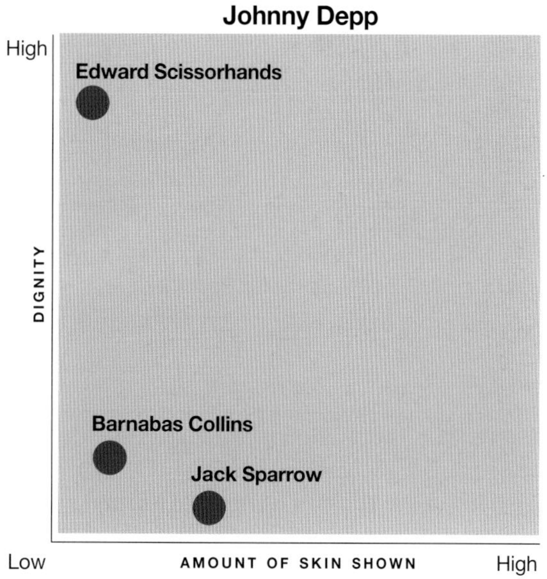
Johnny Depp
High
Edward Scissorhands
DIGNITY
Barnabas Collins
Jack Sparrow
Low
AMOUNT OF SKIN SHOWN
High

Outsmarting Death

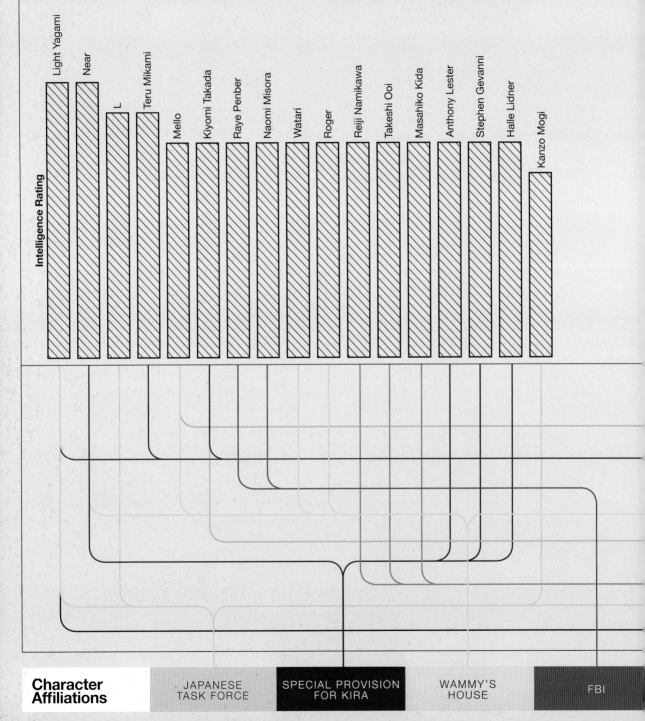

Intelligence Rating

Light Yagami
Near
L
Teru Mikami
Mello
Kiyomi Takada
Raye Penber
Naomi Misora
Watari
Roger
Reiji Namikawa
Takeshi Ooi
Masahiko Kida
Anthony Lester
Stephen Gevanni
Halle Lidner
Kanzo Mogi

Character Affiliations

JAPANESE TASK FORCE

SPECIAL PROVISION FOR KIRA

WAMMY'S HOUSE

FBI

In the manga thriller series *Death Note*, whiz kid Light Yagami uses a magical notebook belonging to a Death God to kill criminals, calling himself "Kira." The police try figuring out who Kira is so they can stop him. The result is an intense game of cat and mouse with allegiances betrayed just as fast as they're made and each side trying to outsmart the other to victory. Below are the intelligence ratings for the significant characters in this 12-volume series, as noted by creators Tsugumi Ohba and Takeshi Obata, and how they're all connected.

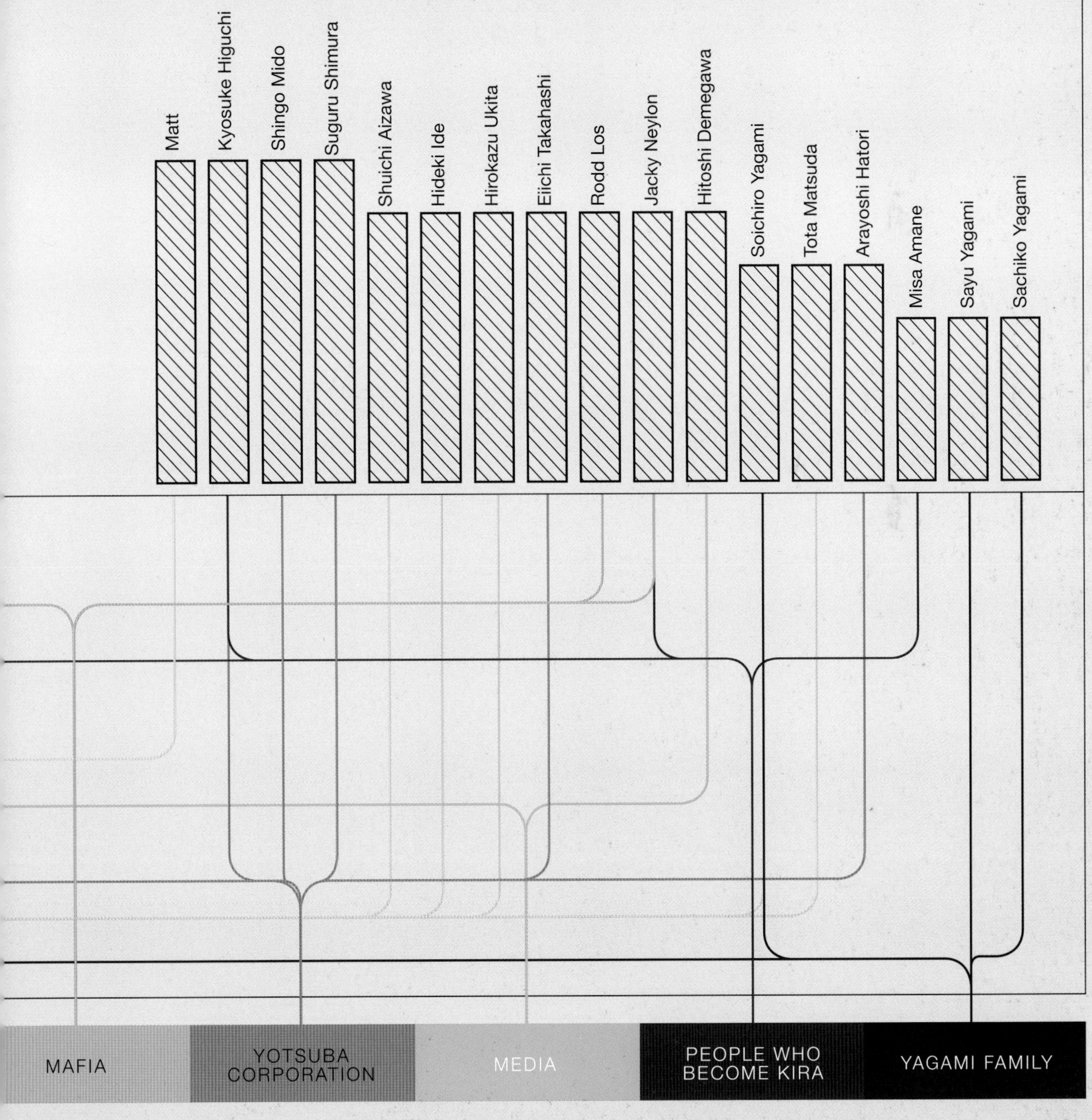

Matt
Kyosuke Higuchi
Shingo Mido
Suguru Shimura
Shuichi Aizawa
Hideki Ide
Hirokazu Ukita
Eiichi Takahashi
Rodd Los
Jacky Neylon
Hitoshi Demegawa
Soichiro Yagami
Tota Matsuda
Arayoshi Hatori
Misa Amane
Sayu Yagami
Sachiko Yagami
MAFIA
YOTSUBA CORPORATION
MEDIA
PEOPLE WHO BECOME KIRA
YAGAMI FAMILY

Boom Boom Pow

Comics have influenced rap more than any other genre of music. Here's a look at where the two intersect.

Match-ups in *Secret Wars*

Philadelphia rapper The Last Emperor released the ultimate comic book rap song in 1997, titled "Secret Wars, Part 1" (a reference to the infamous Marvel crossover series). In the song Last Emperor details an epic battle between rappers and comic book characters. He followed it with "Secret Wars, Part 2" in 2003, which included even more cross-platform fights. Here's who took the title in each.

★ = winner

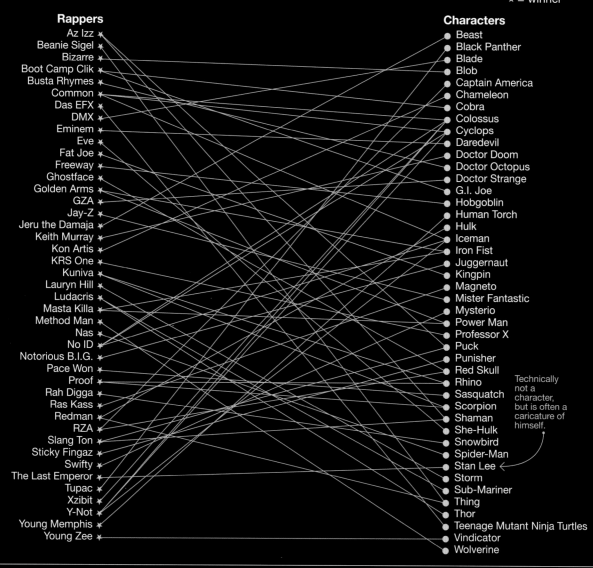

Rappers
Az Izz
Beanie Sigel
Bizarre
Boot Camp Clik
Busta Rhymes
Common
Das EFX
DMX
Eminem
Eve
Fat Joe
Freeway
Ghostface
Golden Arms
GZA
Jay-Z
Jeru the Damaja
Keith Murray
Kon Artis
KRS One
Kuniva
Lauryn Hill
Ludacris
Masta Killa
Method Man
Nas
No ID
Notorious B.I.G.
Pace Won
Proof
Rah Digga
Ras Kass
Redman
RZA
Slang Ton
Sticky Fingaz
Swifty
The Last Emperor
Tupac
Xzibit
Y-Not
Young Memphis
Young Zee
Characters
Beast
Black Panther
Blade
Blob
Captain America
Chameleon
Cobra
Colossus
Cyclops
Daredevil
Doctor Doom
Doctor Octopus
Doctor Strange
G.I. Joe
Hobgoblin
Human Torch
Hulk
Iceman
Iron Fist
Juggernaut
Kingpin
Magneto
Mister Fantastic
Mysterio
Power Man
Professor X
Puck
Punisher
Red Skull
Rhino
Sasquatch
Scorpion
Shaman
She-Hulk
Snowbird
Spider-Man
Stan Lee
Storm
Sub-Mariner
Thing
Thor
Teenage Mutant Ninja Turtles
Vindicator
Wolverine
Technically not a character, but is often a caricature of himself.

Microphone check

The quality of comic books written by rappers:

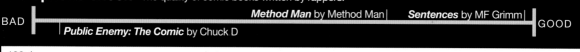

BAD — *Public Enemy: The Comic* by Chuck D — ***Method Man*** by Method Man — ***Sentences*** by MF Grimm — GOOD

Snoop Dogg's "Batman & Robin" (feat. Lady of Rage, RBX), 2002

WORD FREQUENCY

Batman

Robin

Gotham

VILLAINS MENTIONED

Two-Face Catwoman
Riddler   Clayface

Penguin   Mad Hatter
         Mr. Freeze

BAT-GADGETS MENTIONED

Batmobile Bat bomb
Bat switches   Bat cave

Bat phone   Bat gat
         Bat engine

Rappers who take their names from comics

Professor X the Overseer
Professor X is the founder of the X-Men

David Banner
The Hulk's alter ego in the 1978 TV show *The Incredible Hulk*

Mista Sinista
Mister Sinister is a villain of the X-Men

MF Doom
Fantastic Four foe Dr. Doom

X-Ecutioners
This DJ crew was originally called The X-Men until Marvel sued them

DJ Clark Kent
Clark Kent, a.k.a Superman

Big Pun
The Punisher, but much bigger

DJ Green Lantern
Green Lantern, obviously

Jean Grae
Jean Grey is a founding member of the X-Men

Tony Starks
Ghostface Killah's alter ego is pretty close to Iron Man's Tony Stark

Johnny Blaze
Ghost Rider's alter ego (as well as Method Man's)

Eminem's comic history

● Audio ● Print ● Video

1999	**My Name Is** *"Clothes ripped like the Incredible Hulk"*
2000	**Say Goodbye Hollywood** *"Bury my face in comic books, 'cause I don't want to look"*
2001	**Business** *"looks like Batman brought his own Robin"*
2002	**Superman** The title of the 13th track on *The Eminem Show*
	Wanted The appearance of the main character in the comic was based on Eminem. It later became a hit movie.
2003	**Without Me** Wore a Robin costume in the music video
2004	**Rain Man** *"I killed Superman, I killed Super—man"*
2005	**GATman and Robbin** He is featured on this 50 Cent track
2006	**Crack a Bottle** *"Not to mention back with a vengeance so here's the signal, of the bat symbol"*
2007	**My Mom** *"I fall in bed with a bottle of meds and a Heath Ledger bobblehead"* (The Joker)
2008	**The Punisher** Marvel created an Eminem/Punisher digital comic titled *Kill You*
2009	**Cold Wind Blows** *"When the Aquaman drowns and the Human Torch starts swimming"*
2010	**Love the Way You Lie** *"I'm Superman with the wind in his back, She's Lois Lane"*
2011	**On Fire** *"Flows tighter, hot headed as Ghost Rider, cold hearted as Spider-Man throwin' a spider in the snow"*
2012	**Won't Back Down** *"I gave Bruce Wayne a Valium"*

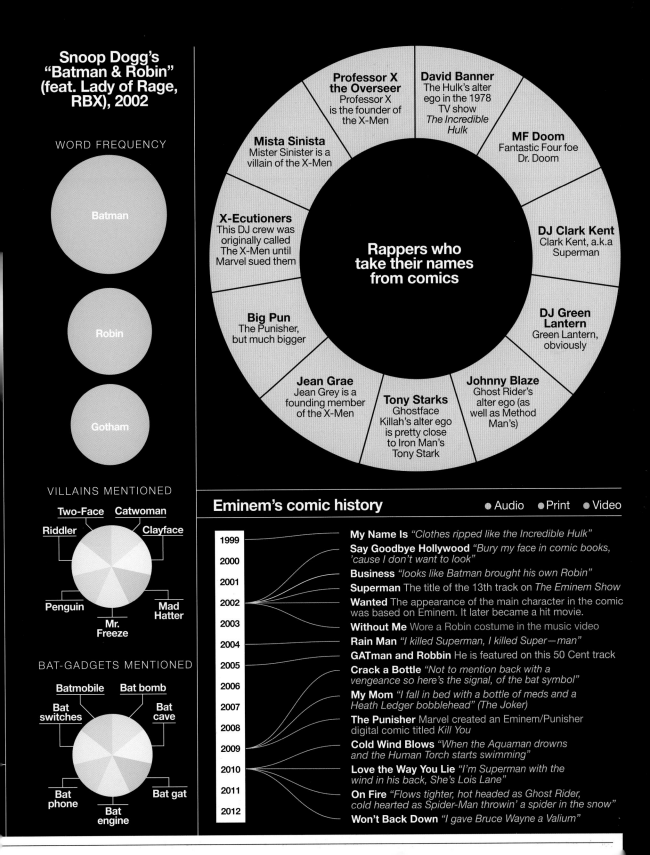

A Personal History of Saying "Good Grief"

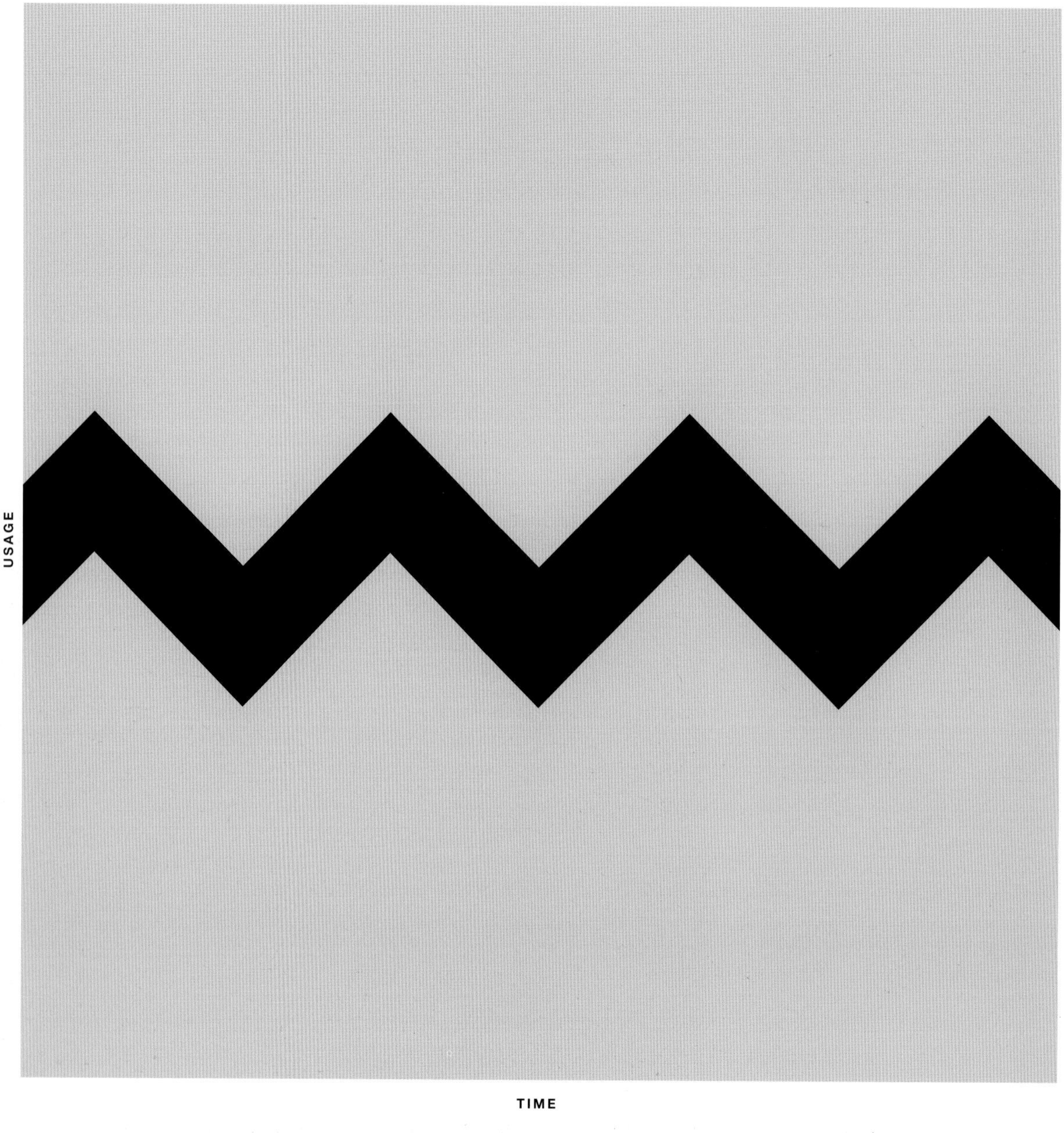
USAGE
TIME

ALTER EGOS

Bobby Digital vs. Batman

In 1998, the rapper RZA, best known for being the unofficial leader of the Wu-Tang Clan, released his first solo album under the pseudonym Bobby Digital, a futuristic superhero. RZA stuck close to the persona and after a while, the rapper's life began looking somewhat familiar.

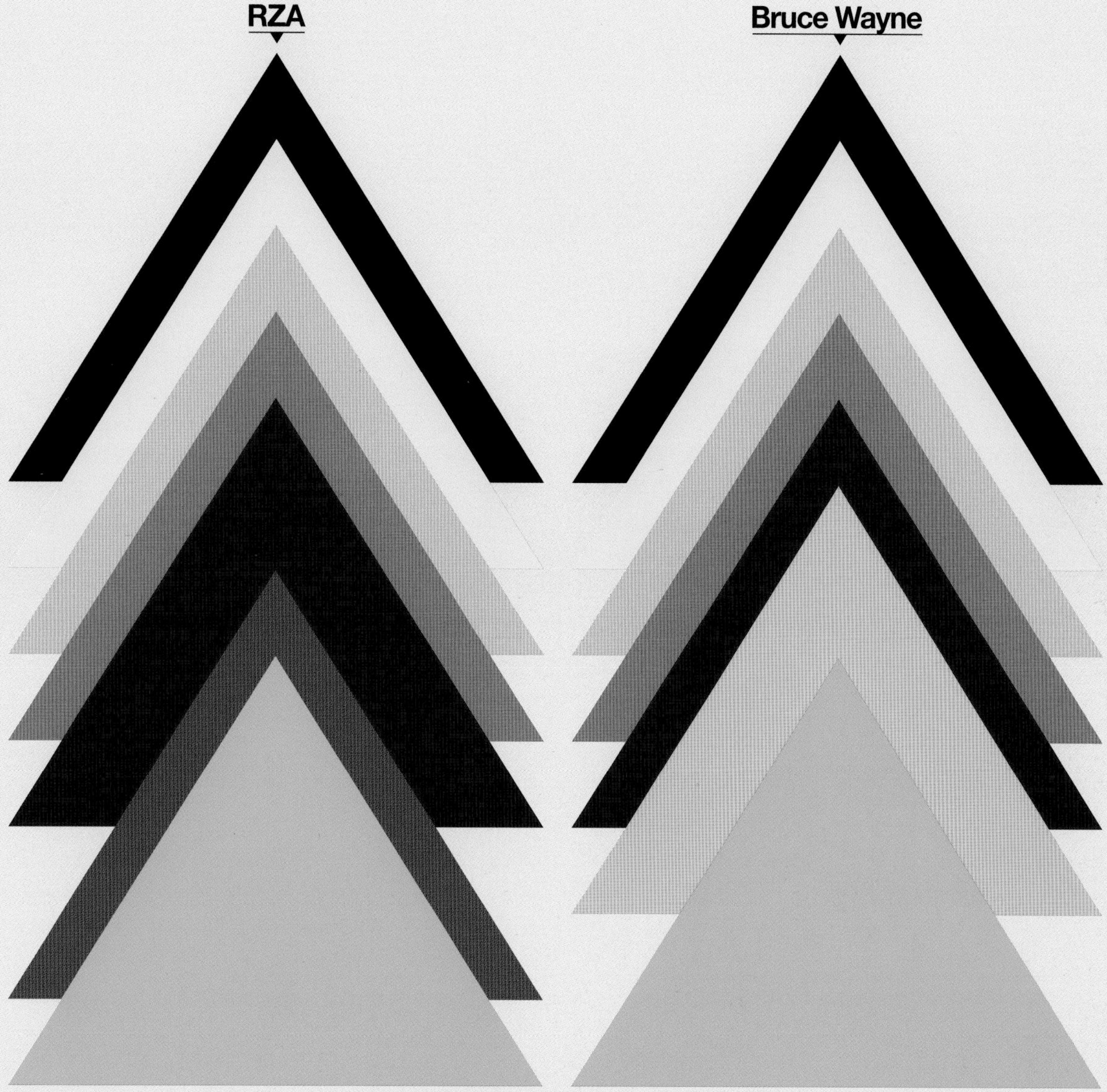

RZA
Bruce Wayne

▲ Superhero alter-ego ▲ Extremely wealthy ▲ Butler on staff ▲ Bomb-proof and bulletproof custom car
▲ Bulletproof and knife-proof super-suit
▲ Crime-fighter ▲ Gold album ▲ Cover by artist Bill Sienkiewicz

Married
Killed this person →

APOKOLIPS

ALL IN THE FAMILY

Mapping the Relationships of the New Gods

NEW GENESIS

When master storyteller Jack Kirby started working for DC Comics in the early '70s, he introduced one of comic's most memorable creations: The Fourth World, and its inhabitants, The New Gods. With action that spanned four titles (*Superman's Pal Jimmy Olsen*, *The Forever People*, *Mister Miracle*, and *The New Gods*), the story follows the ruling families of two planets (New Genesis, led by Highfather, and Apokolips, led by Darkseid) through a messy and murderous battle.

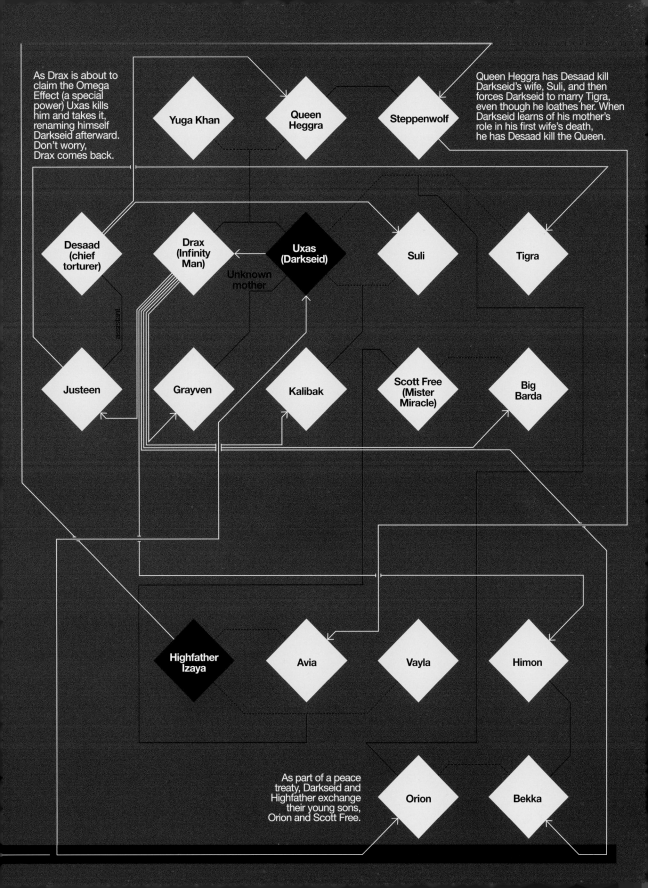

As Drax is about to claim the Omega Effect (a special power) Uxas kills him and takes it, renaming himself Darkseid afterward. Don't worry, Drax comes back.

Queen Heggra has Desaad kill Darkseid's wife, Suli, and then forces Darkseid to marry Tigra, even though he loathes her. When Darkseid learns of his mother's role in his first wife's death, he has Desaad kill the Queen.

Yuga Khan

Queen Heggra

Steppenwolf

Desaad (chief torturer)

Drax (Infinity Man)

Uxas (Darkseid)

Unknown mother

Suli

Tigra

assistant

Justeen

Grayven

Kalibak

Scott Free (Mister Miracle)

Big Barda

Highfather Izaya

Avia

Vayla

Himon

As part of a peace treaty, Darkseid and Highfather exchange their young sons, Orion and Scott Free.

Orion

Bekka

Spy vs.Spy

Soon after he started at *MAD* magazine in 1960, Antonio Prohías introduced one of the most recognizable cartoons, well . . . ever. *Spy vs. Spy* ran for more than 25 years under his hand, starting in January of 1961, and featured two pointy guys constantly trying to off each other. Here's how they matched up.

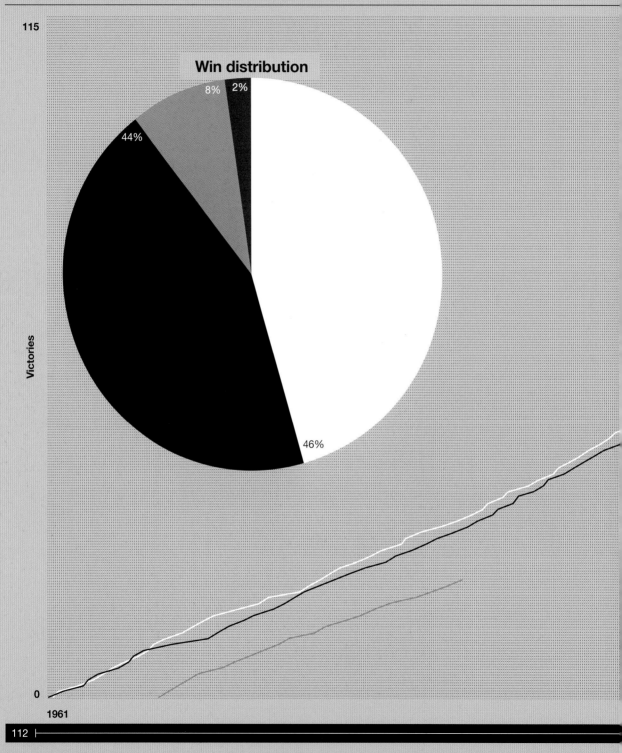

115

Win distribution

2%

8%

44%

46%

Victories

0

1961

Live free and spy hard

Prohías began his career as a political satirist in Cuba. He expressed his distaste for the politics of the new dictator, Fidel Castro, through his cartoons, which led to his firing, spying accusations, and even death threats. He fled to the United States three days before Castro's government took control of the last of the Cuban free press. Prohías used Castro's spy accusations as inspiration for *MAD*'s most popular comic.

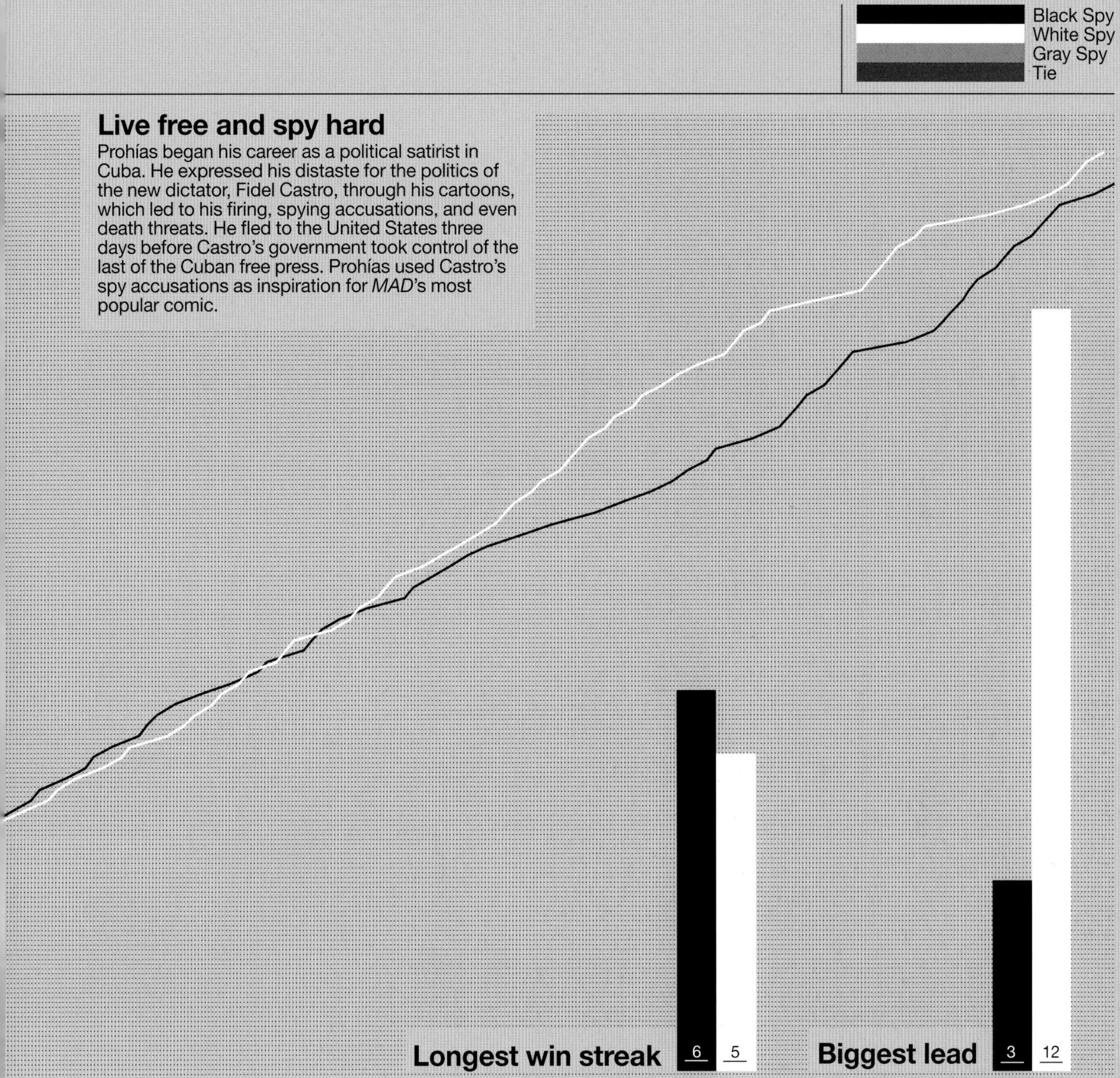
Black Spy
White Spy
Gray Spy
Tie
Longest win streak
6
5
Biggest lead
3
12

The Gray Spy

Prohías introduced a third, female spy in 1962, The Gray Spy, or The Lady in Gray. She won in every appearance, as she used her female prowess to pit the Black and White spies against each other.

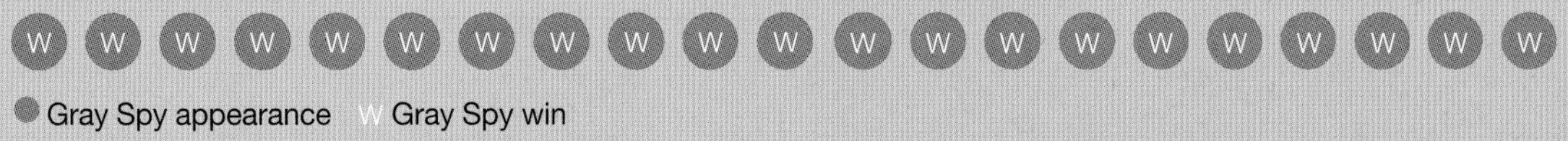
W W W W W W W W W W W W W W W W W W W W W
Gray Spy appearance
W Gray Spy win

1987

Avengers vs. X-Men

Forget long lines, in-seam patdowns, and body scanners at the airport, the Avengers and X-Men man their own jets.

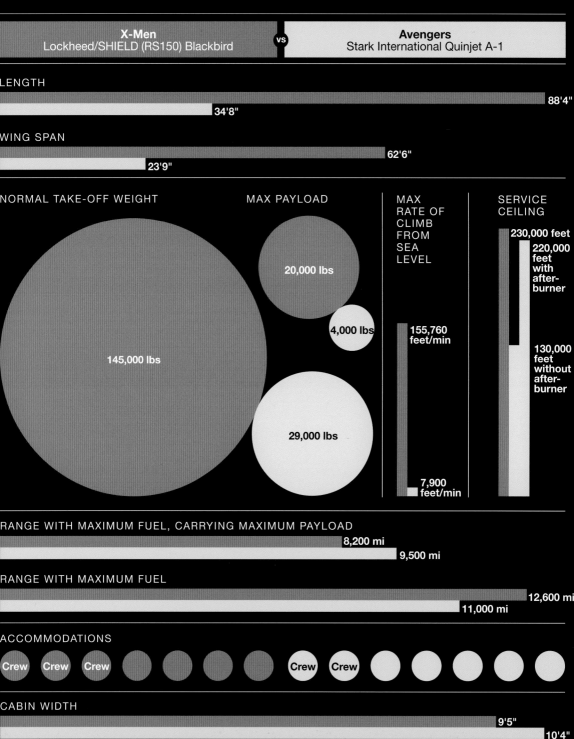

X-Men
Lockheed/SHIELD (RS150) Blackbird

vs

Avengers
Stark International Quinjet A-1

LENGTH
34'8"
88'4"

WING SPAN
23'9"
62'6"

NORMAL TAKE-OFF WEIGHT
145,000 lbs

MAX PAYLOAD
20,000 lbs
4,000 lbs
29,000 lbs

MAX RATE OF CLIMB FROM SEA LEVEL
155,760 feet/min
7,900 feet/min

SERVICE CEILING
230,000 feet
220,000 feet with after-burner
130,000 feet without after-burner

RANGE WITH MAXIMUM FUEL, CARRYING MAXIMUM PAYLOAD
8,200 mi
9,500 mi

RANGE WITH MAXIMUM FUEL
12,600 mi
11,000 mi

ACCOMMODATIONS
Crew Crew Crew
Crew Crew

CABIN WIDTH
9'5"
10'4"

BIRDS OF A FEATHER

Scrooge McDuck's Family Tree

The story of the McDucks actually dates back to AD 122 when the clan was known as the MacDuichs. They dropped the Gaelic spelling 800 years later. The modern history, however, is a different (duck) tale.

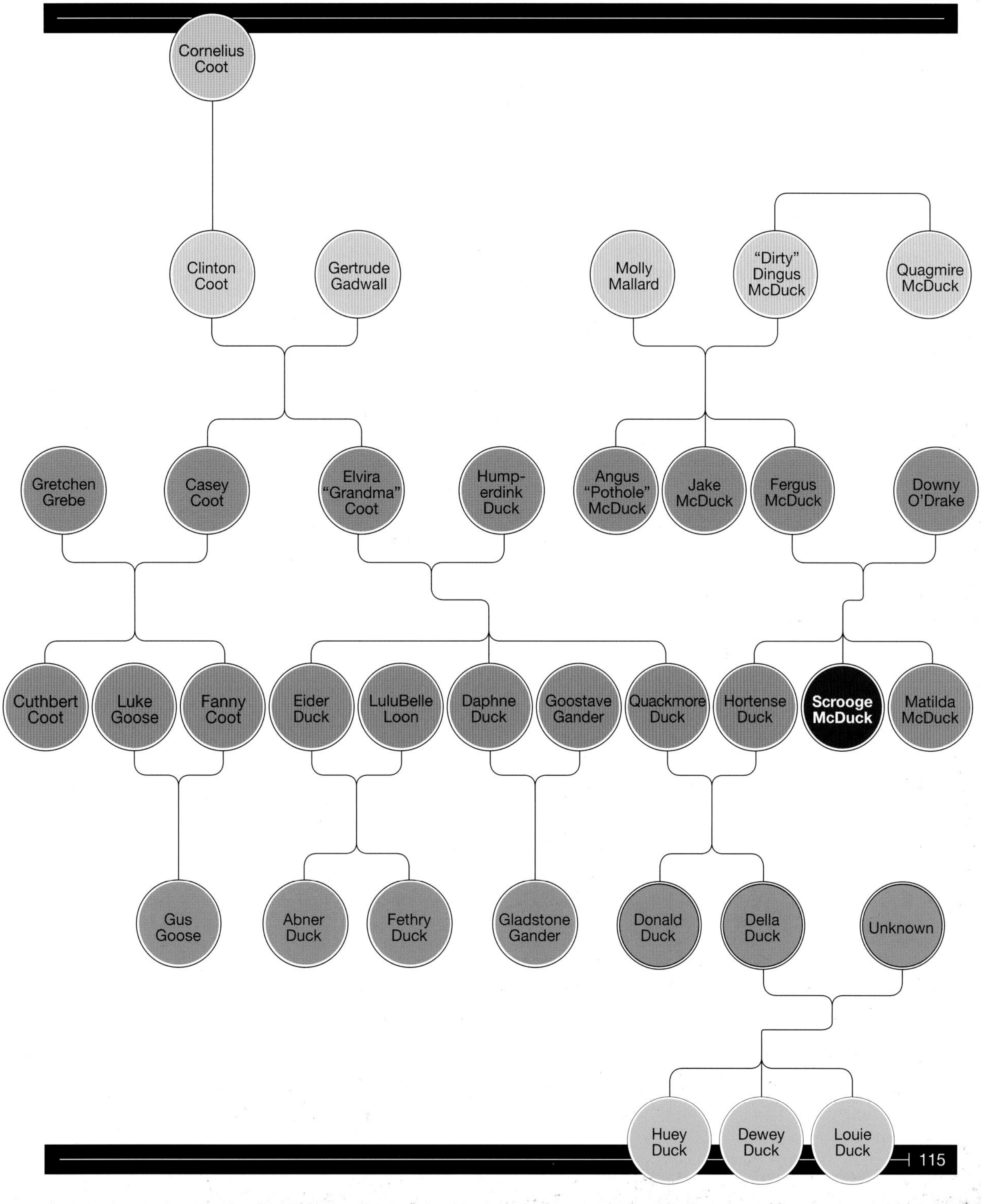

Cornelius Coot
Clinton Coot
Gertrude Gadwall
Molly Mallard
"Dirty" Dingus McDuck
Quagmire McDuck
Gretchen Grebe
Casey Coot
Elvira "Grandma" Coot
Hump-erdink Duck
Angus "Pothole" McDuck
Jake McDuck
Fergus McDuck
Downy O'Drake
Cuthbert Coot
Luke Goose
Fanny Coot
Eider Duck
LuluBelle Loon
Daphne Duck
Goostave Gander
Quackmore Duck
Hortense Duck
Scrooge McDuck
Matilda McDuck
Gus Goose
Abner Duck
Fethry Duck
Gladstone Gander
Donald Duck
Della Duck
Unknown
Huey Duck
Dewey Duck
Louie Duck

Every TV Show Starring Batman

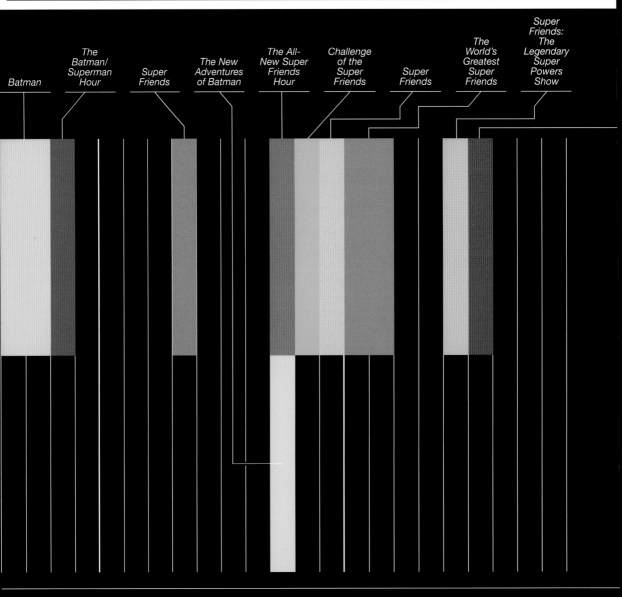

Batman

The Batman/ Superman Hour

Super Friends

The New Adventures of Batman

The All-New Super Friends Hour

Challenge of the Super Friends

Super Friends

The World's Greatest Super Friends

Super Friends: The Legendary Super Powers Show

1970

1980

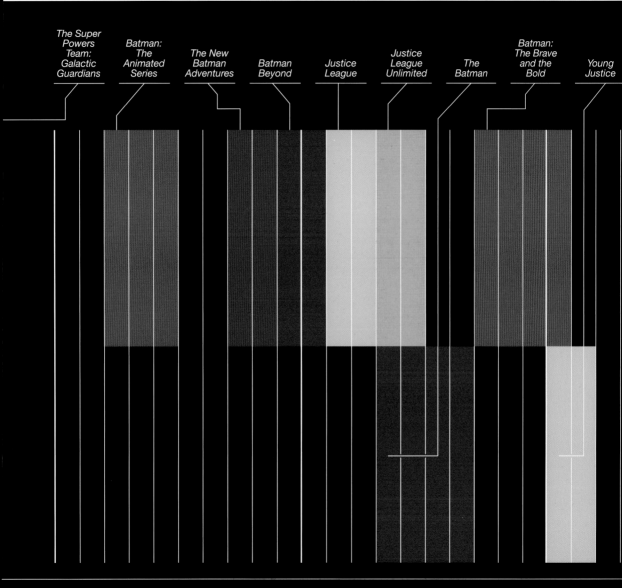

The Super
Powers
Team:
Galactic
Guardians

Batman:
The
Animated
Series

The New
Batman
Adventures

Batman
Beyond

Justice
League

Justice
League
Unlimited

The
Batman

Batman:
The Brave
and the
Bold

Young
Justice

1990
2000
2010

Character Kingdom

A taxonomy of characters, classified by name.

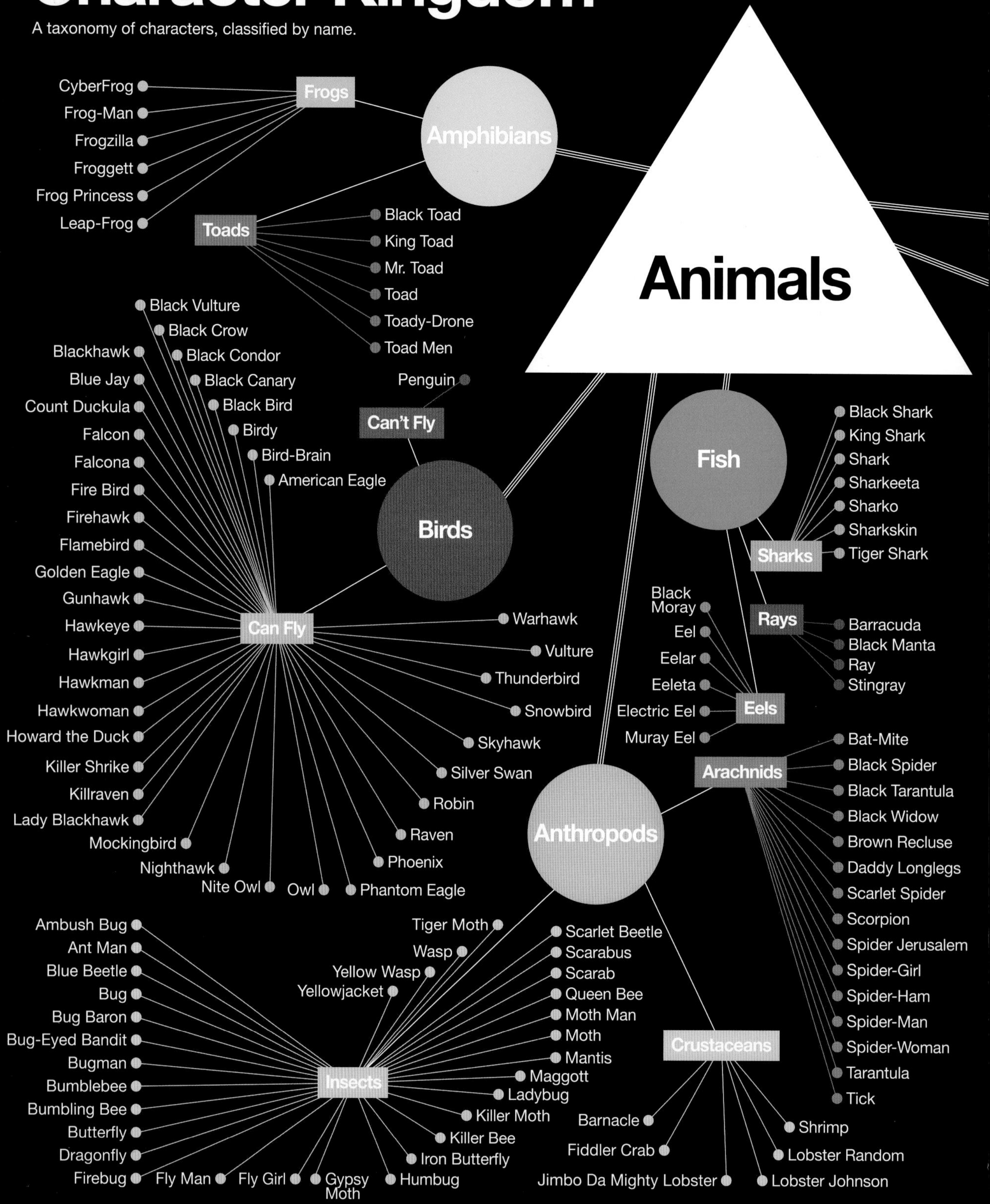

Animals
Amphibians
Frogs
CyberFrog
Frog-Man
Frogzilla
Froggett
Frog Princess
Leap-Frog
Toads
Black Toad
King Toad
Mr. Toad
Toad
Toady-Drone
Toad Men
Birds
Can't Fly
Penguin
Can Fly
Black Vulture
Black Crow
Black Condor
Black Canary
Black Bird
Birdy
Bird-Brain
American Eagle
Blackhawk
Blue Jay
Count Duckula
Falcon
Falcona
Fire Bird
Firehawk
Flamebird
Golden Eagle
Gunhawk
Hawkeye
Hawkgirl
Hawkman
Hawkwoman
Howard the Duck
Killer Shrike
Killraven
Lady Blackhawk
Mockingbird
Nighthawk
Nite Owl
Owl
Phantom Eagle
Phoenix
Raven
Robin
Silver Swan
Skyhawk
Snowbird
Thunderbird
Vulture
Warhawk
Fish
Sharks
Black Shark
King Shark
Shark
Sharkeeta
Sharko
Sharkskin
Tiger Shark
Rays
Barracuda
Black Manta
Ray
Stingray
Eels
Black Moray
Eel
Eelar
Eeleta
Electric Eel
Muray Eel
Anthropods
Arachnids
Bat-Mite
Black Spider
Black Tarantula
Black Widow
Brown Recluse
Daddy Longlegs
Scarlet Spider
Scorpion
Spider Jerusalem
Spider-Girl
Spider-Ham
Spider-Man
Spider-Woman
Tarantula
Tick
Crustaceans
Barnacle
Fiddler Crab
Jimbo Da Mighty Lobster
Lobster Johnson
Lobster Random
Shrimp
Insects
Ambush Bug
Ant Man
Blue Beetle
Bug
Bug Baron
Bug-Eyed Bandit
Bugman
Bumblebee
Bumbling Bee
Butterfly
Dragonfly
Firebug
Fly Man
Fly Girl
Gypsy Moth
Humbug
Iron Butterfly
Killer Bee
Killer Moth
Ladybug
Maggott
Mantis
Moth
Moth Man
Queen Bee
Scarab
Scarabus
Scarlet Beetle
Tiger Moth
Wasp
Yellow Wasp
Yellowjacket

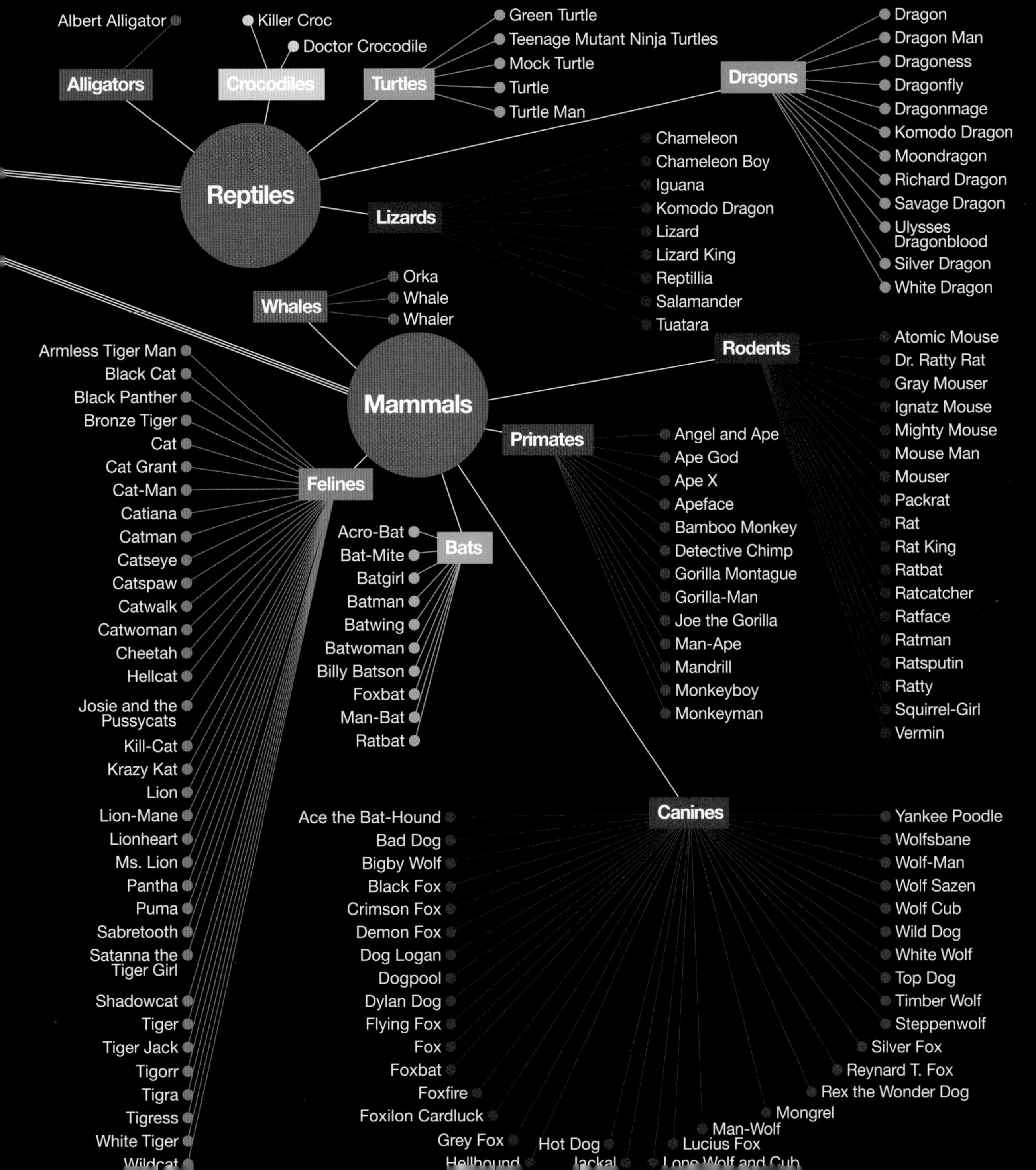
Reptiles
Alligators
Albert Alligator
Crocodiles
Killer Croc
Doctor Crocodile
Turtles
Green Turtle
Teenage Mutant Ninja Turtles
Mock Turtle
Turtle
Turtle Man
Dragons
Dragon
Dragon Man
Dragoness
Dragonfly
Dragonmage
Komodo Dragon
Moondragon
Richard Dragon
Savage Dragon
Ulysses Dragonblood
Silver Dragon
White Dragon
Lizards
Chameleon
Chameleon Boy
Iguana
Komodo Dragon
Lizard
Lizard King
Reptillia
Salamander
Tuatara
Mammals
Whales
Orka
Whale
Whaler
Rodents
Atomic Mouse
Dr. Ratty Rat
Gray Mouser
Ignatz Mouse
Mighty Mouse
Mouse Man
Mouser
Packrat
Rat
Rat King
Ratbat
Ratcatcher
Ratface
Ratman
Ratsputin
Ratty
Squirrel-Girl
Vermin
Primates
Angel and Ape
Ape God
Ape X
Apeface
Bamboo Monkey
Detective Chimp
Gorilla Montague
Gorilla-Man
Joe the Gorilla
Man-Ape
Mandrill
Monkeyboy
Monkeyman
Felines
Armless Tiger Man
Black Cat
Black Panther
Bronze Tiger
Cat
Cat Grant
Cat-Man
Catiana
Catman
Catseye
Catspaw
Catwalk
Catwoman
Cheetah
Hellcat
Josie and the Pussycats
Kill-Cat
Krazy Kat
Lion
Lion-Mane
Lionheart
Ms. Lion
Pantha
Puma
Sabretooth
Satanna the Tiger Girl
Shadowcat
Tiger
Tiger Jack
Tigorr
Tigra
Tigress
White Tiger
Wildcat
Bats
Acro-Bat
Bat-Mite
Batgirl
Batman
Batwing
Batwoman
Billy Batson
Foxbat
Man-Bat
Ratbat
Canines
Ace the Bat-Hound
Bad Dog
Bigby Wolf
Black Fox
Crimson Fox
Demon Fox
Dog Logan
Dogpool
Dylan Dog
Flying Fox
Fox
Foxbat
Foxfire
Foxilon Cardluck
Grey Fox
Hellhound
Hot Dog
Jackal
Lone Wolf and Cub
Lucius Fox
Man-Wolf
Mongrel
Rex the Wonder Dog
Reynard T. Fox
Silver Fox
Steppenwolf
Timber Wolf
Top Dog
White Wolf
Wild Dog
Wolf Cub
Wolf Sazen
Wolf-Man
Wolfsbane
Yankee Poodle

The Punisher's Kill Count

Piling up all The Punisher's bodies from movies and comic books

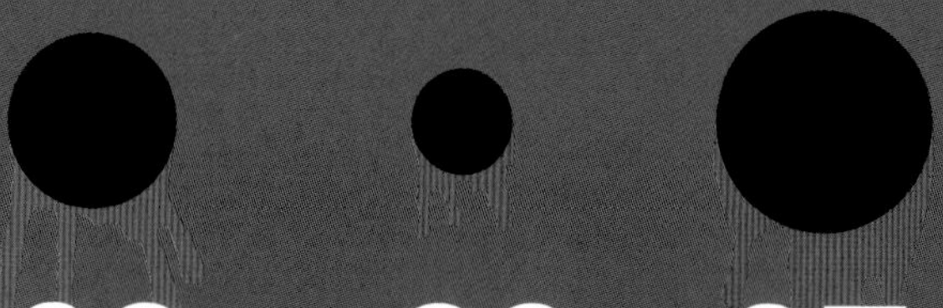

60

The Punisher
(1989)
starring
Dolph
Lundgren

22

The Punisher
(2004)
starring
Thomas Jane

97

Punisher: War Zone
(2008)
starring
Ray Stevenson

48,502

The Punisher
in comic books,
1974–2011

FIGHTING FORCES
Oppression and Rebellion in *Persepolis*

Persepolis is the true story of Marjane Satrapi, a young girl growing up during the Iranian Revolution in the 1980s. Satrapi is a free spirit growing up in an oppressive world. Despite an environment that's closing in on her and her independent-minded parents, Satrapi isn't afraid to give as good as she gets.

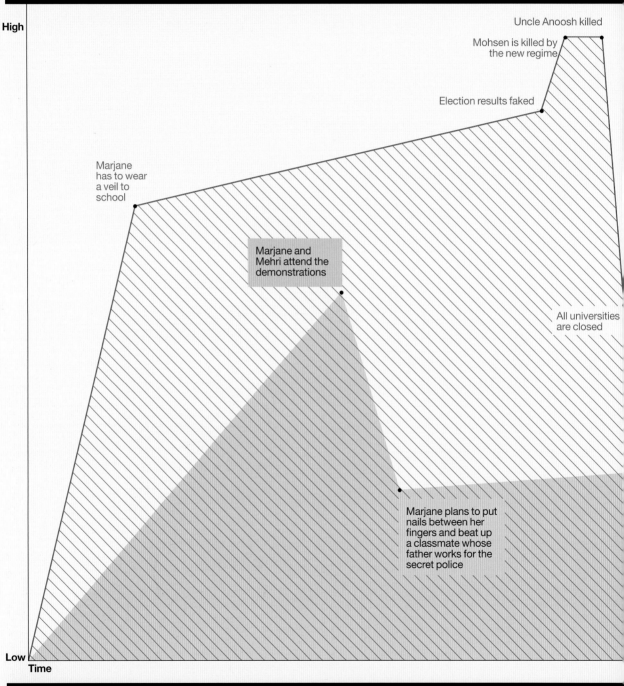

High

Uncle Anoosh killed

Mohsen is killed by the new regime

Election results faked

Marjane has to wear a veil to school

Marjane and Mehri attend the demonstrations

All universities are closed

Marjane plans to put nails between her fingers and beat up a classmate whose father works for the secret police

Low

Time

SPOILER ALERT

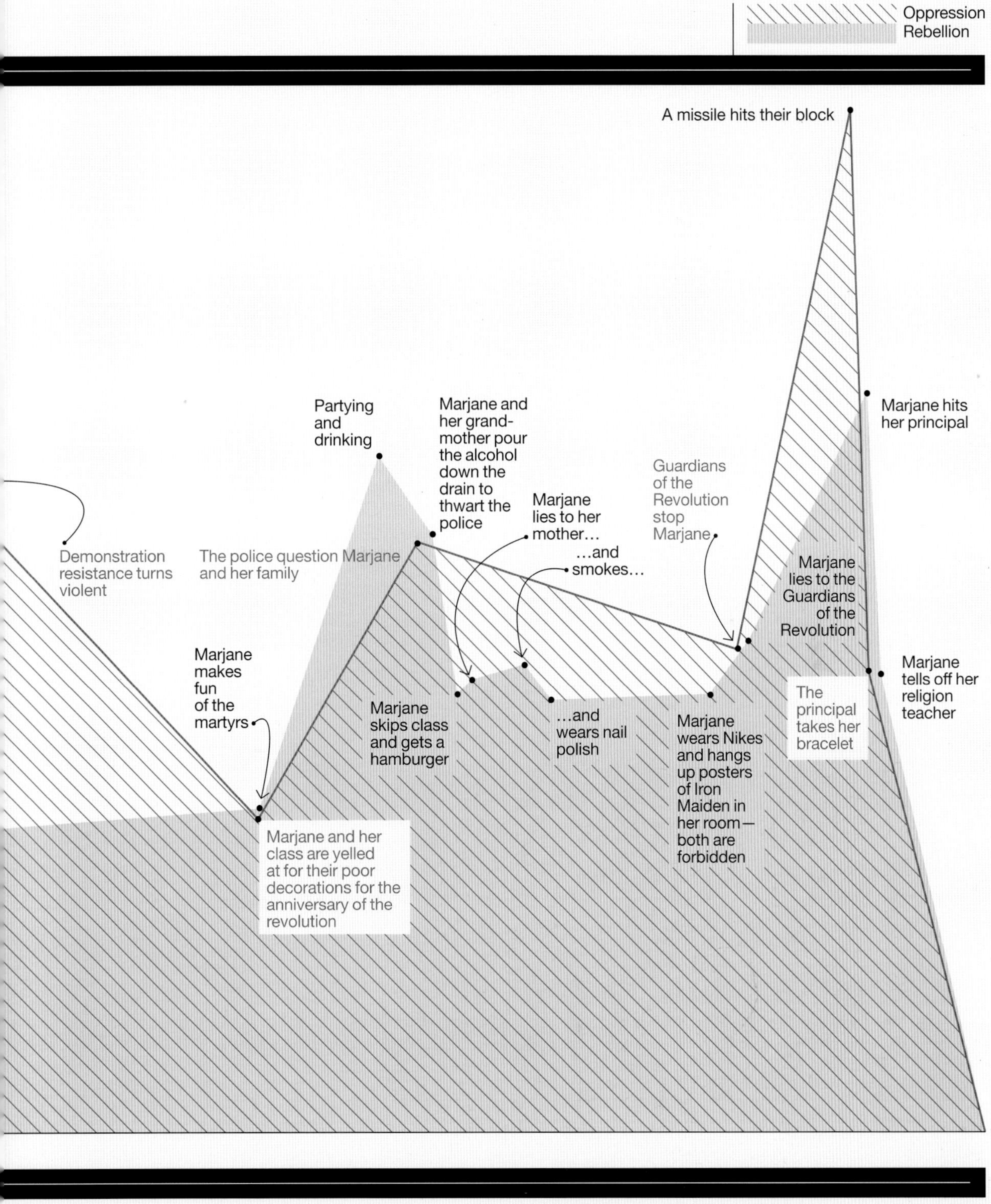
Oppression
Rebellion
A missile hits their block
Partying and drinking
Marjane and her grand-mother pour the alcohol down the drain to thwart the police
Marjane hits her principal
Guardians of the Revolution stop Marjane
Marjane lies to her mother…
…and smokes…
Demonstration resistance turns violent
The police question Marjane and her family
Marjane lies to the Guardians of the Revolution
Marjane makes fun of the martyrs
Marjane tells off her religion teacher
The principal takes her bracelet
Marjane skips class and gets a hamburger
…and wears nail polish
Marjane wears Nikes and hangs up posters of Iron Maiden in her room—both are forbidden
Marjane and her class are yelled at for their poor decorations for the anniversary of the revolution

Mutant Manhattan

A guide to New York locations in the Marvel Comics universe

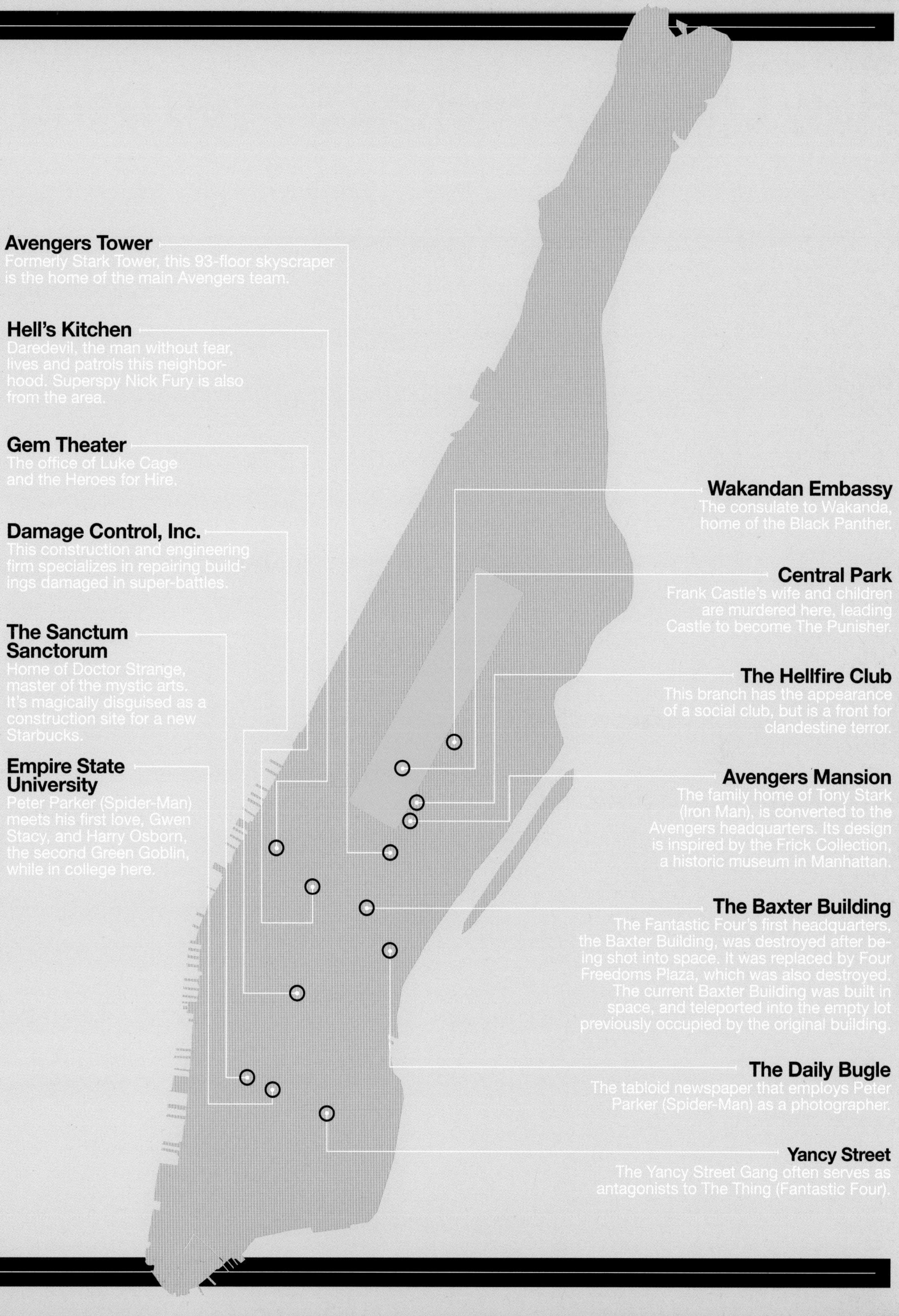
Avengers Tower
Formerly Stark Tower, this 93-floor skyscraper is the home of the main Avengers team.
Hell's Kitchen
Daredevil, the man without fear, lives and patrols this neighborhood. Superspy Nick Fury is also from the area.
Gem Theater
The office of Luke Cage and the Heroes for Hire.
Damage Control, Inc.
This construction and engineering firm specializes in repairing buildings damaged in super-battles.
The Sanctum Sanctorum
Home of Doctor Strange, master of the mystic arts. It's magically disguised as a construction site for a new Starbucks.
Empire State University
Peter Parker (Spider-Man) meets his first love, Gwen Stacy, and Harry Osborn, the second Green Goblin, while in college here.
Wakandan Embassy
The consulate to Wakanda, home of the Black Panther.
Central Park
Frank Castle's wife and children are murdered here, leading Castle to become The Punisher.
The Hellfire Club
This branch has the appearance of a social club, but is a front for clandestine terror.
Avengers Mansion
The family home of Tony Stark (Iron Man), is converted to the Avengers headquarters. Its design is inspired by the Frick Collection, a historic museum in Manhattan.
The Baxter Building
The Fantastic Four's first headquarters, the Baxter Building, was destroyed after being shot into space. It was replaced by Four Freedoms Plaza, which was also destroyed. The current Baxter Building was built in space, and teleported into the empty lot previously occupied by the original building.
The Daily Bugle
The tabloid newspaper that employs Peter Parker (Spider-Man) as a photographer.
Yancy Street
The Yancy Street Gang often serves as antagonists to The Thing (Fantastic Four).

TO THE GRAVE AND BACK
How Long Characters Stayed Dead

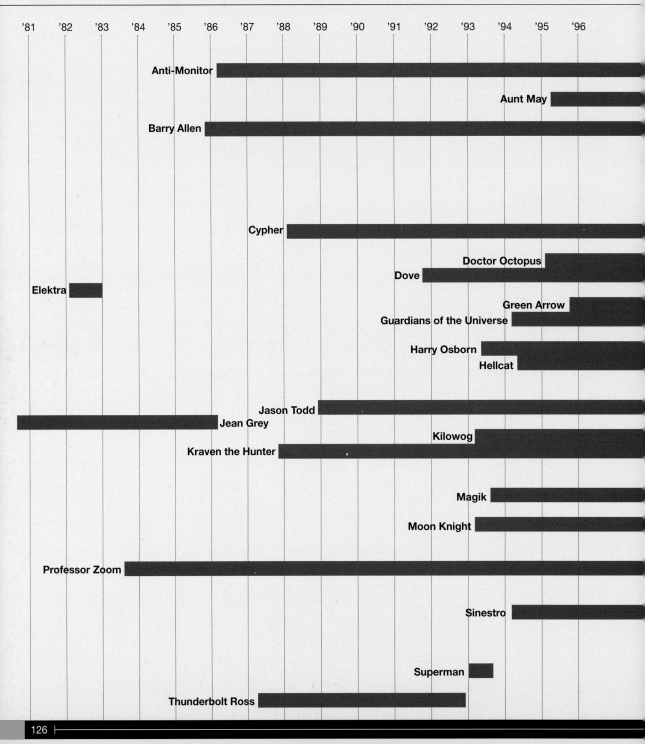

'81 '82 '83 '84 '85 '86 '87 '88 '89 '90 '91 '92 '93 '94 '95 '96

Anti-Monitor

Aunt May

Barry Allen

Cypher

Doctor Octopus

Dove

Elektra

Green Arrow

Guardians of the Universe

Harry Osborn

Hellcat

Jason Todd

Jean Grey

Kilowog

Kraven the Hunter

Magik

Moon Knight

Professor Zoom

Sinestro

Superman

Thunderbolt Ross

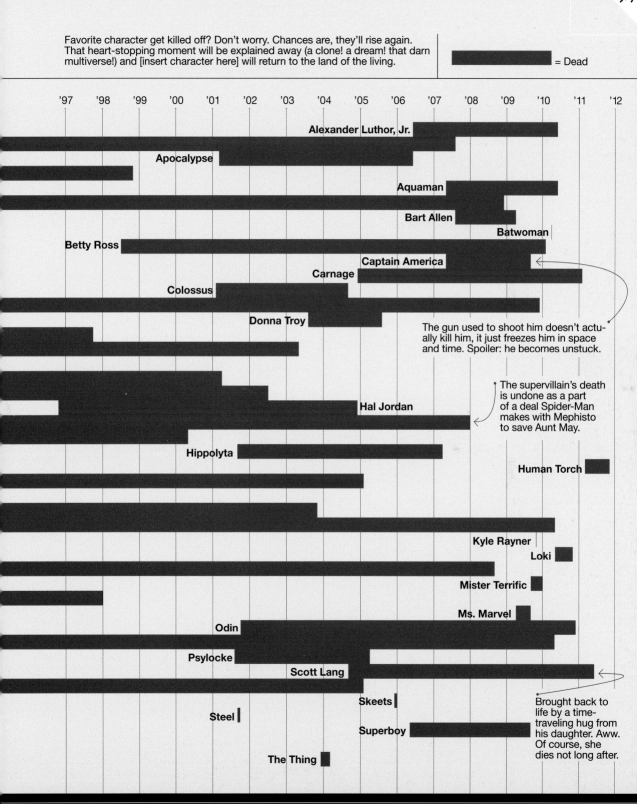

Favorite character get killed off? Don't worry. Chances are, they'll rise again. That heart-stopping moment will be explained away (a clone! a dream! that darn multiverse!) and [insert character here] will return to the land of the living.

= Dead

'97 '98 '99 '00 '01 '02 '03 '04 '05 '06 '07 '08 '09 '10 '11 '12

Alexander Luthor, Jr.

Apocalypse

Aquaman

Bart Allen

Batwoman

Betty Ross

Captain America

Carnage

Colossus

Donna Troy

Hal Jordan

The gun used to shoot him doesn't actually kill him, it just freezes him in space and time. Spoiler: he becomes unstuck.

Hippolyta

The supervillain's death is undone as a part of a deal Spider-Man makes with Mephisto to save Aunt May.

Human Torch

Kyle Rayner

Loki

Mister Terrific

Ms. Marvel

Odin

Psylocke

Scott Lang

Skeets

Steel

Superboy

The Thing

Brought back to life by a time-traveling hug from his daughter. Aww. Of course, she dies not long after.

CHOOSE YOUR OWN ADVENTURE

The *MAD* Magazine Mystery Record

CHORUS:

It's a great big, beautiful, wonderful, incredible, super-spectacular day

And your heart is humming with good times coming

And you got that happy feeling things are going your way

All the bells are ringing and a little bird's singing while he sits on your windowsill

Saying yessiree, I can surely see, it will plainly be, most definitely

A super-spectacular day!

Untillllllll. . .

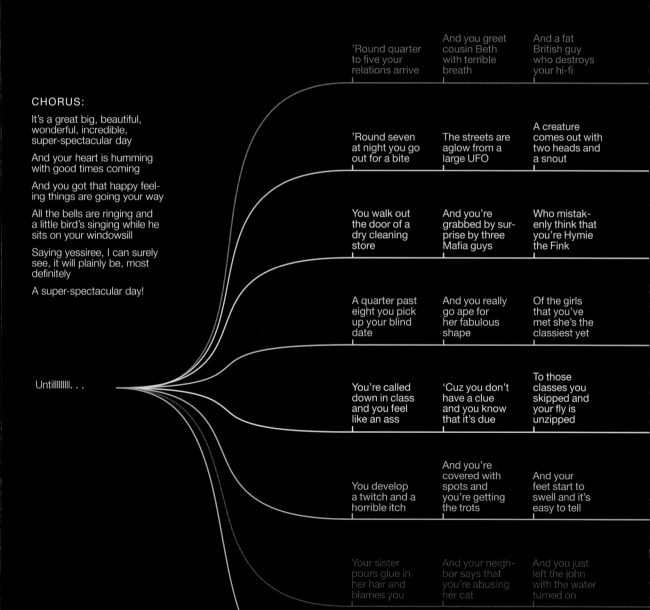

'Round quarter to five your relations arrive	And you greet cousin Beth with terrible breath	And a fat British guy who destroys your hi-fi
'Round seven at night you go out for a bite	The streets are aglow from a large UFO	A creature comes out with two heads and a snout
You walk out the door of a dry cleaning store	And you're grabbed by surprise by three Mafia guys	Who mistakenly think that you're Hymie the Fink
A quarter past eight you pick up your blind date	And you really go ape for her fabulous shape	Of the girls that you've met she's the classiest yet
You're called down in class and you feel like an ass	'Cuz you don't have a clue and you know that it's due	To those classes you skipped and your fly is unzipped
You develop a twitch and a horrible itch	And you're covered with spots and you're getting the trots	And your feet start to swell and it's easy to tell
Your sister pours glue in her hair and blames you	And your neighbor says that you're abusing her cat	And you just left the john with the water turned on

In the summer of 1980, *MAD* magazine tucked an exclusive flexi-disc record within its pages. Depending on where the needle landed on it, the record would play one of eight variations of the song, "It's a Super-Spectacular Day."

And your great-uncle Fred who gets drunk in your bed	And your third cousin Dick who is mentally sick	And his creepy friend Joe and six more you don't know	And you're sure there and then as you're shafted again. . .
It talks like a frog and throws up on your dog	It thinks you are great and wants you for its mate	You're sealed in a case and go flying in space	And you silently say as the Earth fades away. . .
They break your right arm and do bodily harm	And you're writhing in pain and you try to explain	That your name is Jerome and you're on your way home	And you let out a sigh as you're left there to die. . .
And she's pretty and bright and it's love at first sight	And it's really a shame she's not feeling the same	'Cuz she thinks you're a schmuck and she says "lots of luck"	And you sob in despair as she gives you the air. . .
And your acne has spread to the back of your head	And some jerk spreads the word that you're some kind of nerd	And you fight in the hall and punch through a wall	And there isn't a doubt as they're flunking you out. . .
From this hideous wheeze that some awful disease	So you call an M.D. and he says, "Don't ask me	If it gets any worse you can speak to my nurse"	And you manage to say as you wither away. . .
And the house gets all wet and your mother's upset	And you'd die if you knew what your dad's gonna do	And your python gets loose and you know it's no use	And you cry there in fear and it's now very clear. . .
And you run out of gas while you're trying to pass	And you're stalled on the tracks and you try to relax	But the train's coming through and it's heading for you	And you have a quick flash as you brace for the crash. . .

. . . that it's not such a super-spectacular day!

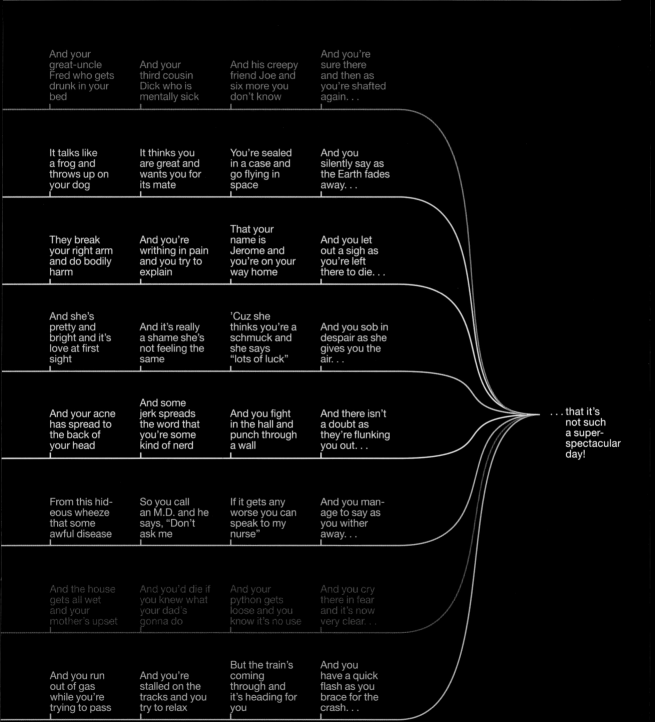

FAST COMPANY

The Four Faces of The Flash

Since 1940, four different people have put on the famous red costume—and sometimes at the same time. Blame alternate realities, a return from the grave, and time travel. It's confusing! Here's a guide to the fastest men alive.

■ THE FLASH   ☐ KID FLASH   ■ IMPULSE

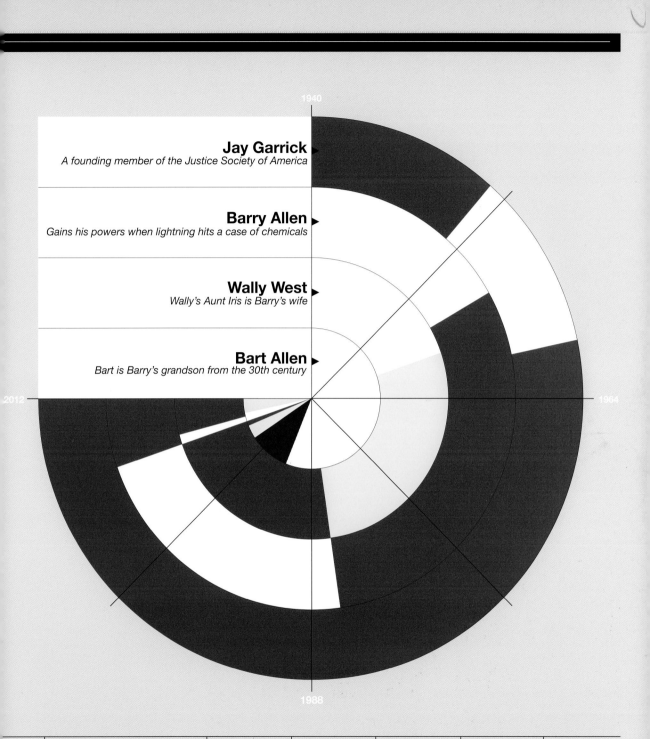

Jay Garrick
A founding member of the Justice Society of America

Barry Allen
Gains his powers when lightning hits a case of chemicals

Wally West
Wally's Aunt Iris is Barry's wife

Bart Allen
Bart is Barry's grandson from the 30th century

1940

2012

1964

1988

1951
Jay retires after the House Un-American Activities Committee investigates the JSA for Communists and asks for their identities.

1959
Wally starts his career as Barry's side-kick.

1961
Jay is revealed to actually be a hero on Earth-2, an alternate reality.

1985
Barry dies during the *Crisis on Infinite Earths*.

2006
Wally and his family leave for another dimension and return after his twins rapidly age.

2007
Bart dies and returns a few years later as his teenage self from the future.

A *Watchmen* Primer

Originally published by DC Comics as a limited 12-issue series in 1986, *Watchmen* is widely regarded as the best comic . . . ever. The story, written by Alan Moore and drawn by Dave Gibbons, spans generations of superhero teams, as much of a critique of the genre as an exploration of it.

The *Watchmen* effect

Watchmen changed everything. It showed just how layered and how adult a comic book could be—and the industry took notice. After its publication books became significantly less jokey.

Dark
Light
Publication of *Watchmen*
1929
2013

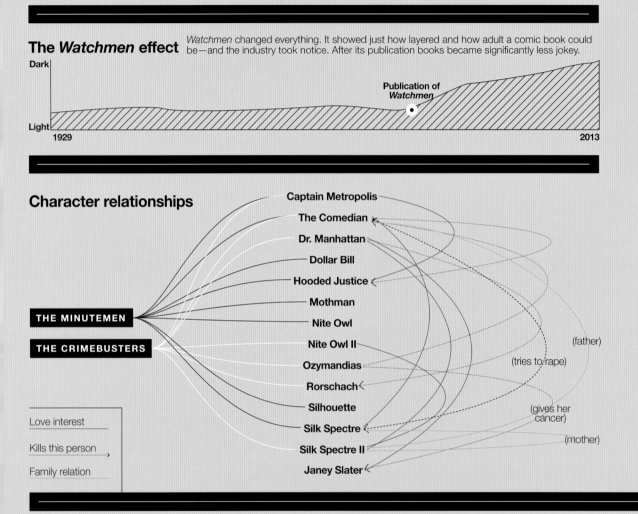

Character relationships

Captain Metropolis
The Comedian
Dr. Manhattan
Dollar Bill
Hooded Justice
Mothman
Nite Owl
Nite Owl II
Ozymandias
Rorschach
Silhouette
Silk Spectre
Silk Spectre II
Janey Slater
THE MINUTEMEN
THE CRIMEBUSTERS
(father)
(tries to rape)
(gives her cancer)
(mother)
Love interest
Kills this person
Family relation

Watchmen timeline, 1935–1985

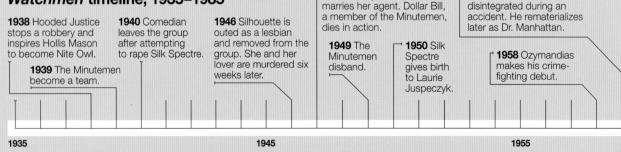

1938 Hooded Justice stops a robbery and inspires Hollis Mason to become Nite Owl.

1939 The Minutemen become a team.

1940 Comedian leaves the group after attempting to rape Silk Spectre.

1946 Silhouette is outed as a lesbian and removed from the group. She and her lover are murdered six weeks later.

1947 Silk Spectre retires and marries her agent. Dollar Bill, a member of the Minutemen, dies in action.

1949 The Minutemen disband.

1950 Silk Spectre gives birth to Laurie Juspeczyk.

1958 Ozymandias makes his crime-fighting debut.

1959 Jon Osterman is disintegrated during an accident. He rematerializes later as Dr. Manhattan.

1935
1945
1955

Characters origins

Alan Moore's original pitch for *Watchmen* had included characters that DC Comics acquired from Charlton Comics a few years prior. Realizing their inclusion in *Watchmen* would render many unusable thereafter, Moore's editor, Dick Giordano, suggested creating original characters. Moore did just that, but based his cast on the Charlton lot. Here's where he pulled his inspiration.

BLUE BEETLE
CAPTAIN ATOM
NIGHTSHADE
PEACEMAKER
THE QUESTION
THUNDERBOLT

THE COMEDIAN
DR. MANHATTAN
NITE OWL
OZYMANDIAS
RORSCHACH
SILK SPECTRE

The smiley face

Watchmen's most iconic image is the smiley face button belonging to the Comedian. When the Comedian dies in the opening pages, his blood splatters in a dripping line on the smiley face. The smiley face imagery is a direct visual metaphor to the face of the doomsday clock that is prominently featured in each issue. The circle and line imagery also appears in many subtle forms throughout the series, including a radar screen, goggles and the sun. Here's how many times you can spot the symbolism in each issue.

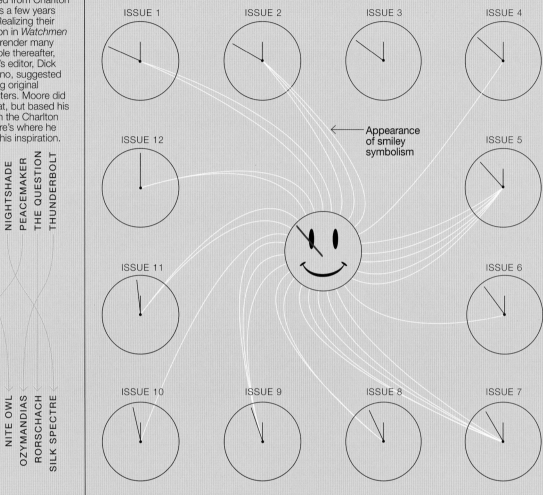

ISSUE 1 · ISSUE 2 · ISSUE 3 · ISSUE 4 · ISSUE 12 · ISSUE 5 · ISSUE 11 · ISSUE 6 · ISSUE 10 · ISSUE 9 · ISSUE 8 · ISSUE 7

← Appearance of smiley symbolism

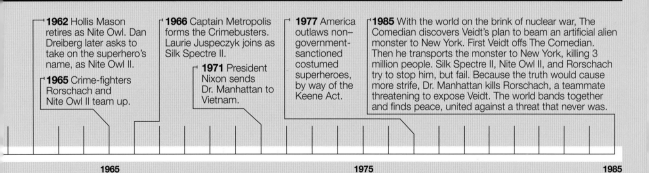

1962 Hollis Mason retires as Nite Owl. Dan Dreiberg later asks to take on the superhero's name, as Nite Owl II.

1965 Crime-fighters Rorschach and Nite Owl II team up.

1966 Captain Metropolis forms the Crimebusters. Laurie Juspeczyk joins as Silk Spectre II.

1971 President Nixon sends Dr. Manhattan to Vietnam.

1977 America outlaws non–government-sanctioned costumed superheroes, by way of the Keene Act.

1985 With the world on the brink of nuclear war, The Comedian discovers Veidt's plan to beam an artificial alien monster to New York. First Veidt offs The Comedian. Then he transports the monster to New York, killing 3 million people. Silk Spectre II, Nite Owl II, and Rorschach try to stop him, but fail. Because the truth would cause more strife, Dr. Manhattan kills Rorschach, a teammate threatening to expose Veidt. The world bands together and finds peace, united against a threat that never was.

1965 · 1975 · 1985

AMAZONIAN PRIME

70 Years of Wonder Woman's Legs

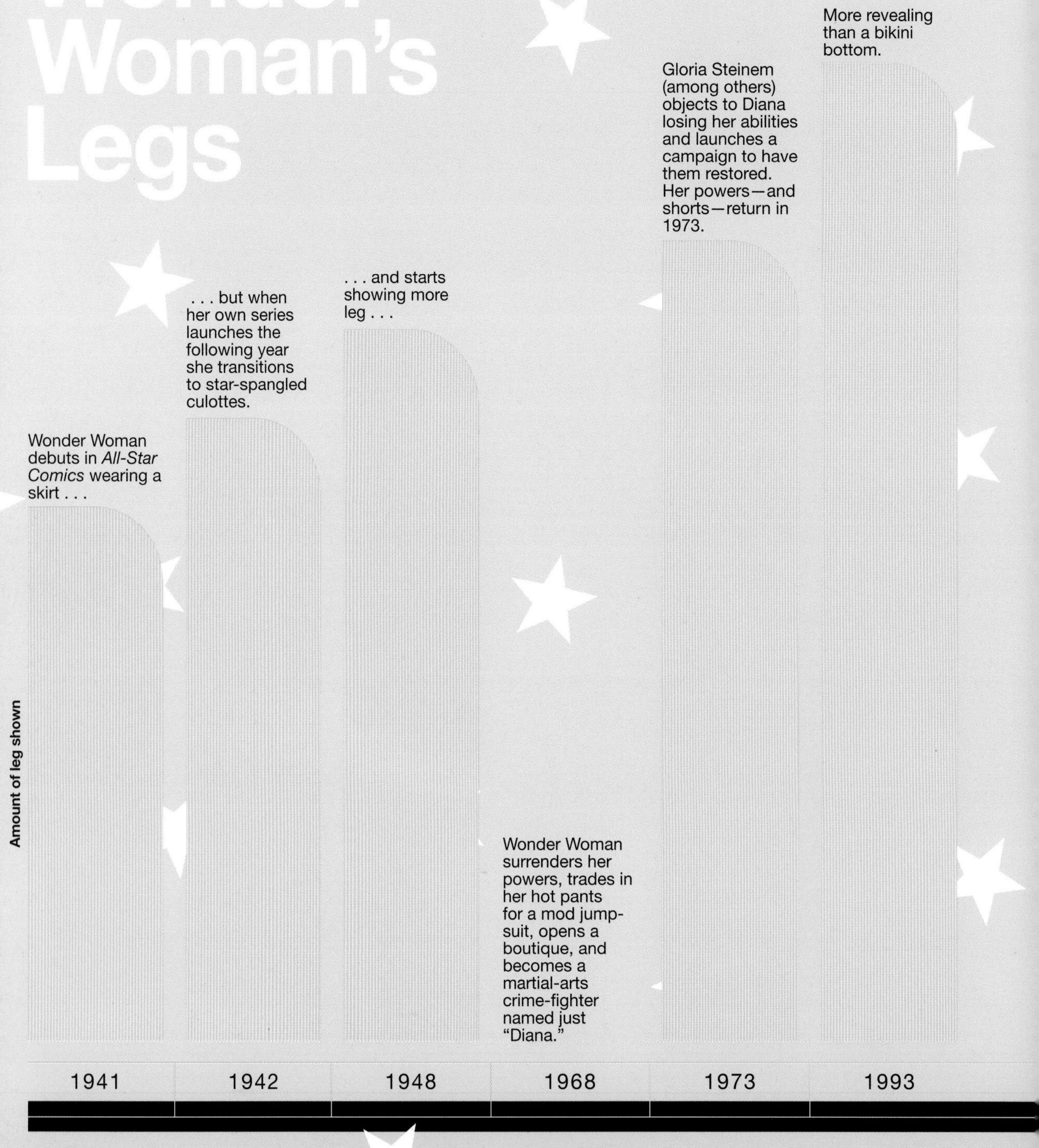
Amount of leg shown
Wonder Woman debuts in *All-Star Comics* wearing a skirt . . .
. . . but when her own series launches the following year she transitions to star-spangled culottes.
. . . and starts showing more leg . . .
Wonder Woman surrenders her powers, trades in her hot pants for a mod jump-suit, opens a boutique, and becomes a martial-arts crime-fighter named just "Diana."
Gloria Steinem (among others) objects to Diana losing her abilities and launches a campaign to have them restored. Her powers—and shorts—return in 1973.
More revealing than a bikini bottom.
1941
1942
1948
1968
1973
1993

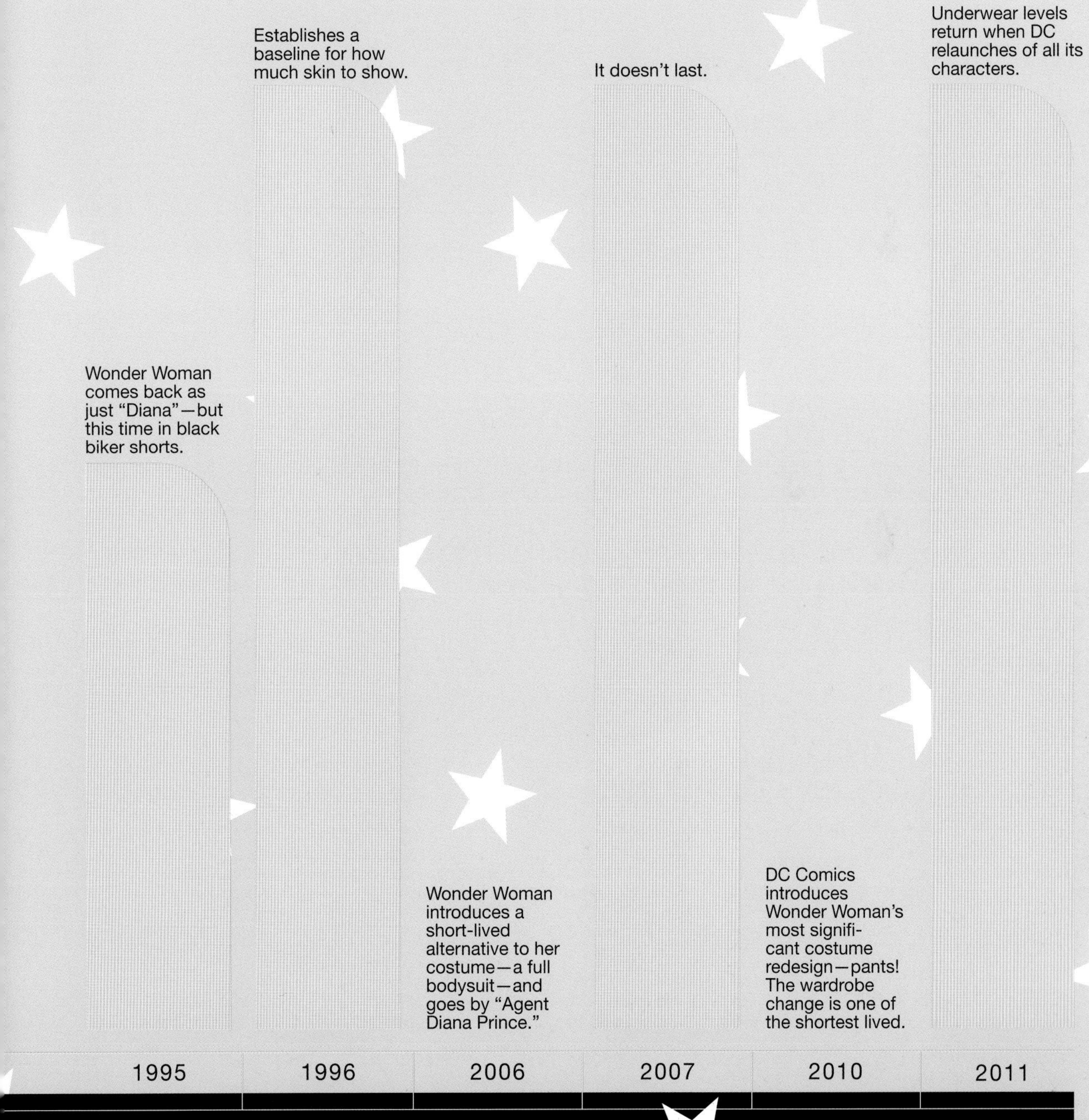
1995
Wonder Woman comes back as just "Diana"—but this time in black biker shorts.
1996
Establishes a baseline for how much skin to show.
2006
Wonder Woman introduces a short-lived alternative to her costume—a full bodysuit—and goes by "Agent Diana Prince."
2007
It doesn't last.
2010
DC Comics introduces Wonder Woman's most signifi-cant costume redesign—pants! The wardrobe change is one of the shortest lived.
2011
Underwear levels return when DC relaunches of all its characters.

RECURRING CHARACTER
Chris Evans

The actor has the notable distinction of having appeared in more comic book movies than any actor before him. While we're going to ignore the questions of quality (what's up, not-so-*Fantastic Four*?), some of his performances have fared better at the box office than others.

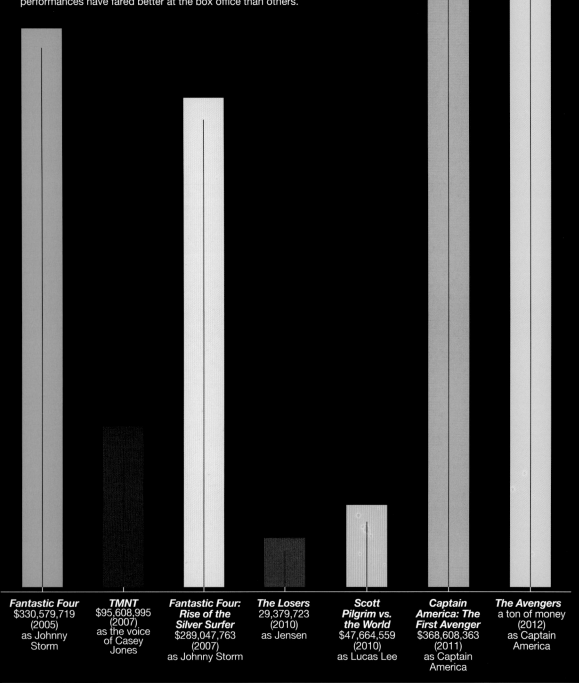

| *Fantastic Four*
$330,579,719
(2005)
as Johnny Storm | *TMNT*
$95,608,995
(2007)
as the voice
of Casey
Jones | *Fantastic Four:
Rise of the
Silver Surfer*
$289,047,763
(2007)
as Johnny Storm | *The Losers*
29,379,723
(2010)
as Jensen | *Scott
Pilgrim vs.
the World*
$47,664,559
(2010)
as Lucas Lee | *Captain
America: The
First Avenger*
$368,608,363
(2011)
as Captain
America | *The Avengers*
a ton of money
(2012)
as Captain
America |

How to Spot a Vigilante

This class of superheroes has more in common than just their ability to kick major ass.

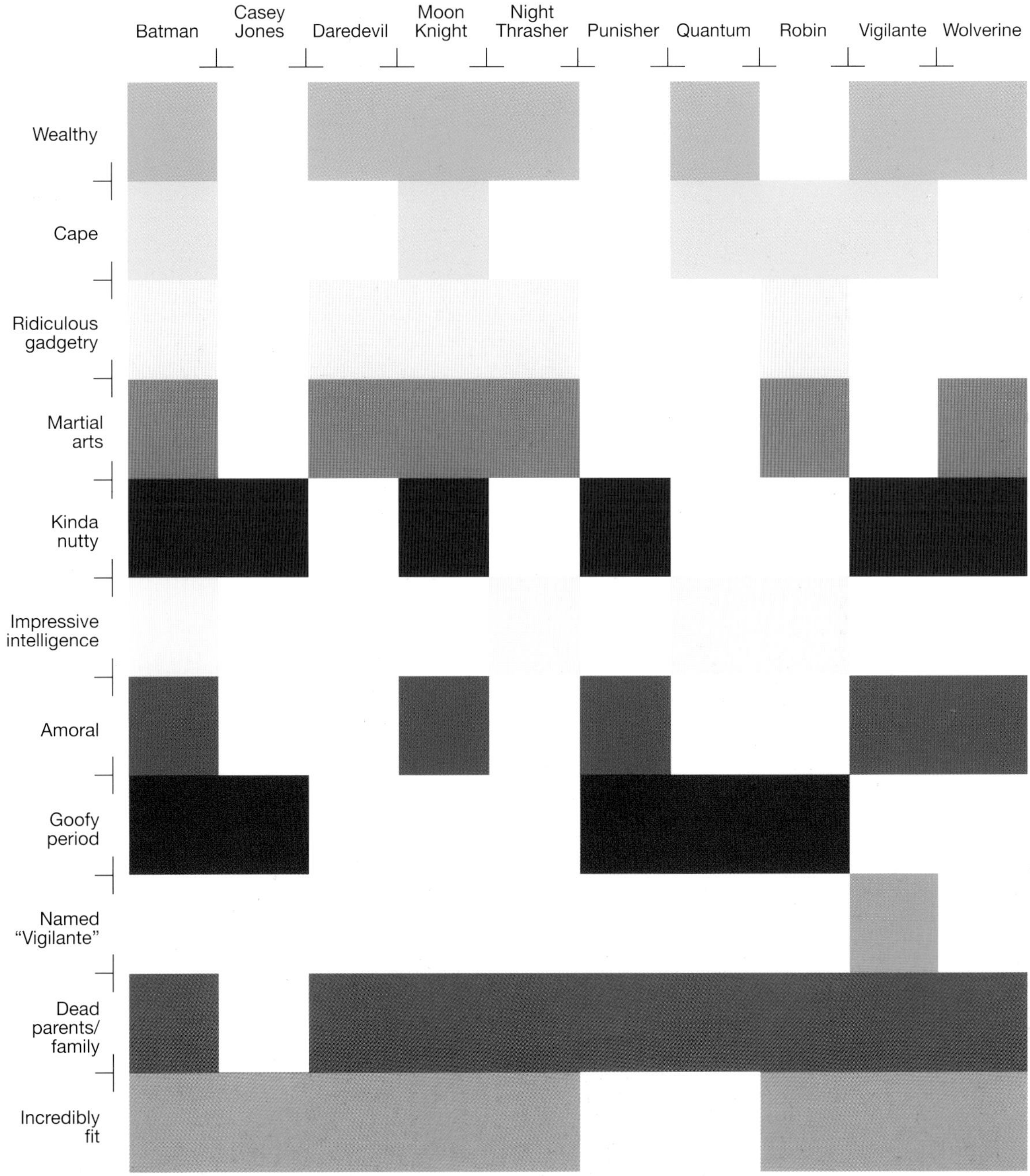

Batman
Casey Jones
Daredevil
Moon Knight
Night Thrasher
Punisher
Quantum
Robin
Vigilante
Wolverine
Wealthy
Cape
Ridiculous gadgetry
Martial arts
Kinda nutty
Impressive intelligence
Amoral
Goofy period
Named "Vigilante"
Dead parents/ family
Incredibly fit

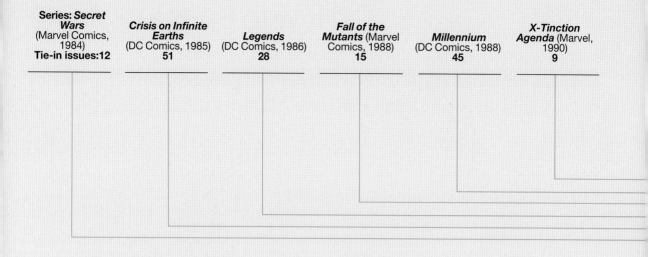

Series: *Secret Wars* (Marvel Comics, 1984)
Tie-in issues:12

Crisis on Infinite Earths (DC Comics, 1985)
51

Legends (DC Comics, 1986)
28

Fall of the Mutants (Marvel Comics, 1988)
15

Millennium (DC Comics, 1988)
45

X-Tinction Agenda (Marvel, 1990)
9

NOT STANDARD ISSUE

An Explanation of Crossover Issues and Their Tie-Ins

Big events that span multiple series are a boon to sales, but the stories tend to be so expansive that they require additional issues just to explain what the heck is going on. These extras are called tie-ins. Here's how many tie-ins were needed to explain each series crossover.

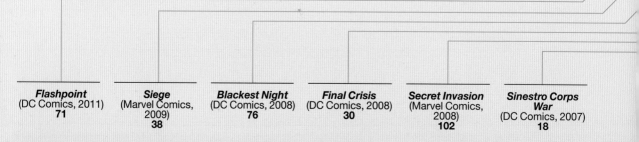

Flashpoint (DC Comics, 2011)
71

Siege (Marvel Comics, 2009)
38

Blackest Night (DC Comics, 2008)
76

Final Crisis (DC Comics, 2008)
30

Secret Invasion (Marvel Comics, 2008)
102

Sinestro Corps War (DC Comics, 2007)
18

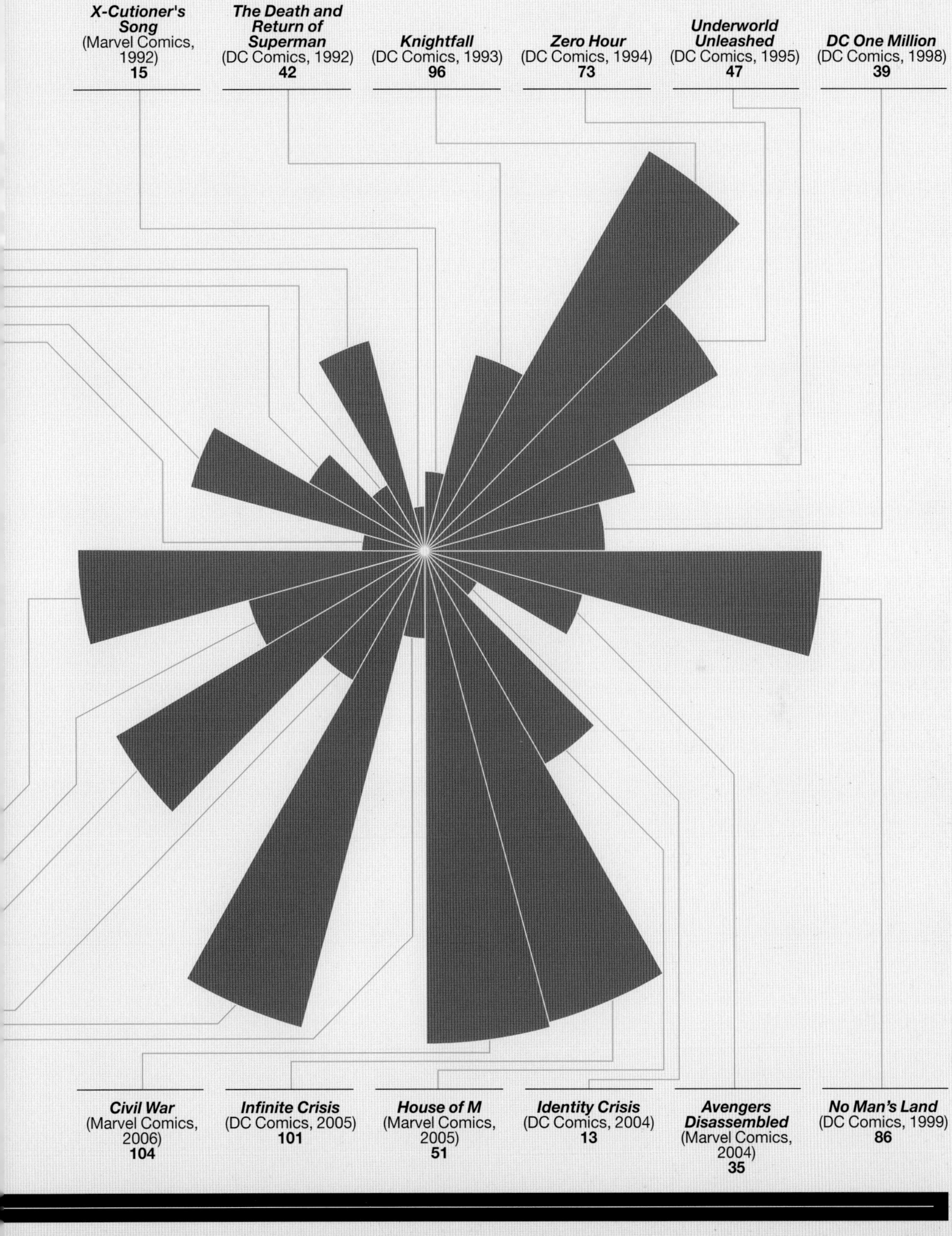

X-Cutioner's Song (Marvel Comics, 1992) 15
The Death and Return of Superman (DC Comics, 1992) 42
Knightfall (DC Comics, 1993) 96
Zero Hour (DC Comics, 1994) 73
Underworld Unleashed (DC Comics, 1995) 47
DC One Million (DC Comics, 1998) 39
Civil War (Marvel Comics, 2006) 104
Infinite Crisis (DC Comics, 2005) 101
House of M (Marvel Comics, 2005) 51
Identity Crisis (DC Comics, 2004) 13
Avengers Disassembled (Marvel Comics, 2004) 35
No Man’s Land (DC Comics, 1999) 86

Tintin's Travels

Hergé's *The Adventures of Tintin* stars the titular Tintin, a young investigative reporter who travels all over the world—and sometimes out of it—in search of a story.

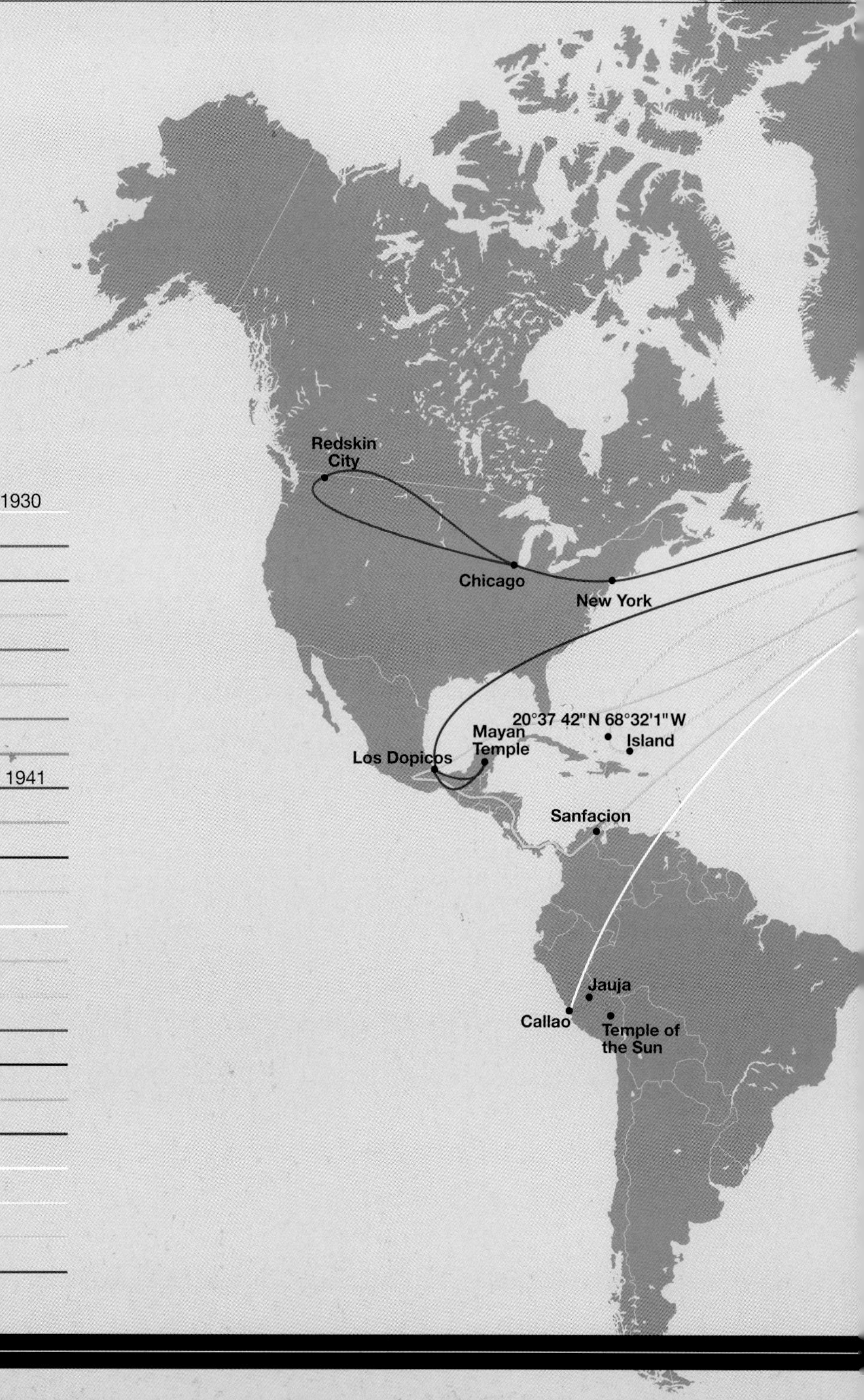

Redskin City
Chicago
New York
20°37 42" N 68°32'1" W
Island
Mayan Temple
Los Dopicos
Sanfacion
Jauja
Callao
Temple of the Sun

BOOK:

Tintin in the Land of the Soviets 1930
Tintin in the Congo 1931
Tintin in America 1932
Cigars of the Pharaoh 1934
The Blue Lotus 1936
The Broken Ear 1937
The Black Island 1938
King Ottokar's Sceptre 1939
The Crab with the Golden Claws 1941
The Shooting Star 1942
The Secret of the Unicorn 1943
Red Rackham's Treasure 1944
The Seven Crystal Balls 1948
Prisoners of the Sun 1949
Land of Black Gold 1950
Destination Moon 1953
Explorers on the Moon 1953
The Calculus Affair 1956
The Red Sea Sharks 1958
Tintin in Tibet 1960
The Castafiore Emerald 1963
Flight 714 1968
Tintin and the Picaros 1976

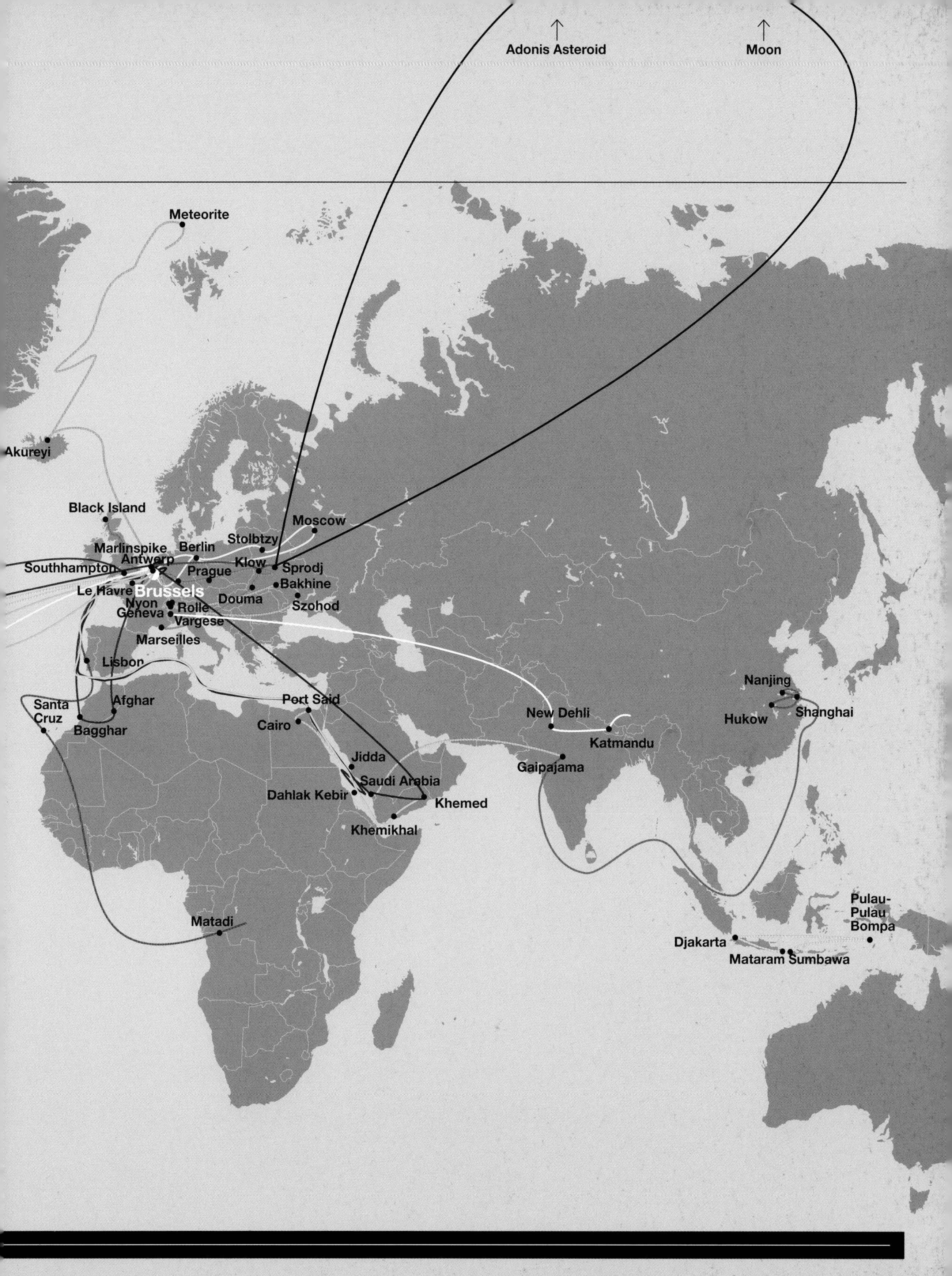
Adonis Asteroid
Moon
Meteorite
Akureyi
Black Island
Moscow
Stolbtzy
Marlinspike
Berlin
Antwerp
Southhampton
Klow
Sprodj
Prague
Bakhine
Le Havre
Brussels
Douma
Nyon
Rolle
Szohod
Geneva
Vargese
Marseilles
Lisbon
Afghar
Port Said
Santa Cruz
Bagghar
Cairo
Nanjing
New Dehli
Hukow
Shanghai
Katmandu
Jidda
Gaipajama
Saudi Arabia
Dahlak Kebir
Khemed
Khemikhal
Pulau-Pulau Bompa
Matadi
Djakarta
Mataram
Sumbawa

Tintin Publication History

1930

Tintin in the Land of the Soviets is published in book form, written by Georges Remi under the pen name Hergé.

Tintin in the Congo appears in book form in black and white. Its stereotypical depiction of the Congolese is still controversial today.

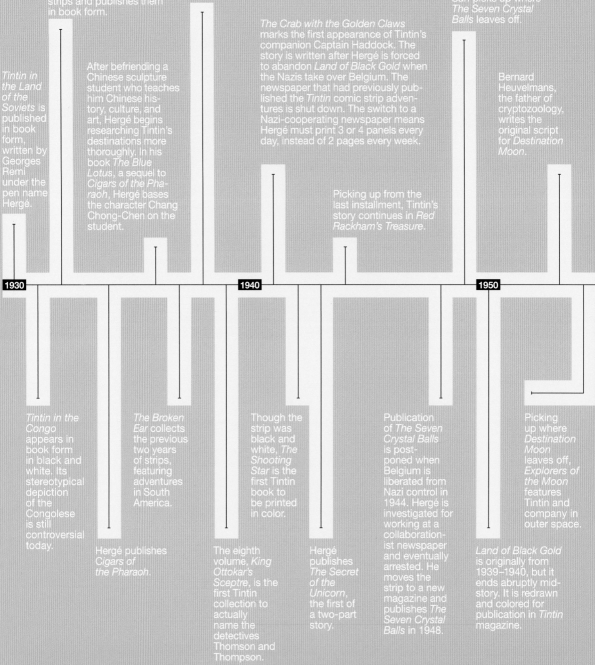

Hergé collects his black and white *Tintin in America* strips and publishes them in book form.

Hergé publishes *Cigars of the Pharaoh.*

After befriending a Chinese sculpture student who teaches him Chinese history, culture, and art, Hergé begins researching Tintin's destinations more thoroughly. In his book *The Blue Lotus*, a sequel to *Cigars of the Pharaoh*, Hergé bases the character Chang Chong-Chen on the student.

The Broken Ear collects the previous two years of strips, featuring adventures in South America.

Hergé prints *The Black Island*, the only book in which Tintin physically disciplines his trusty dog Snowy.

The eighth volume, *King Ottokar's Sceptre*, is the first Tintin collection to actually name the detectives Thomson and Thompson.

1940

The Crab with the Golden Claws marks the first appearance of Tintin's companion Captain Haddock. The story is written after Hergé is forced to abandon *Land of Black Gold* when the Nazis take over Belgium. The newspaper that had previously published the *Tintin* comic strip adventures is shut down. The switch to a Nazi-cooperating newspaper means Hergé must print 3 or 4 panels every day, instead of 2 pages every week.

Though the strip was black and white, *The Shooting Star* is the first Tintin book to be printed in color.

Hergé publishes *The Secret of the Unicorn*, the first of a two-part story.

Picking up from the last installment, Tintin's story continues in *Red Rackham's Treasure.*

Publication of *The Seven Crystal Balls* is postponed when Belgium is liberated from Nazi control in 1944. Hergé is investigated for working at a collaborationist newspaper and eventually arrested. He moves the strip to a new magazine and publishes *The Seven Crystal Balls* in 1948.

Prisoners of the Sun picks up where *The Seven Crystal Balls* leaves off.

1950

Land of Black Gold is originally from 1939–1940, but it ends abruptly midstory. It is redrawn and colored for publication in *Tintin* magazine.

Bernard Heuvelmans, the father of cryptozoology, writes the original script for *Destination Moon*.

Picking up where *Destination Moon* leaves off, *Explorers of the Moon* features Tintin and company in outer space.

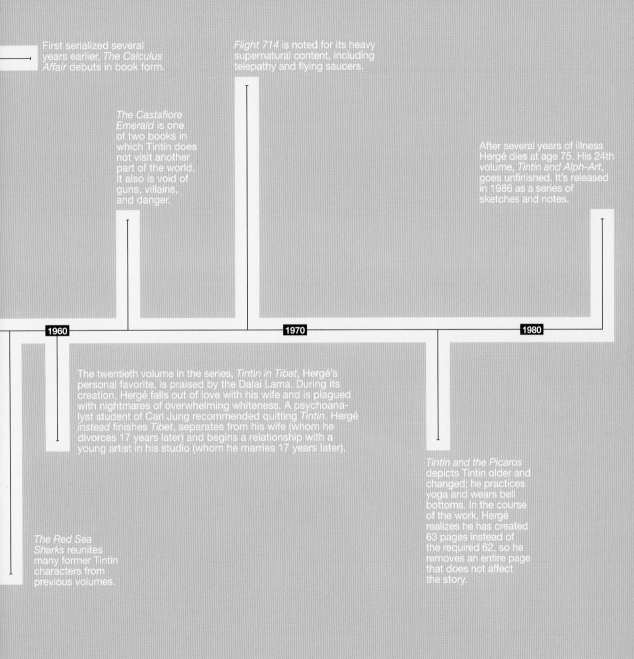

First serialized several years earlier, *The Calculus Affair* debuts in book form.

The Red Sea Sharks reunites many former Tintin characters from previous volumes.

1960

The twentieth volume in the series, *Tintin in Tibet*, Hergé's personal favorite, is praised by the Dalai Lama. During its creation, Hergé falls out of love with his wife and is plagued with nightmares of overwhelming whiteness. A psychoanalyst student of Carl Jung recommended quitting *Tintin*. Hergé *instead* finishes *Tibet*, separates from his wife (whom he divorces 17 years later) and begins a relationship with a young artist in his studio (whom he marries 17 years later).

The Castafiore Emerald is one of two books in which Tintin does not visit another part of the world. It also is void of guns, villains, and danger.

Flight 714 is noted for its heavy supernatural content, including telepathy and flying saucers.

1970

Tintin and the Picaros depicts Tintin older and changed; he practices yoga and wears bell bottoms. In the course of the work, Hergé realizes he has created 63 pages instead of the required 62, so he removes an entire page that does not affect the story.

1980

After several years of illness Hergé dies at age 75. His 24th volume, *Tintin and Alph-Art*, goes unfinished. It's released in 1986 as a series of sketches and notes.

REVISIONIST HISTORY

30 Years of Changing Tintin

1943
Hergé re-edits and colors *The Crab with the Golden Claws*. He also adds four arbitrary full-page panels since the original strips didn't have enough material to fill the 62-page quota set by the publisher.

1946
Hergé redraws and colors *Tintin in the Congo* in his new *ligne claire* style. He also scraps nearly half the pages, adds cameos by Thomson and Thompson, and removes several references to Belgian rule in Africa.

1955
Hergé re-draws and colors *Cigars of the Pharaoh*. He cuts full pages including the scenes where Tintin dons makeup to pass as a Muslim and where Snowy plays a gramophone to warn his owner of an approaching cobra.

1961
The original strips that make up this volume ran during Germany's occupation of Belgium. Amidst accusations that Hergé is anti-Semitic, he removes several offensive Jewish characters and all references to God in *The Shooting Star*.

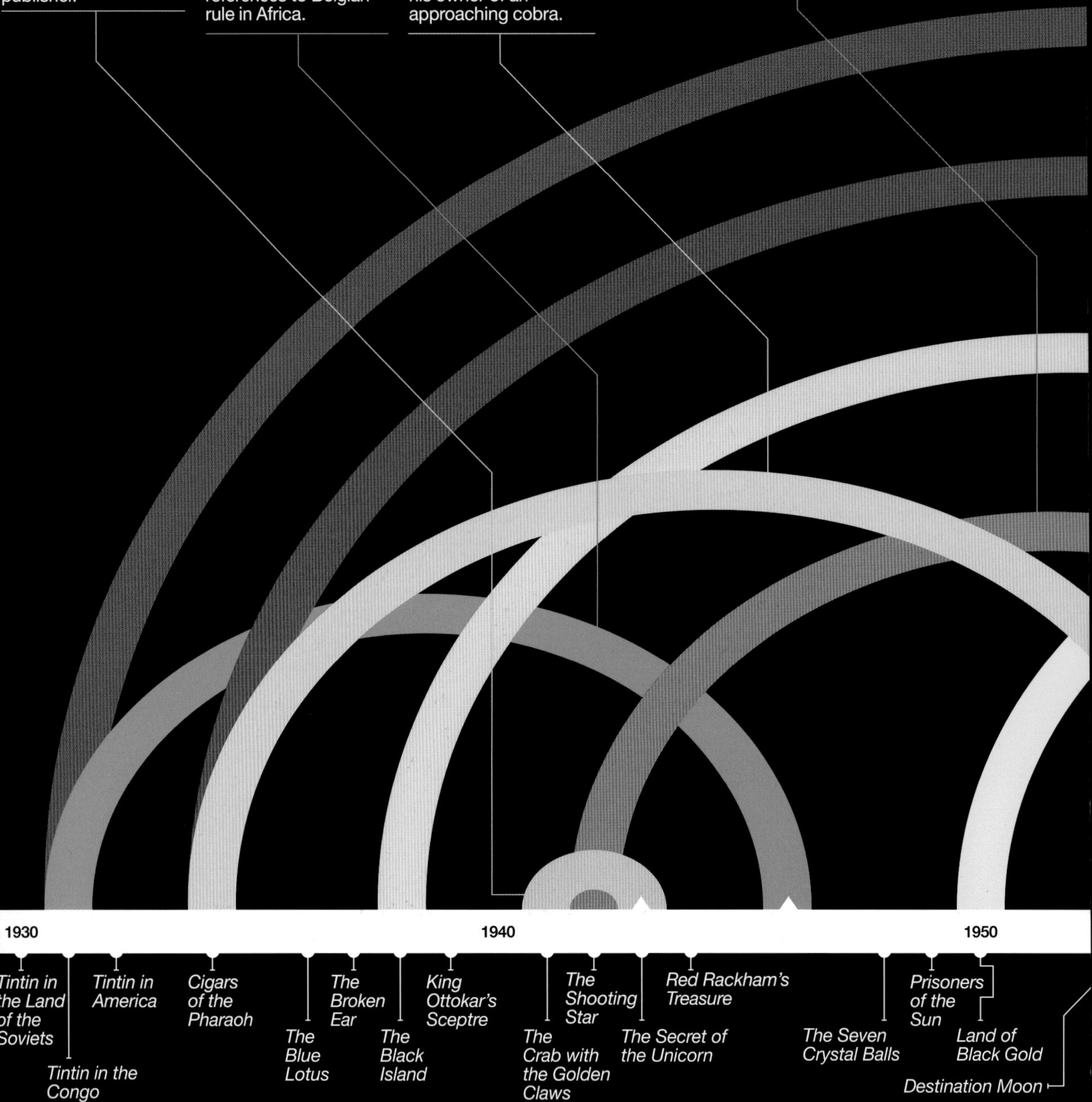

1930
1940
1950
Tintin in the Land of the Soviets
Tintin in the Congo
Tintin in America
Cigars of the Pharaoh
The Blue Lotus
The Broken Ear
The Black Island
King Ottokar's Sceptre
The Crab with the Golden Claws
The Shooting Star
The Secret of the Unicorn
Red Rackham's Treasure
The Seven Crystal Balls
Prisoners of the Sun
Land of Black Gold
Destination Moon

Millions of people have read *Tintin*, but the stories they picked up may not have been the same ones originally published. The reason: Tintin creator Hergé often went back to rewrite, re-draw, and re-edit his famous series. Sometimes he did it for space, sometimes to add color, and sometimes to subdue controversy.

1962
After complaints, Hergé removes the Air India logo from plane crash debris that appears in *Tintin in Tibet*.

1966
The Black Island is updated to portray Great Britain more accurately, including names, police uniforms, locations, and modern vehicles.

1971
Hergé again updates *Cigars of the Pharaoh* when it is translated into English. Hergé redraws a scene where a Sheik shows Tintin that he's reading *Destination Moon*, a Tintin volume published 19 years after *Cigars'* original release.

1972
Land of Black Gold changes locations. Palestine turns into the fictional Arab state of Khemed and actual Arabic is inserted into the dialogue in place of nonsensical imagined script.

1975
Hergé again re-draws a page from *Tintin in the Congo* for Scandinavian publishers. He changes a scene where Tintin kills a rhinoceros by drilling a hole in its back, filling it with gunpowder, and lighting it on fire. In the updated version, the rhino runs away scared after accidentally firing Tintin's gun.

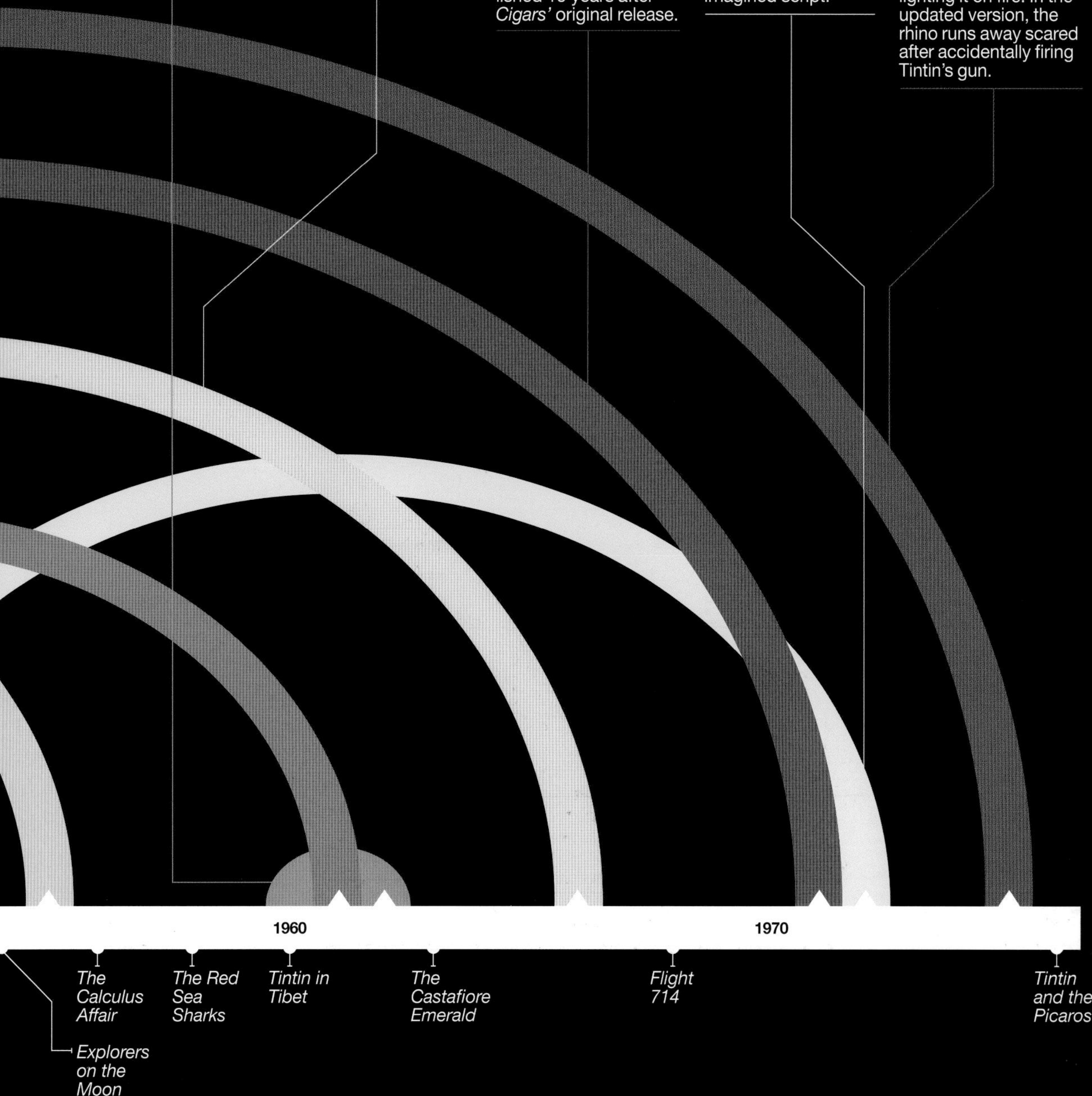

1960
1970
The Calculus Affair
The Red Sea Sharks
Tintin in Tibet
The Castafiore Emerald
Flight 714
Tintin and the Picaros
Explorers on the Moon

BOOK REPORT

The Library of Congress Comic Collection

The Library of Congress's mission, according to official policy, is to create a "comprehensive record of the Platinum, Golden, and Silver Ages of US comic book publishing (representing the formative years of comic book development as well as current trends)." They collect a lot; but they also miss a lot. Here's how they go about beefing up their collection.

How thoroughly the library collects different subjects

Basic
Materials introducing the subject

Intermediary
Enough to support undergrad instruction

Advanced
All important reference works

Comprehensive
All significant works

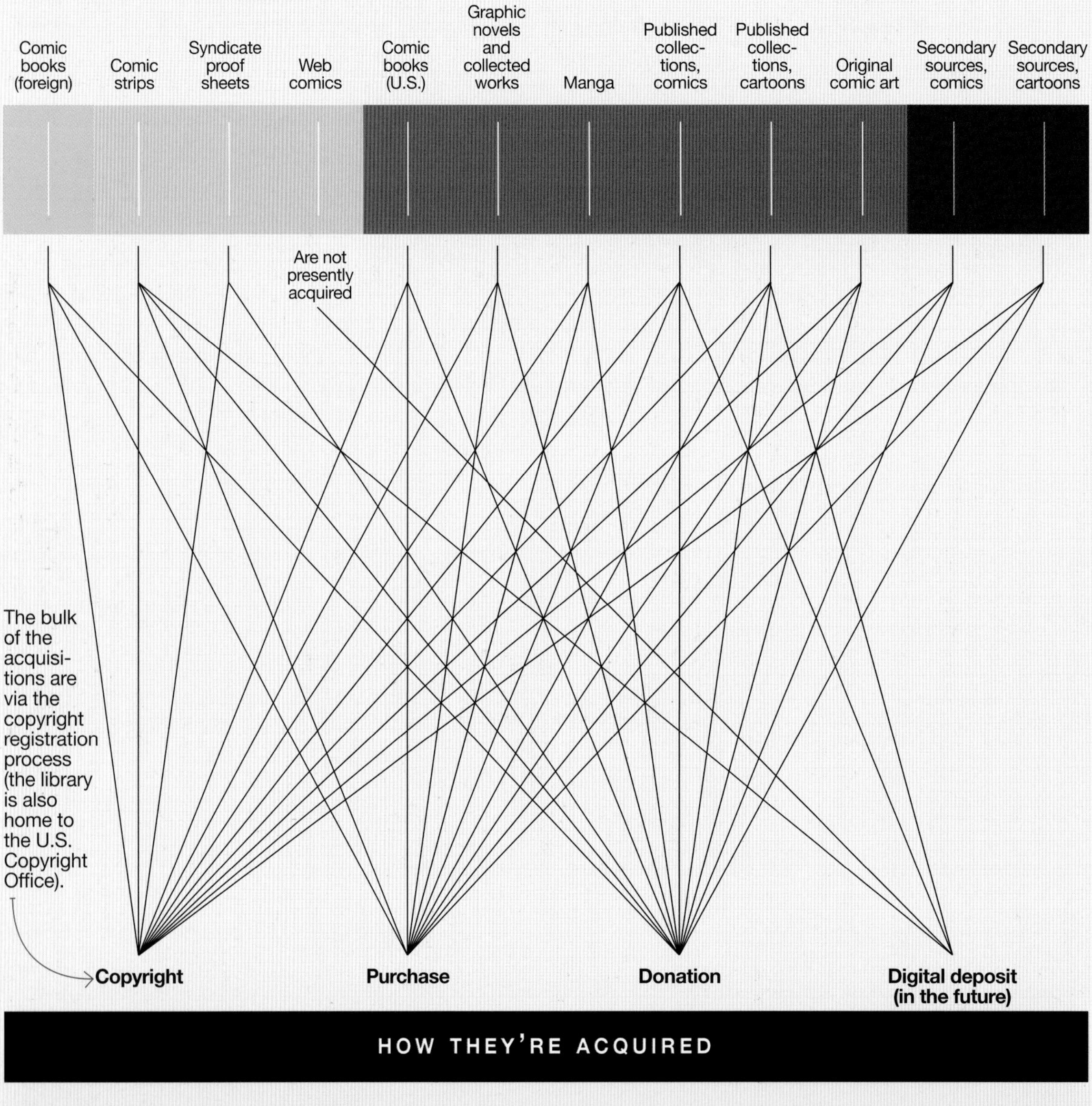
Comic books (foreign)
Comic strips
Syndicate proof sheets
Web comics
Comic books (U.S.)
Graphic novels and collected works
Manga
Published collec-tions, comics
Published collec-tions, cartoons
Original comic art
Secondary sources, comics
Secondary sources, cartoons
Are not presently acquired
The bulk of the acquisi-tions are via the copyright registration process (the library is also home to the U.S. Copyright Office).
Copyright
Purchase
Donation
Digital deposit (in the future)
HOW THEY'RE ACQUIRED

The Schedule of a Manga Artist

In Japan, giant magazines hundreds of pages thick are printed every week. To meet the page count, comic book artists work some pretty crazy hours. Here's a week in the life of one artist.

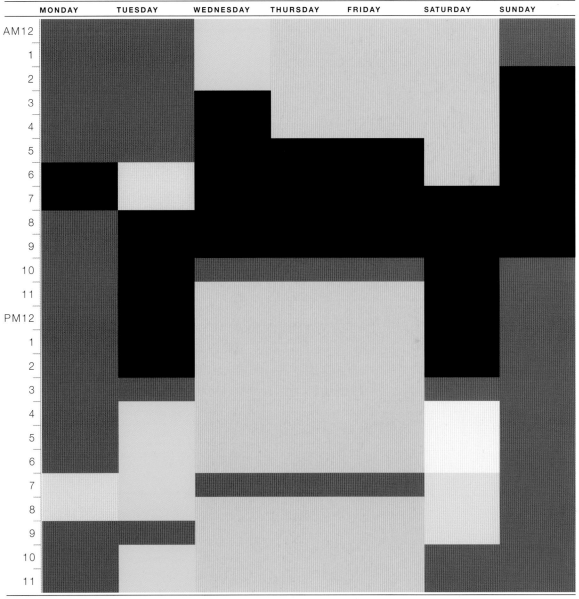

	MONDAY	TUESDAY	WEDNESDAY	THURSDAY	FRIDAY	SATURDAY	SUNDAY

Legend:
- Work on rough pages
- Assistants help production
- Meet with the editor
- Work on cover or color pages
- Sleeping
- Meal break
- Free time

COVER TO COVER

Marvel and DC's Price History

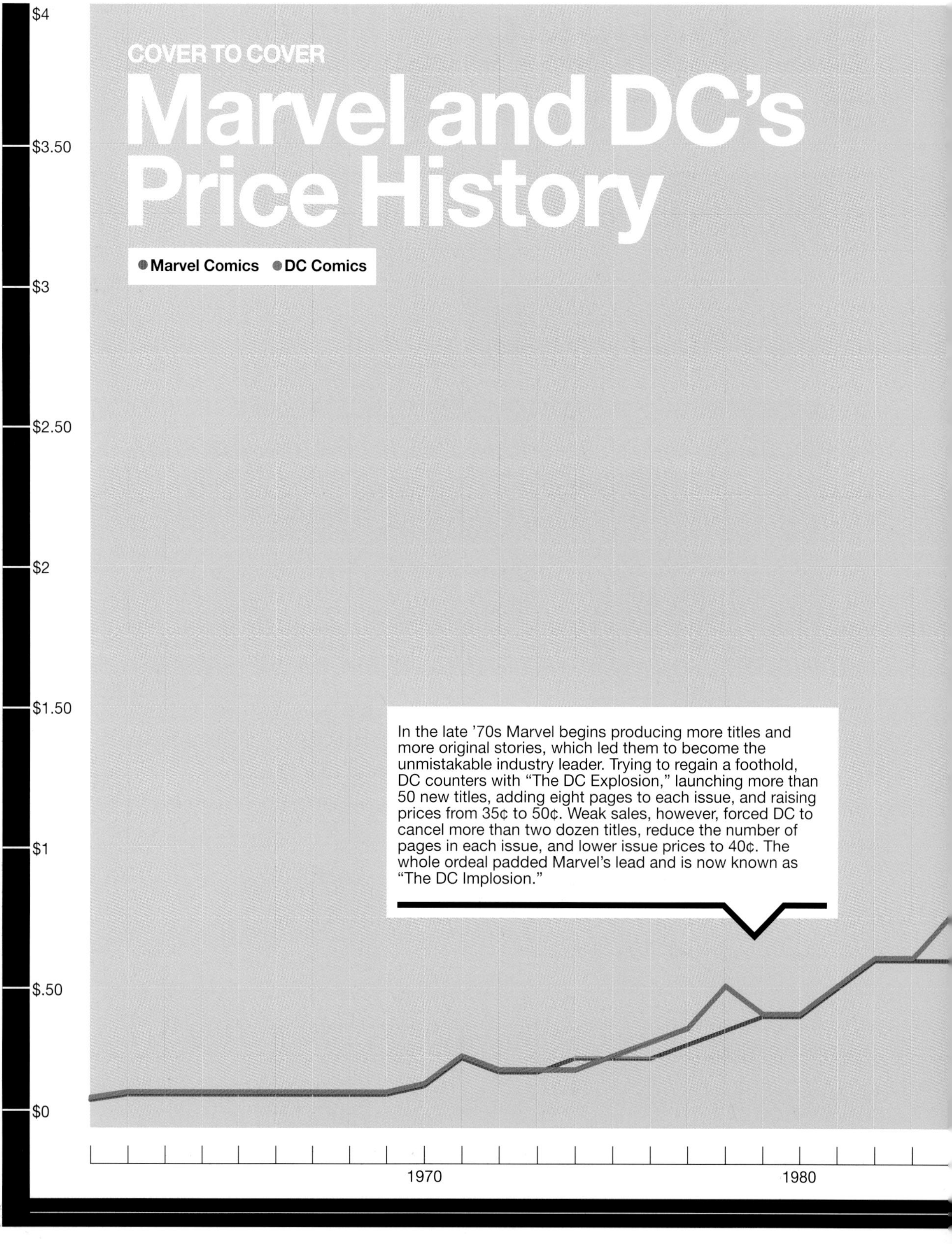

● Marvel Comics ● DC Comics
$4
$3.50
$3
$2.50
$2
$1.50
$1
$.50
$0
1970
1980

In the late '70s Marvel begins producing more titles and more original stories, which led them to become the unmistakable industry leader. Trying to regain a foothold, DC counters with "The DC Explosion," launching more than 50 new titles, adding eight pages to each issue, and raising prices from 35¢ to 50¢. Weak sales, however, forced DC to cancel more than two dozen titles, reduce the number of pages in each issue, and lower issue prices to 40¢. The whole ordeal padded Marvel's lead and is now known as "The DC Implosion."

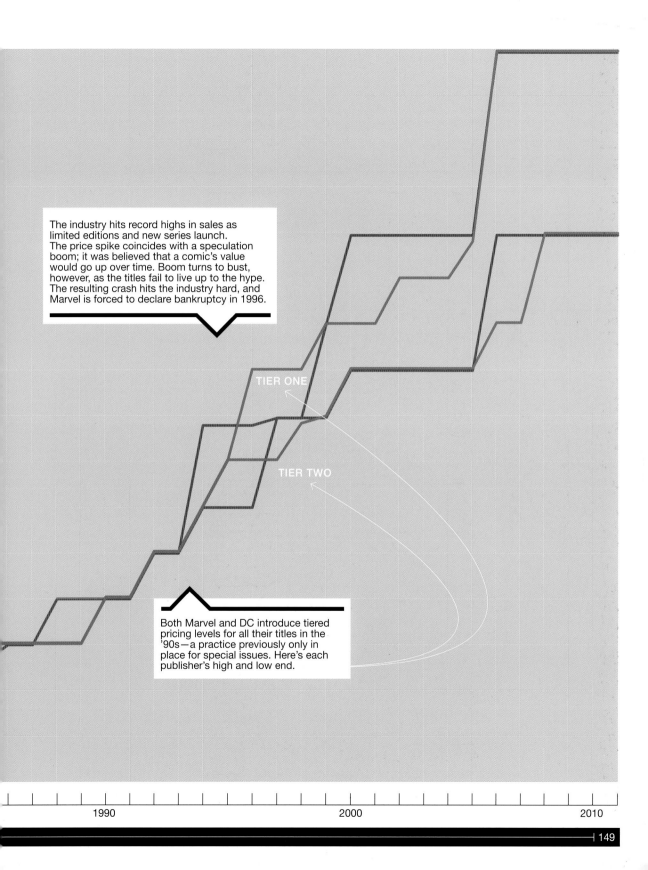

The industry hits record highs in sales as limited editions and new series launch. The price spike coincides with a speculation boom; it was believed that a comic's value would go up over time. Boom turns to bust, however, as the titles fail to live up to the hype. The resulting crash hits the industry hard, and Marvel is forced to declare bankruptcy in 1996.

TIER ONE

TIER TWO

Both Marvel and DC introduce tiered pricing levels for all their titles in the '90s—a practice previously only in place for special issues. Here's each publisher's high and low end.

1990   2000   2010

Size Matters

Here's how Marvel and DC's super cities (and a few small countries) stack up against real-world urban development.

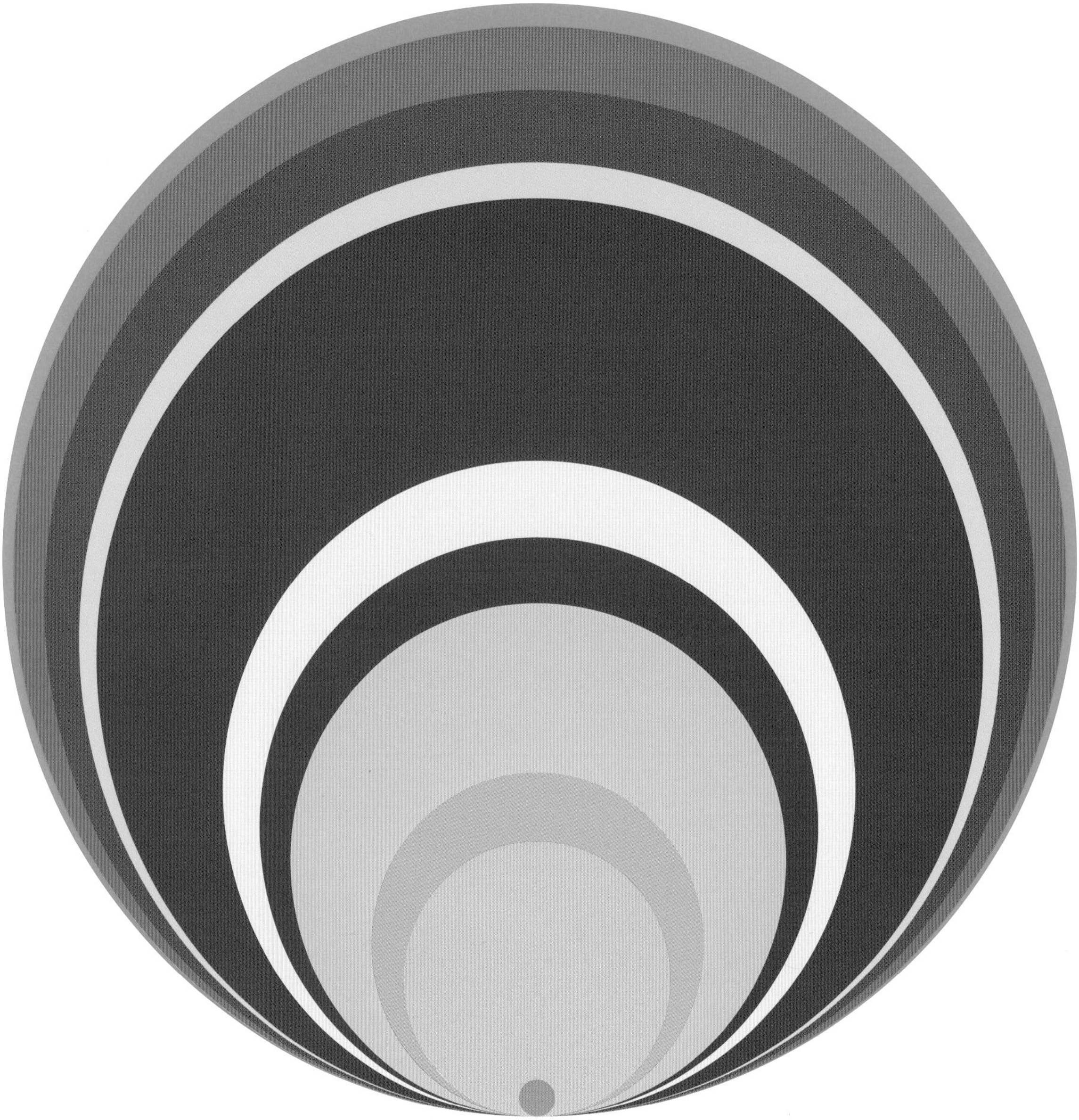

Atlantis 9,000 **Kingdom of Latveria** 500,000 **Coast City** 781,071 **Star City** 1,735,714
Paris 2,211,297 **Chicago** 2,833,321 **Gotham City** 5,554,285 **Kingdom of Wakanda** 6,000,000
Metropolis 6,942,857 **London** 7,830,000 **New York** 8,175,133

Assorted *Peanuts*

Best friends, brothers, and budding love in Charles Schulz's long-running strip.

Best friends
Love interest
Family

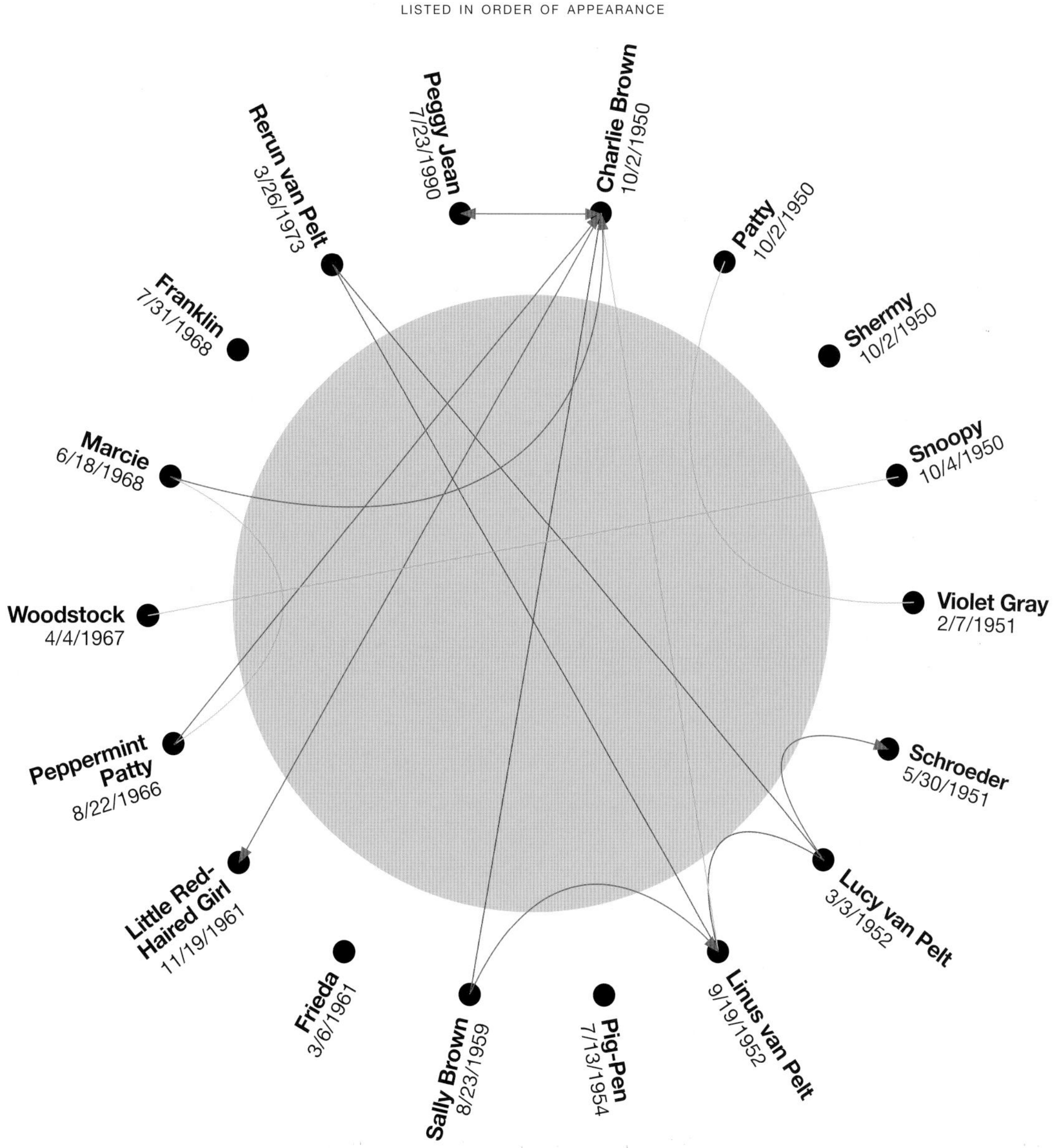
LISTED IN ORDER OF APPEARANCE
Charlie Brown
10/2/1950
Patty
10/2/1950
Shermy
10/2/1950
Snoopy
10/4/1950
Violet Gray
2/7/1951
Schroeder
5/30/1951
Lucy van Pelt
3/3/1952
Linus van Pelt
9/19/1952
Pig-Pen
7/13/1954
Sally Brown
8/23/1959
Frieda
3/6/1961
Little Red-Haired Girl
11/19/1961
Peppermint Patty
8/22/1966
Woodstock
4/4/1967
Marcie
6/18/1968
Franklin
7/31/1968
Rerun van Pelt
3/26/1973
Peggy Jean
7/23/1990

Marvel Universe Trading Cards

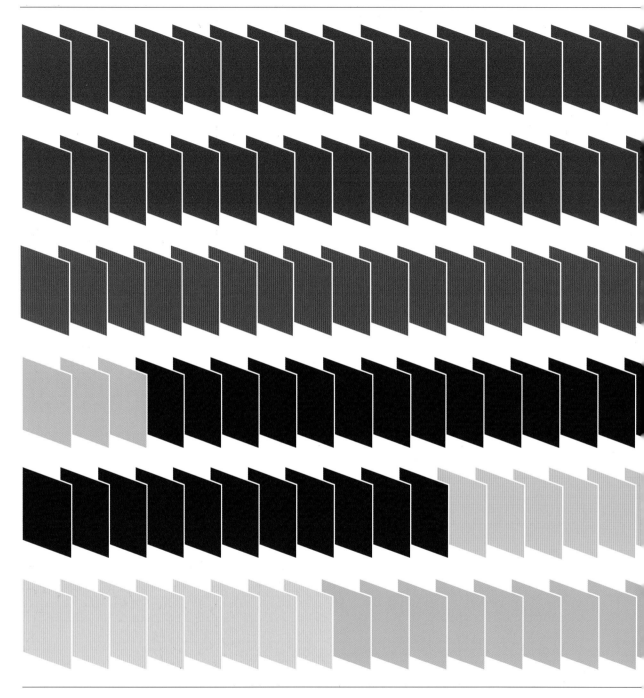

| Superheroes | Supervillains | Rookies | Famous Battles | Most Valuable Comics | Team Pictures |

Just as the comic book industry enjoyed booming sales in the '90s, so did collectible trading cards. It started when Marvel Comics released their first set in 1990. The 167-card set featured notable characters, famous battles, and even 12-cards featuring Spider-Man interviewing his peers.

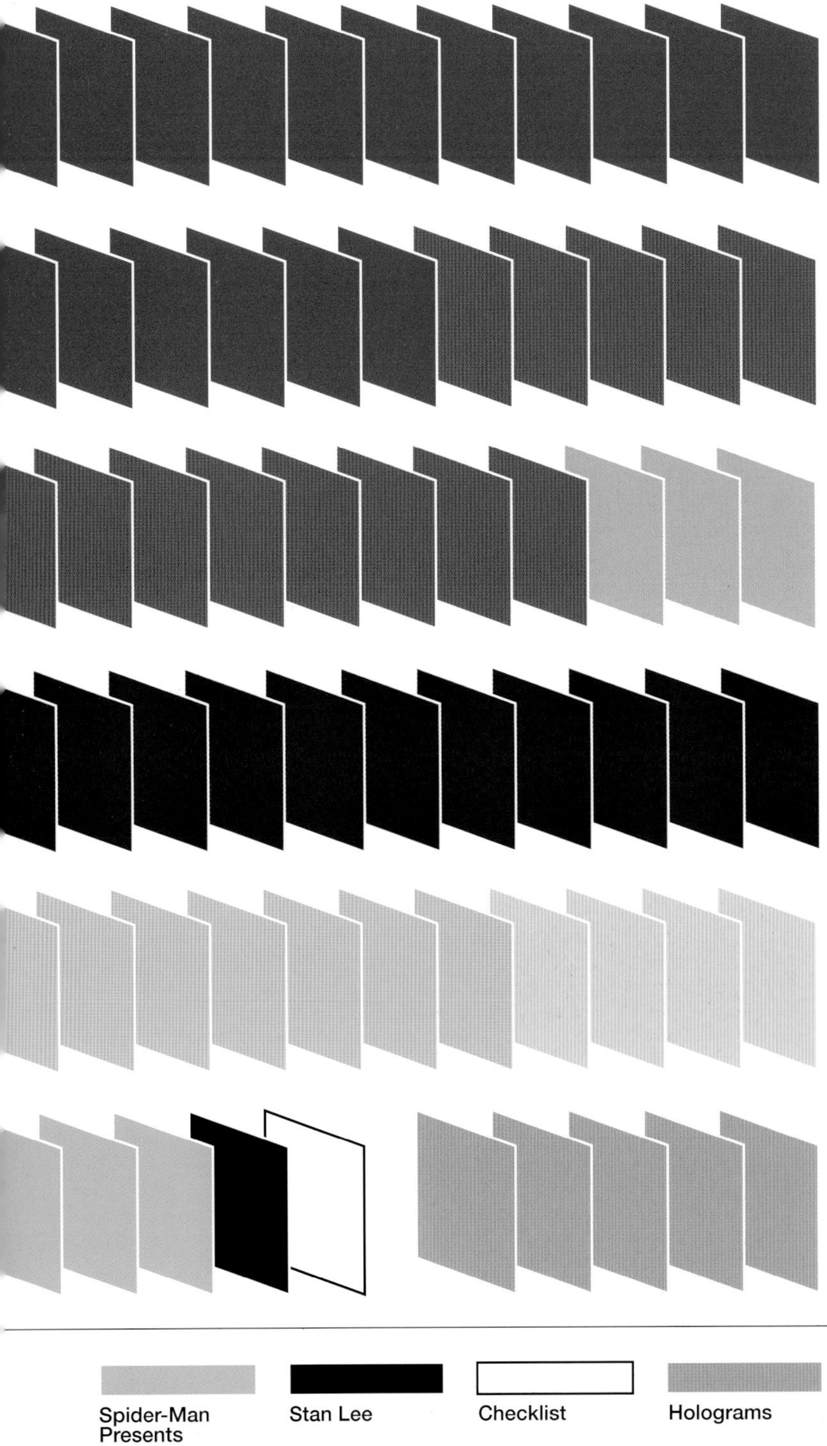

Spider-Man Presents
Stan Lee
Checklist
Holograms

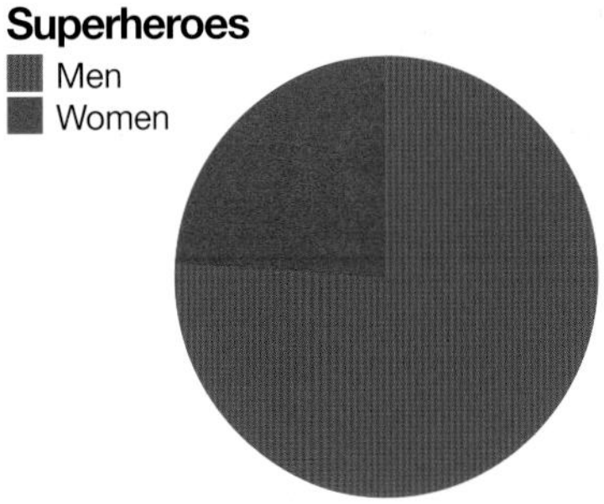

Superheroes
Men
Women

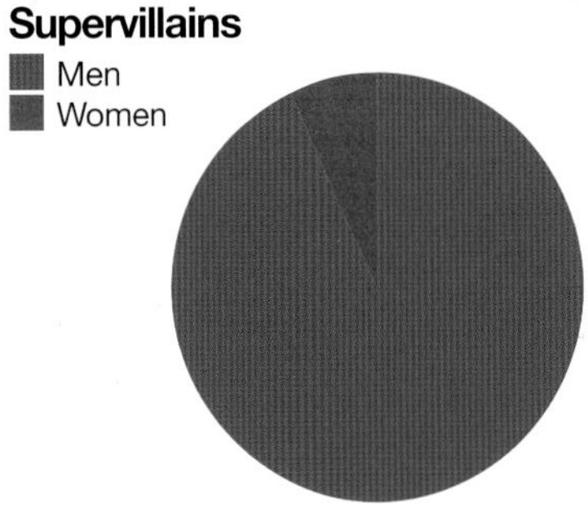

Supervillains
Men
Women

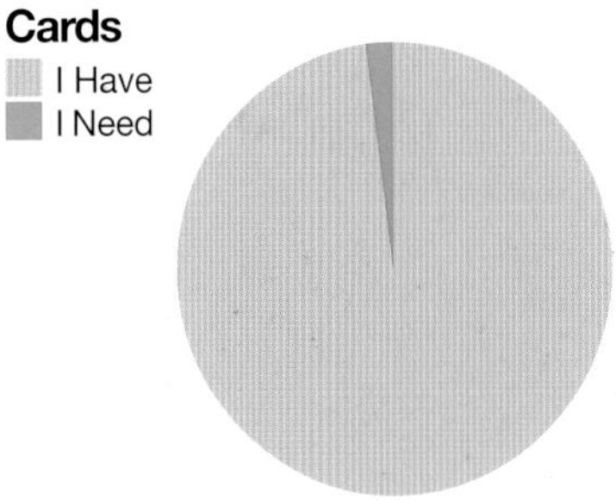

Cards
I Have
I Need

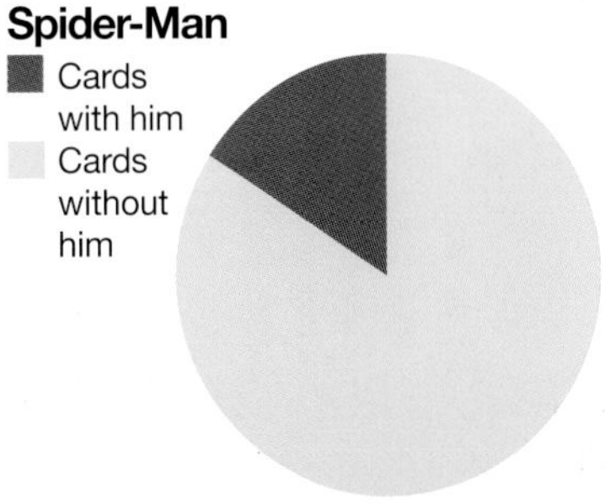

Spider-Man
Cards with him
Cards without him

Gotham City Police Department Utility Bill

When the city needs to call in its big gun,
it does so at a big price.

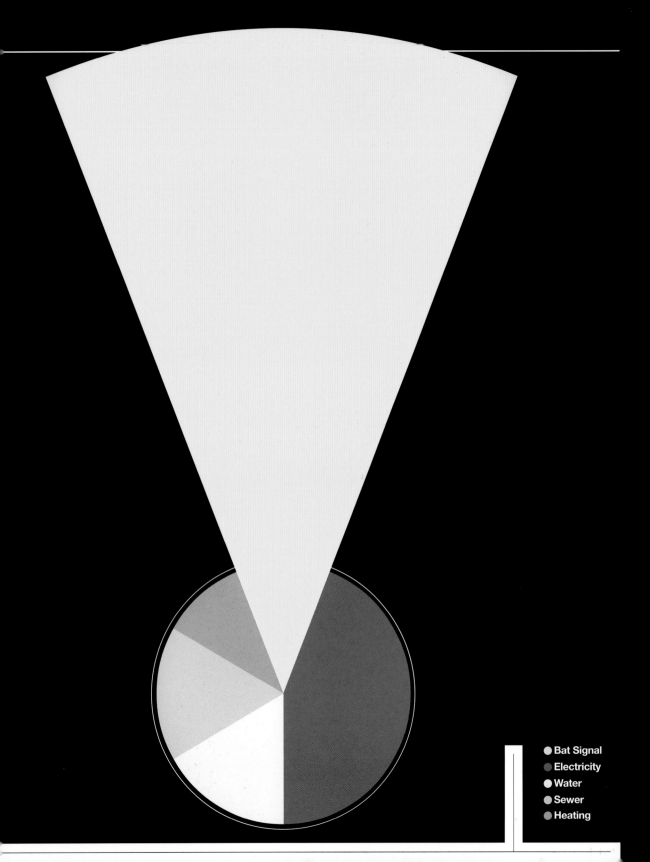

● Bat Signal
● Electricity
● Water
● Sewer
● Heating

Power Pack

Super strength is not the only asset artists have given Power Girl.

AVERAGE
WOMAN'S
BREAST SIZE

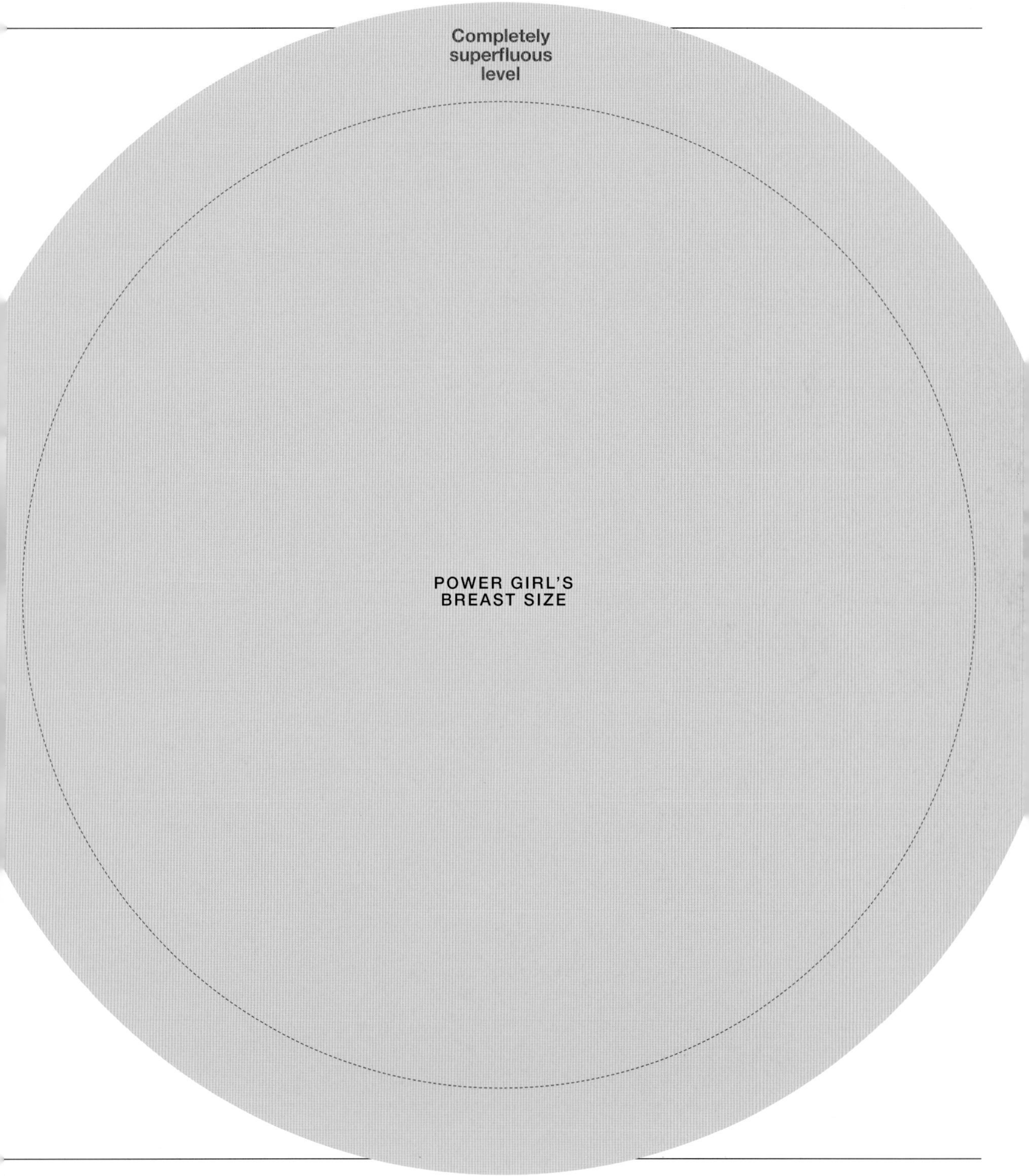
Completely superfluous level
POWER GIRL'S BREAST SIZE

If You Were The Punisher, What Would You Do?

A glimpse into the mind of Frank Castle, a man searching for someone who deserves to die.

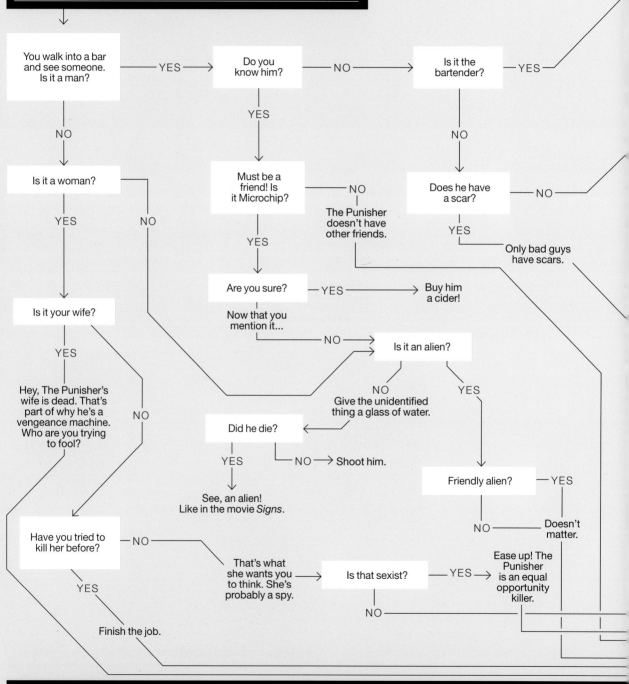

You walk into a bar and see someone. Is it a man? — YES → Do you know him? — NO → Is it the bartender? — YES

You walk into a bar and see someone. Is it a man? — NO → Is it a woman?

Do you know him? — YES → Must be a friend! Is it Microchip?

Is it the bartender? — NO → Does he have a scar?

Must be a friend! Is it Microchip? — NO → The Punisher doesn't have other friends.

Must be a friend! Is it Microchip? — YES → Are you sure?

Does he have a scar? — YES → Only bad guys have scars.

Does he have a scar? — NO

Is it a woman? — YES → Is it your wife?

Is it a woman? — NO

Are you sure? — YES → Buy him a cider!

Are you sure? — Now that you mention it... — NO → Is it an alien?

Is it your wife? — YES → Hey, The Punisher's wife is dead. That's part of why he's a vengeance machine. Who are you trying to fool?

Is it your wife? — NO

Is it an alien? — NO → Give the unidentified thing a glass of water. → Did he die?

Is it an alien? — YES → Friendly alien?

Did he die? — YES → See, an alien! Like in the movie *Signs*.

Did he die? — NO → Shoot him.

Friendly alien? — YES → Doesn't matter.

Friendly alien? — NO

Have you tried to kill her before? — NO → That's what she wants you to think. She's probably a spy. → Is that sexist?

Have you tried to kill her before? — YES → Finish the job.

Is that sexist? — YES → Ease up! The Punisher is an equal opportunity killer.

Is that sexist? — NO

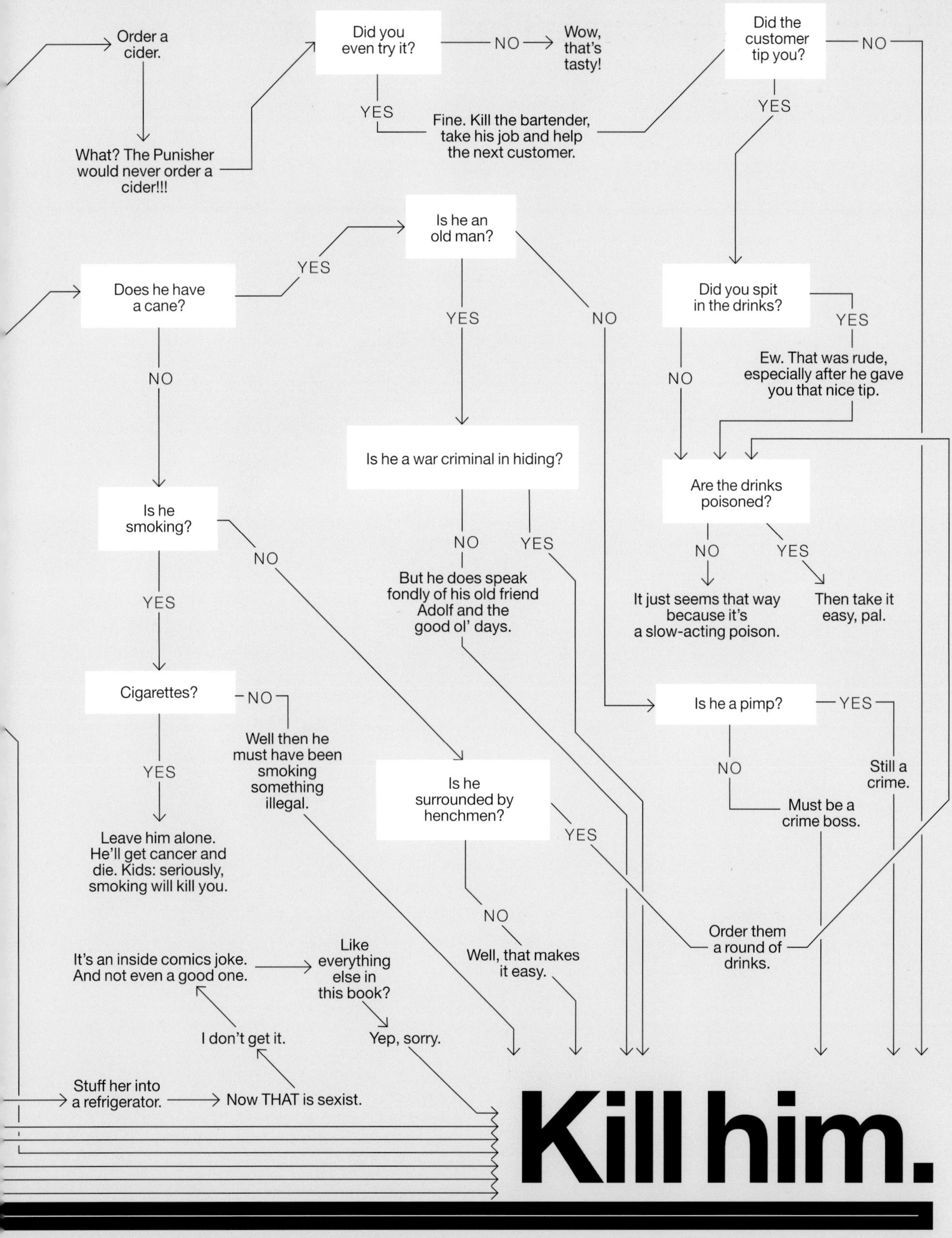

Order a cider.
What? The Punisher would never order a cider!!!
Did you even try it?
NO
Wow, that's tasty!
YES
Fine. Kill the bartender, take his job and help the next customer.
Did the customer tip you?
NO
YES
Is he an old man?
YES
Does he have a cane?
YES
NO
NO
Did you spit in the drinks?
YES
NO
Ew. That was rude, especially after he gave you that nice tip.
Is he a war criminal in hiding?
Are the drinks poisoned?
Is he smoking?
NO
NO
YES
NO
YES
But he does speak fondly of his old friend Adolf and the good ol' days.
It just seems that way because it's a slow-acting poison.
Then take it easy, pal.
YES
Cigarettes?
NO
Well then he must have been smoking something illegal.
Is he a pimp?
YES
NO
Still a crime.
YES
Is he surrounded by henchmen?
YES
Must be a crime boss.
Leave him alone. He'll get cancer and die. Kids: seriously, smoking will kill you.
NO
Order them a round of drinks.
It's an inside comics joke. And not even a good one.
Like everything else in this book?
Well, that makes it easy.
I don't get it.
Yep, sorry.
Stuff her into a refrigerator.
Now THAT is sexist.
Kill him.

Gotham City Police Department

The Major Crimes Unit in the DC Comics series *Gotham Central* deals with the toughest cases in the Police Department—including all superhero and supervillain issues. Here's how the squad has paired up to fight crime . . . and each other.

Legend:
- Partner
- Love Interest
- First Shift (day)
- Second Shift (night)
- Support

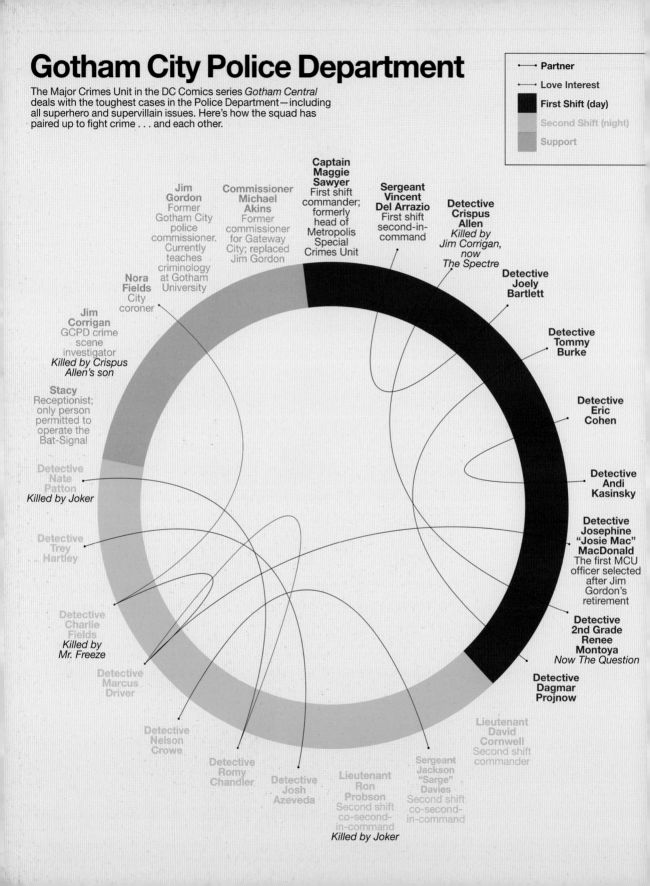

Captain Maggie Sawyer
First shift commander; formerly head of Metropolis Special Crimes Unit

Sergeant Vincent Del Arrazio
First shift second-in-command

Detective Crispus Allen
Killed by Jim Corrigan, now The Spectre

Detective Joely Bartlett

Detective Tommy Burke

Detective Eric Cohen

Detective Andi Kasinsky

Detective Josephine "Josie Mac" MacDonald
The first MCU officer selected after Jim Gordon's retirement

Detective 2nd Grade Renee Montoya
Now The Question

Detective Dagmar Projnow

Lieutenant David Cornwell
Second shift commander

Sergeant Jackson "Sarge" Davies
Second shift co-second-in-command

Lieutenant Ron Probson
Second shift co-second-in-command
Killed by Joker

Detective Josh Azeveda

Detective Romy Chandler

Detective Nelson Crowe

Detective Marcus Driver

Detective Charlie Fields
Killed by Mr. Freeze

Detective Trey Hartley

Detective Nate Patton
Killed by Joker

Stacy
Receptionist; only person permitted to operate the Bat-Signal

Jim Corrigan
GCPD crime scene investigator
Killed by Crispus Allen's son

Nora Fields
City coroner

Jim Gordon
Former Gotham City police commissioner. Currently teaches criminology at Gotham University

Commissioner Michael Akins
Former commissioner for Gateway City; replaced Jim Gordon

The Most Quotable Lines from *300*

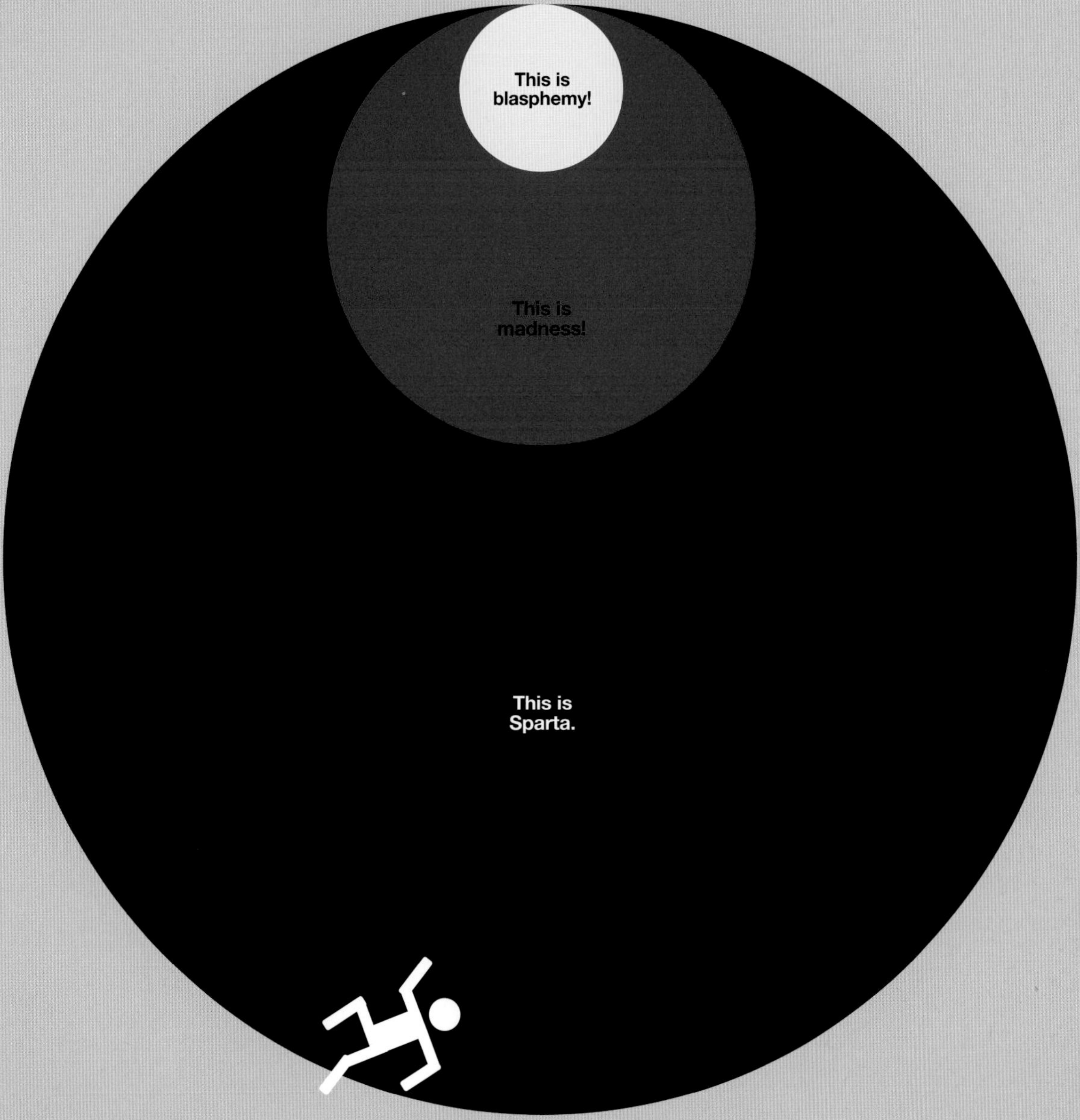
This is blasphemy!
This is madness!
This is Sparta.

Lifespans of Characters in *The Walking Dead*

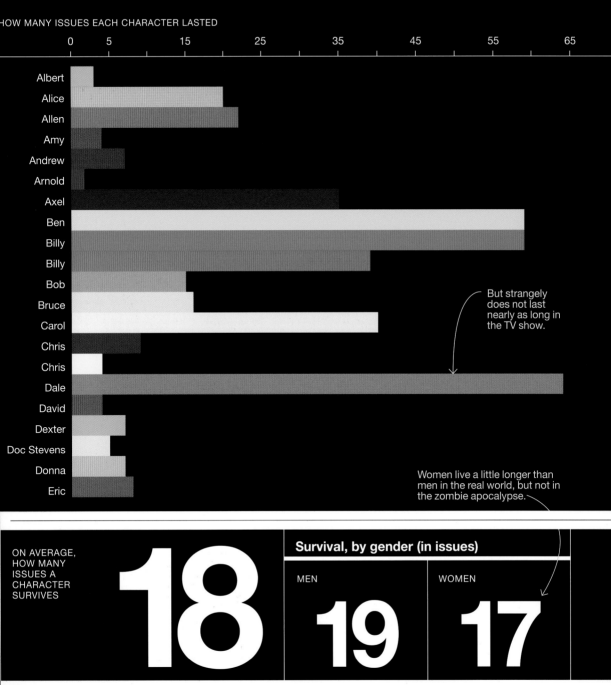

HOW MANY ISSUES EACH CHARACTER LASTED

	0	5	15	25	35	45	55	65

Albert
Alice
Allen
Amy
Andrew
Arnold
Axel
Ben
Billy
Billy
Bob
Bruce
Carol
Chris
Chris
Dale
David
Dexter
Doc Stevens
Donna
Eric

But strangely does not last nearly as long in the TV show.

Women live a little longer than men in the real world, but not in the zombie apocalypse.

ON AVERAGE, HOW MANY ISSUES A CHARACTER SURVIVES	**18**	Survival, by gender (in issues)	
		MEN	WOMEN
		19	**17**

It's hard to stay alive for long when all your neighbors are either zombies or the people freaked out by them. Here's a breakdown of the first 75 issues of *The Walking Dead*, tracking how long characters survived after they were introduced.

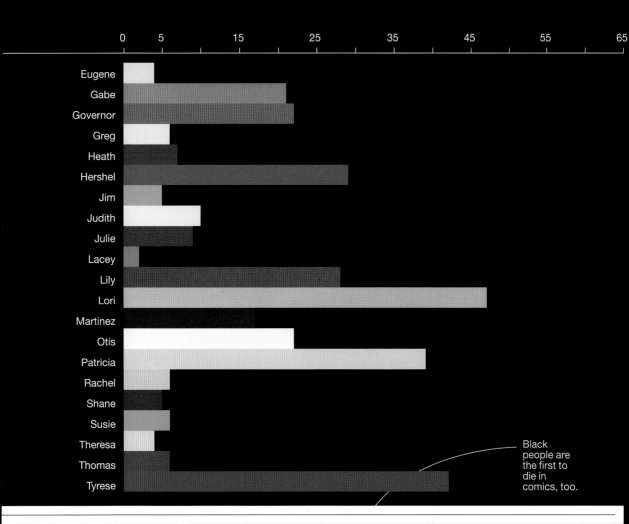

0 5 15 25 35 45 55 65	

Eugene
Gabe
Governor
Greg
Heath
Hershel
Jim
Judith
Julie
Lacey
Lily
Lori
Martinez
Otis
Patricia
Rachel
Shane
Susie
Theresa
Thomas
Tyrese

Black people are the first to die in comics, too.

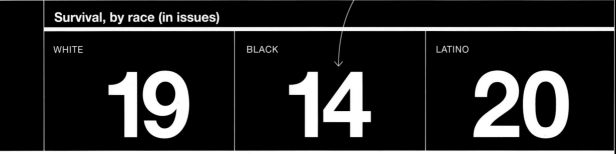

Survival, by race (in issues)

WHITE	BLACK	LATINO
19	**14**	**20**

A Peek Inside the Jean Grey School for Higher Learning

When the X-Men first debuted, the mutants, then teenagers, all studied at Professor Charles Xavier's School for Gifted Youngsters. As the X-Men drew more enemies, the school came under constant attack. Needing a change of scenery, the X-Men eventually moved their headquarters from Salem, New York to San Francisco, California. But Wolverine decided to stay put, rebuilding the old facility under a new moniker (an ode to his one-time teammate Jean Grey, RIP) and reopening it in 2011 with a brand new faculty.

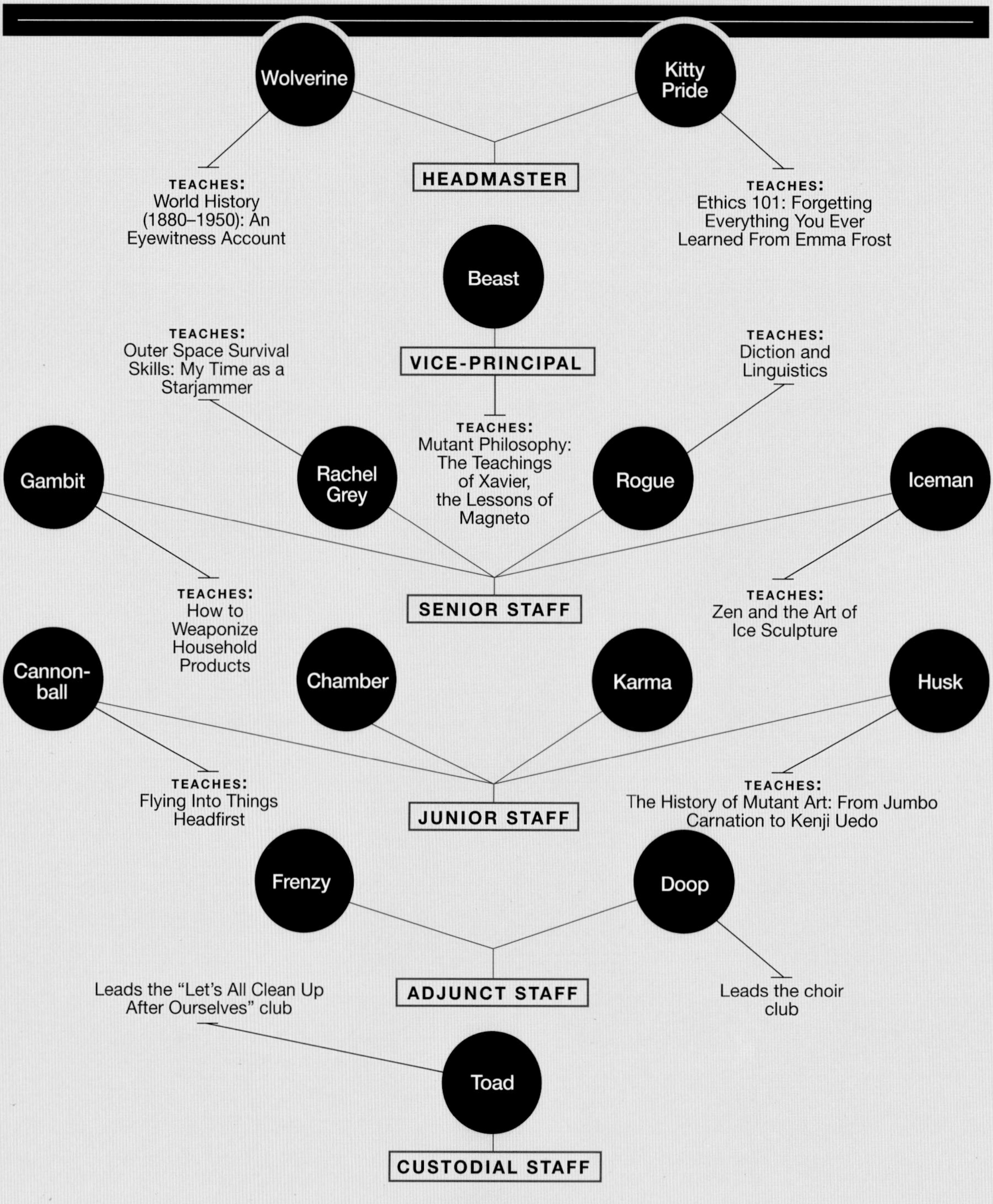

Wolverine
Kitty Pride
TEACHES: World History (1880–1950): An Eyewitness Account
HEADMASTER
TEACHES: Ethics 101: Forgetting Everything You Ever Learned From Emma Frost
Beast
TEACHES: Outer Space Survival Skills: My Time as a Starjammer
VICE-PRINCIPAL
TEACHES: Diction and Linguistics
TEACHES: Mutant Philosophy: The Teachings of Xavier, the Lessons of Magneto
Gambit
Rachel Grey
Rogue
Iceman
TEACHES: How to Weaponize Household Products
SENIOR STAFF
TEACHES: Zen and the Art of Ice Sculpture
Cannon-ball
Chamber
Karma
Husk
TEACHES: Flying Into Things Headfirst
JUNIOR STAFF
TEACHES: The History of Mutant Art: From Jumbo Carnation to Kenji Uedo
Frenzy
Doop
Leads the "Let's All Clean Up After Ourselves" club
ADJUNCT STAFF
Leads the choir club
Toad
CUSTODIAL STAFF

How Fans Voted to Kill Robin

In late 1988 the DC Comics brass became aware of the public's unfavorable opinion of the current Robin, Jason Todd. So that September, DC set up a phone line to determine the fate of Batman's sidekick and instructed fans to call 1-900-720-2660 to save Robin, or 1-900-720-2666 to kill him. With the phone lines open for two days and each call costing 50¢, more than 10,000 people voted.

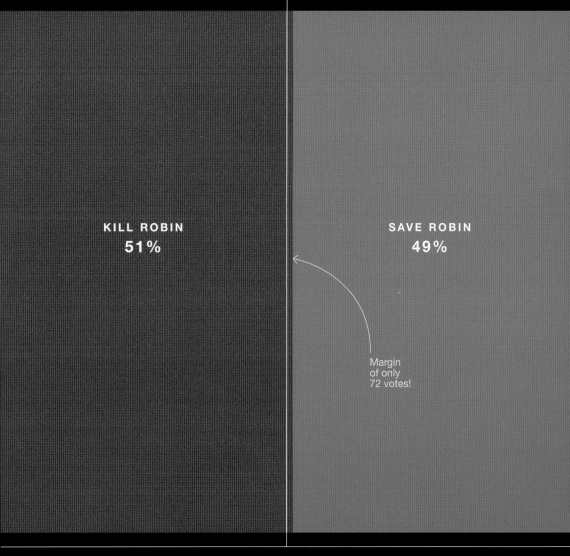

KILL ROBIN
51%

SAVE ROBIN
49%

Margin of only 72 votes!

According to then *Batman* editor Denny O'Neil, one man programmed his phone to dial the "kill" number every 90 seconds for 8 hours, which could have generated enough votes to sway the outcome (and cost the caller $160).

Archie's Ample, Awesome, and Awful Alliteration

Riverdale's Archie Andrews is best known
for being in the middle of a love triangle between
Betty, the girl next door, and Veronica, the
one-percenter. But his acquaintances are vast,
and have similar sounding names.

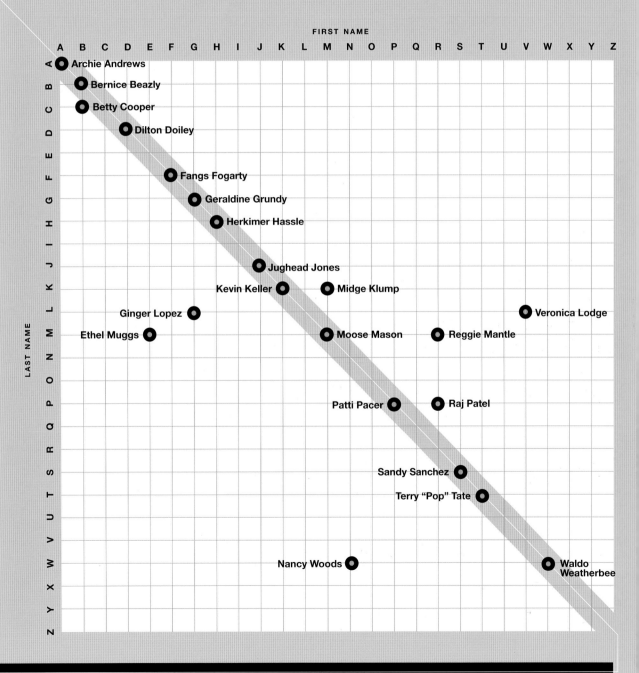

FIRST NAME

A B C D E F G H I J K L M N O P Q R S T U V W X Y Z

LAST NAME

A — Archie Andrews
B — Bernice Beazly
C — Betty Cooper
D — Dilton Doiley
F — Fangs Fogarty
G — Geraldine Grundy
H — Herkimer Hassle
J — Jughead Jones
K — Kevin Keller   Midge Klump
L — Ginger Lopez   Veronica Lodge
M — Ethel Muggs   Moose Mason   Reggie Mantle
P — Patti Pacer   Raj Patel
S — Sandy Sanchez
T — Terry "Pop" Tate
W — Nancy Woods   Waldo Weatherbee

What Makes
Nick Fury
So Intimidating

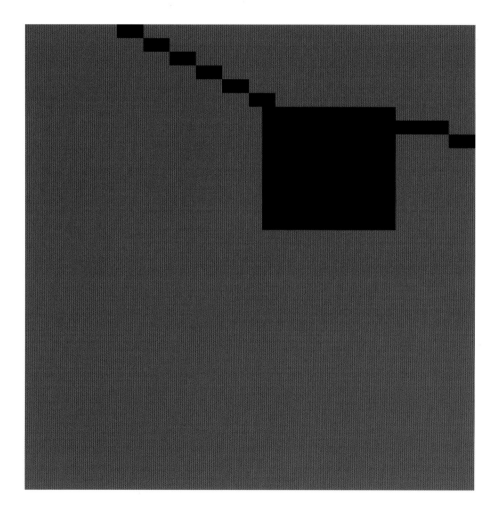

 Head of the nation's most
powerful security force

■ Eyepatch

Reasons to Like Cyclops

■ Team leader   □ Cool sunglasses   ■ Dude gets the hottest X-women even though he's kind of a stiff

How DC Characters Rank in HeroClix

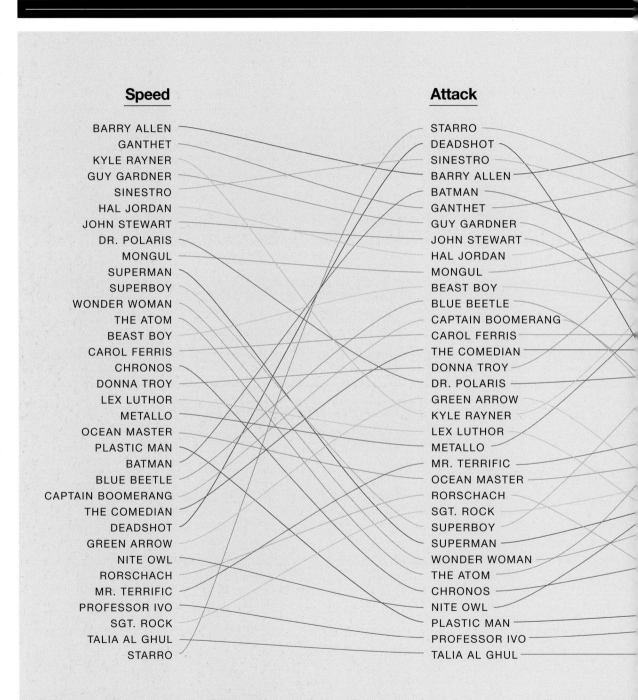

Speed

BARRY ALLEN
GANTHET
KYLE RAYNER
GUY GARDNER
SINESTRO
HAL JORDAN
JOHN STEWART
DR. POLARIS
MONGUL
SUPERMAN
SUPERBOY
WONDER WOMAN
THE ATOM
BEAST BOY
CAROL FERRIS
CHRONOS
DONNA TROY
LEX LUTHOR
METALLO
OCEAN MASTER
PLASTIC MAN
BATMAN
BLUE BEETLE
CAPTAIN BOOMERANG
THE COMEDIAN
DEADSHOT
GREEN ARROW
NITE OWL
RORSCHACH
MR. TERRIFIC
PROFESSOR IVO
SGT. ROCK
TALIA AL GHUL
STARRO

Attack

STARRO
DEADSHOT
SINESTRO
BARRY ALLEN
BATMAN
GANTHET
GUY GARDNER
JOHN STEWART
HAL JORDAN
MONGUL
BEAST BOY
BLUE BEETLE
CAPTAIN BOOMERANG
CAROL FERRIS
THE COMEDIAN
DONNA TROY
DR. POLARIS
GREEN ARROW
KYLE RAYNER
LEX LUTHOR
METALLO
MR. TERRIFIC
OCEAN MASTER
RORSCHACH
SGT. ROCK
SUPERBOY
SUPERMAN
WONDER WOMAN
THE ATOM
CHRONOS
NITE OWL
PLASTIC MAN
PROFESSOR IVO
TALIA AL GHUL

Launched in 2002, HeroClix is a game where players battle each other with miniature comic character figurines. Each figure has ratings for Speed, Attack, Defense and Damage dealt, which are updated during gameplay. They're interesting because the ratings don't exactly align to the comics—in fact, they can't, because DC Comics doesn't use official power ratings the same way that Marvel Comics does (see page 184).

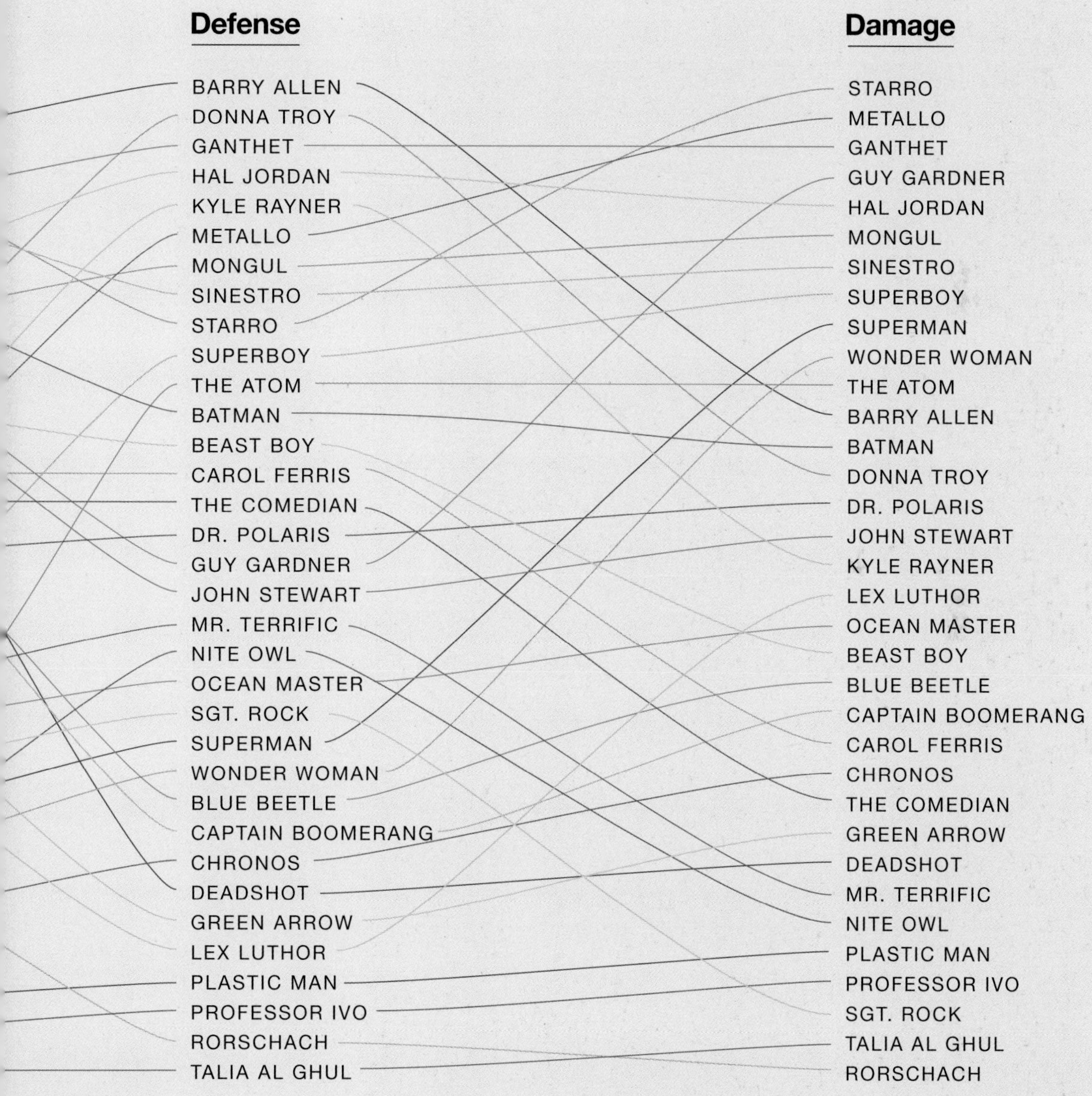

Defense
BARRY ALLEN
DONNA TROY
GANTHET
HAL JORDAN
KYLE RAYNER
METALLO
MONGUL
SINESTRO
STARRO
SUPERBOY
THE ATOM
BATMAN
BEAST BOY
CAROL FERRIS
THE COMEDIAN
DR. POLARIS
GUY GARDNER
JOHN STEWART
MR. TERRIFIC
NITE OWL
OCEAN MASTER
SGT. ROCK
SUPERMAN
WONDER WOMAN
BLUE BEETLE
CAPTAIN BOOMERANG
CHRONOS
DEADSHOT
GREEN ARROW
LEX LUTHOR
PLASTIC MAN
PROFESSOR IVO
RORSCHACH
TALIA AL GHUL
Damage
STARRO
METALLO
GANTHET
GUY GARDNER
HAL JORDAN
MONGUL
SINESTRO
SUPERBOY
SUPERMAN
WONDER WOMAN
THE ATOM
BARRY ALLEN
BATMAN
DONNA TROY
DR. POLARIS
JOHN STEWART
KYLE RAYNER
LEX LUTHOR
OCEAN MASTER
BEAST BOY
BLUE BEETLE
CAPTAIN BOOMERANG
CAROL FERRIS
CHRONOS
THE COMEDIAN
GREEN ARROW
DEADSHOT
MR. TERRIFIC
NITE OWL
PLASTIC MAN
PROFESSOR IVO
SGT. ROCK
TALIA AL GHUL
RORSCHACH

Shell Boy

The other Turtles constantly make fun of Donatello. Here's why:

 He spends his time
studying science

He spends his time
playing with his staff

Five Easy Pieces

Captain America has repeatedly broken his shield. Fingers crossed he took out the extended warranty.

1982
Damage: Molecule Man destroys the shield, Iron Man's armor, Thor's hammer, and the Silver Surfer's surfboard.
Repair: Molecule Man reassembles them all save for the armor, which is too complex.

1985
Damage: While wielding the power of the Beyonder, Dr. Doom partially destroys the shield.
Repair: The villain Klaw's shockwave power inadvertently realigns the nano-structure of the taped-together shield.

1991
Damage: Thanos punches the shield while in possession of the Infinity Gauntlet. (It has magic powers).
Repair: Nebula obtains the gauntlet and command-Zs all of Thanos's damage.

2004
Damage: Wielding the Odinforce, Thor dents the shield with Mjolnir, his hammer.
Repair: Thor later hammers out the dents.

2011
Damage: Snapped in half by the Serpent, the Asgardian god of fear.
Repair: Iron Man reconstructs the shield using the mystical Asgardian metal *Uru*.

BAT-RELATIONSHIPS

The World of the Caped Crusade

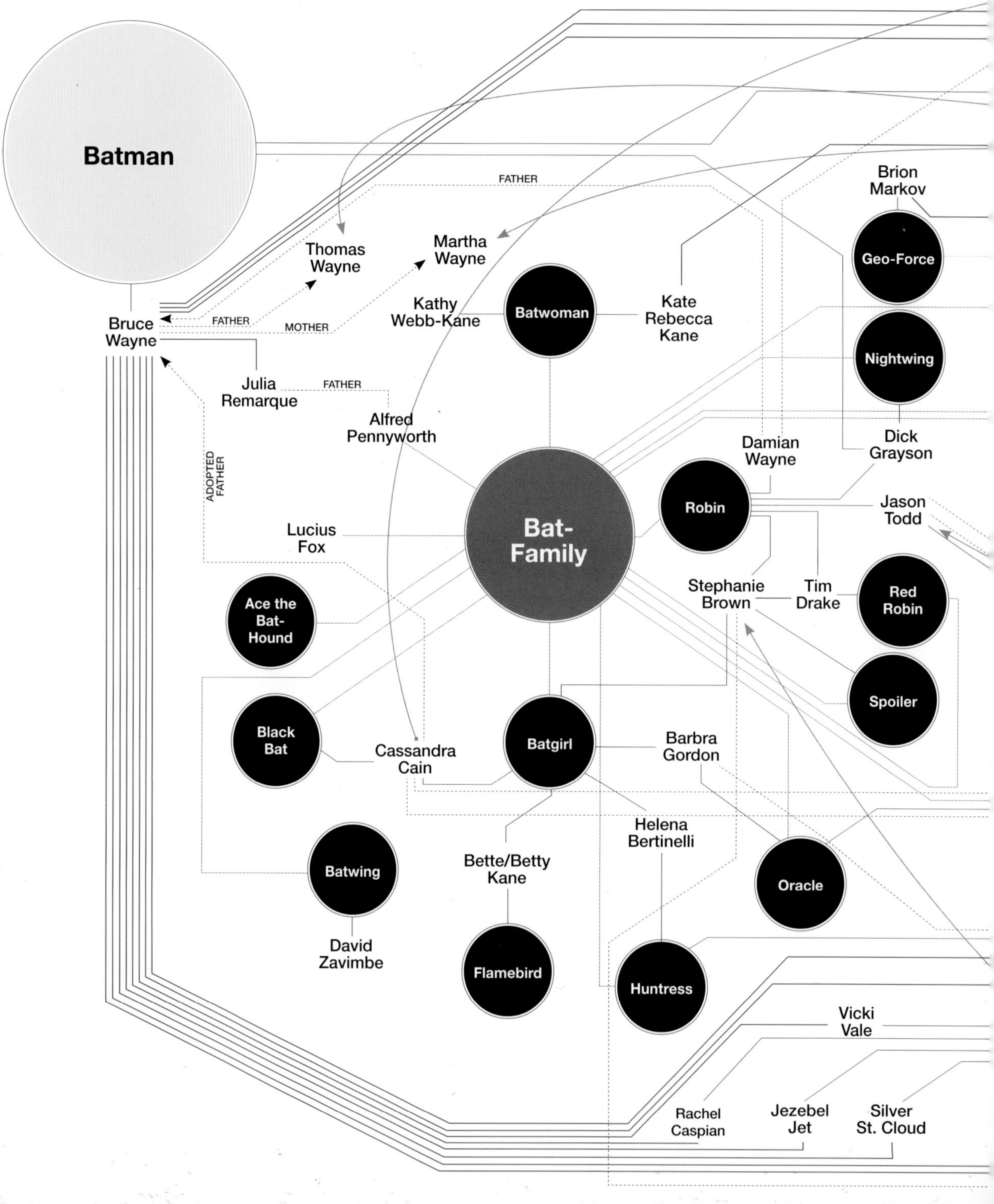
Batman
Bruce Wayne
Thomas Wayne
Martha Wayne
FATHER
FATHER
MOTHER
FATHER
ADOPTED FATHER
Julia Remarque
FATHER
Alfred Pennyworth
Kathy Webb-Kane
Batwoman
Kate Rebecca Kane
Brion Markov
Geo-Force
Nightwing
Dick Grayson
Damian Wayne
Robin
Jason Todd
Bat-Family
Lucius Fox
Ace the Bat-Hound
Stephanie Brown
Tim Drake
Red Robin
Spoiler
Black Bat
Cassandra Cain
Batgirl
Barbra Gordon
Helena Bertinelli
Batwing
David Zavimbe
Bette/Betty Kane
Flamebird
Oracle
Huntress
Vicki Vale
Rachel Caspian
Jezebel Jet
Silver St. Cloud

PANEL TO SCREEN

The History of Comic Book Movies

Taking illustrated stories to the screen hasn't always been as prominent or as commercially successful as it is today—more than half of all comic book movies were made in the past decade. Below compares the domestic box office returns (top) to the Rotten Tomatoes score (bottom) of every widely released movie based on a comic book.

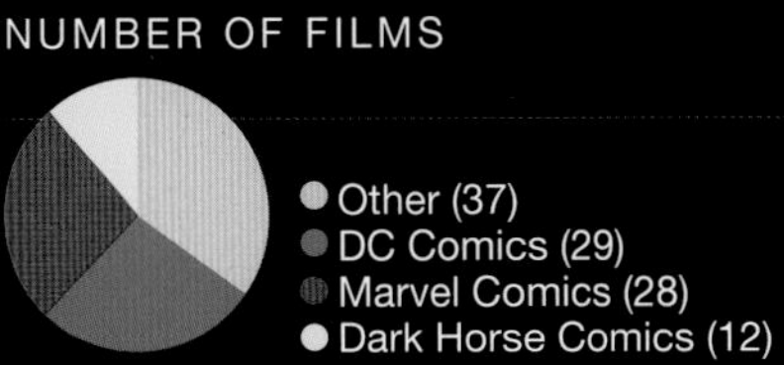

NUMBER OF FILMS
Other (37)
DC Comics (29)
Marvel Comics (28)
Dark Horse Comics (12)

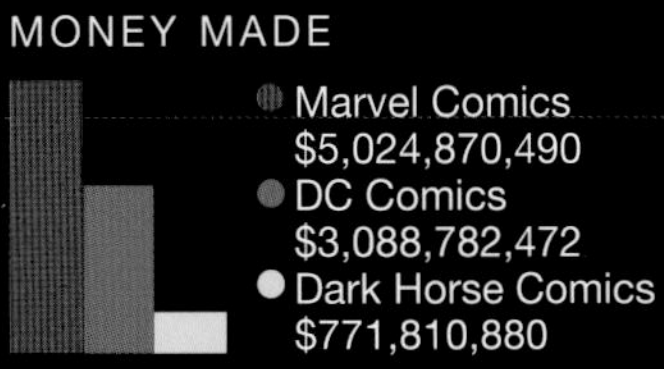

MONEY MADE
Marvel Comics $5,024,870,490
DC Comics $3,088,782,472
Dark Horse Comics $771,810,880

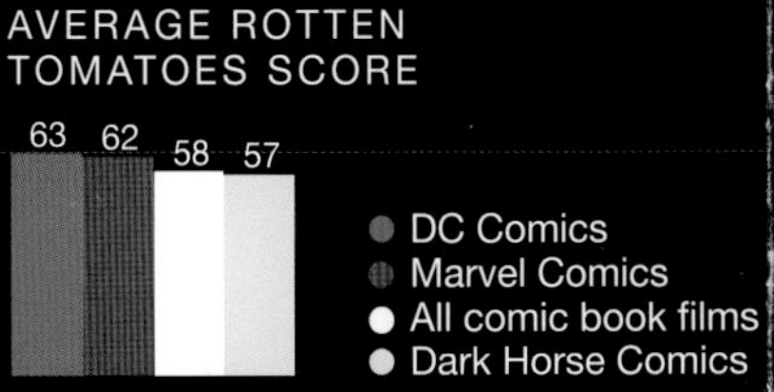

AVERAGE ROTTEN TOMATOES SCORE
63
62
58
57
DC Comics
Marvel Comics
All comic book films
Dark Horse Comics

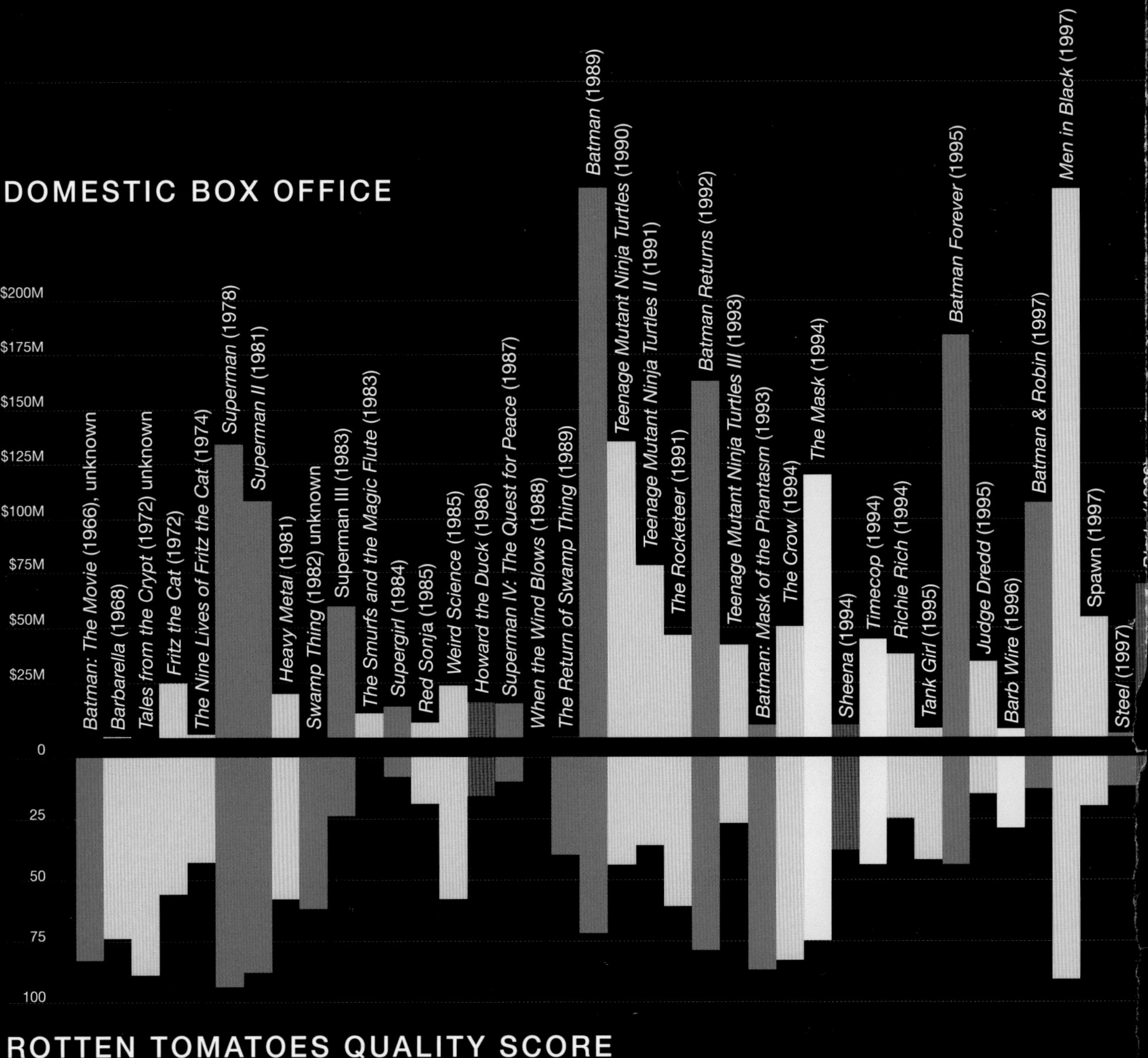

DOMESTIC BOX OFFICE
$200M
$175M
$150M
$125M
$100M
$75M
$50M
$25M
0
Batman: The Movie (1966), unknown
Barbarella (1968)
Tales from the Crypt (1972) unknown
Fritz the Cat (1972)
The Nine Lives of Fritz the Cat (1974)
Superman (1978)
Superman II (1981)
Heavy Metal (1981)
Swamp Thing (1982) unknown
Superman III (1983)
The Smurfs and the Magic Flute (1983)
Supergirl (1984)
Red Sonja (1985)
Weird Science (1985)
Howard the Duck (1986)
Superman IV: The Quest for Peace (1987)
When the Wind Blows (1988)
The Return of Swamp Thing (1989)
Batman (1989)
Teenage Mutant Ninja Turtles (1990)
Teenage Mutant Ninja Turtles II (1991)
The Rocketeer (1991)
Batman Returns (1992)
Teenage Mutant Ninja Turtles III (1993)
Batman: Mask of the Phantasm (1993)
The Crow (1994)
The Mask (1994)
Sheena (1994)
Timecop (1994)
Richie Rich (1994)
Tank Girl (1995)
Batman Forever (1995)
Judge Dredd (1995)
Barb Wire (1996)
Batman & Robin (1997)
Men in Black (1997)
Spawn (1997)
Steel (1997)
25
50
75
100
ROTTEN TOMATOES QUALITY SCORE

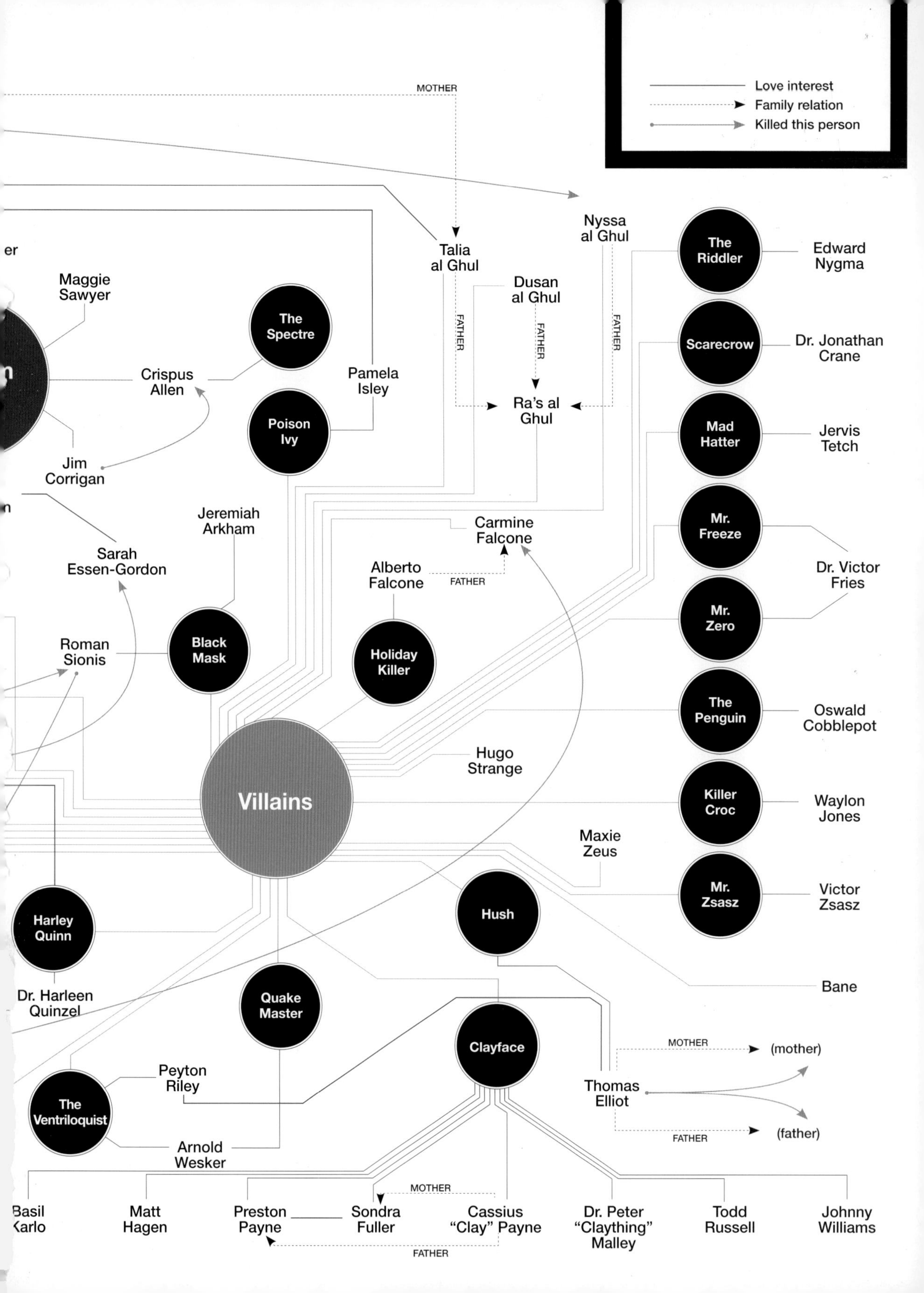

Love interest
Family relation
Killed this person
MOTHER
er
Maggie Sawyer
The Spectre
Crispus Allen
Pamela Isley
Poison Ivy
Jim Corrigan
Talia al Ghul
Nyssa al Ghul
Dusan al Ghul
FATHER
FATHER
FATHER
Ra's al Ghul
The Riddler
Edward Nygma
Scarecrow
Dr. Jonathan Crane
Mad Hatter
Jervis Tetch
Mr. Freeze
Mr. Zero
Dr. Victor Fries
Jeremiah Arkham
Carmine Falcone
Alberto Falcone
FATHER
Sarah Essen-Gordon
Roman Sionis
Black Mask
Holiday Killer
The Penguin
Oswald Cobblepot
Hugo Strange
Villains
Killer Croc
Waylon Jones
Maxie Zeus
Mr. Zsasz
Victor Zsasz
Hush
Harley Quinn
Dr. Harleen Quinzel
Bane
Quake Master
Clayface
MOTHER
(mother)
Thomas Elliot
FATHER
(father)
Peyton Riley
The Ventriloquist
Arnold Wesker
Basil Karlo
Matt Hagen
Preston Payne
Sondra Fuller
MOTHER
Cassius "Clay" Payne
FATHER
Dr. Peter "Claything" Malley
Todd Russell
Johnny Williams

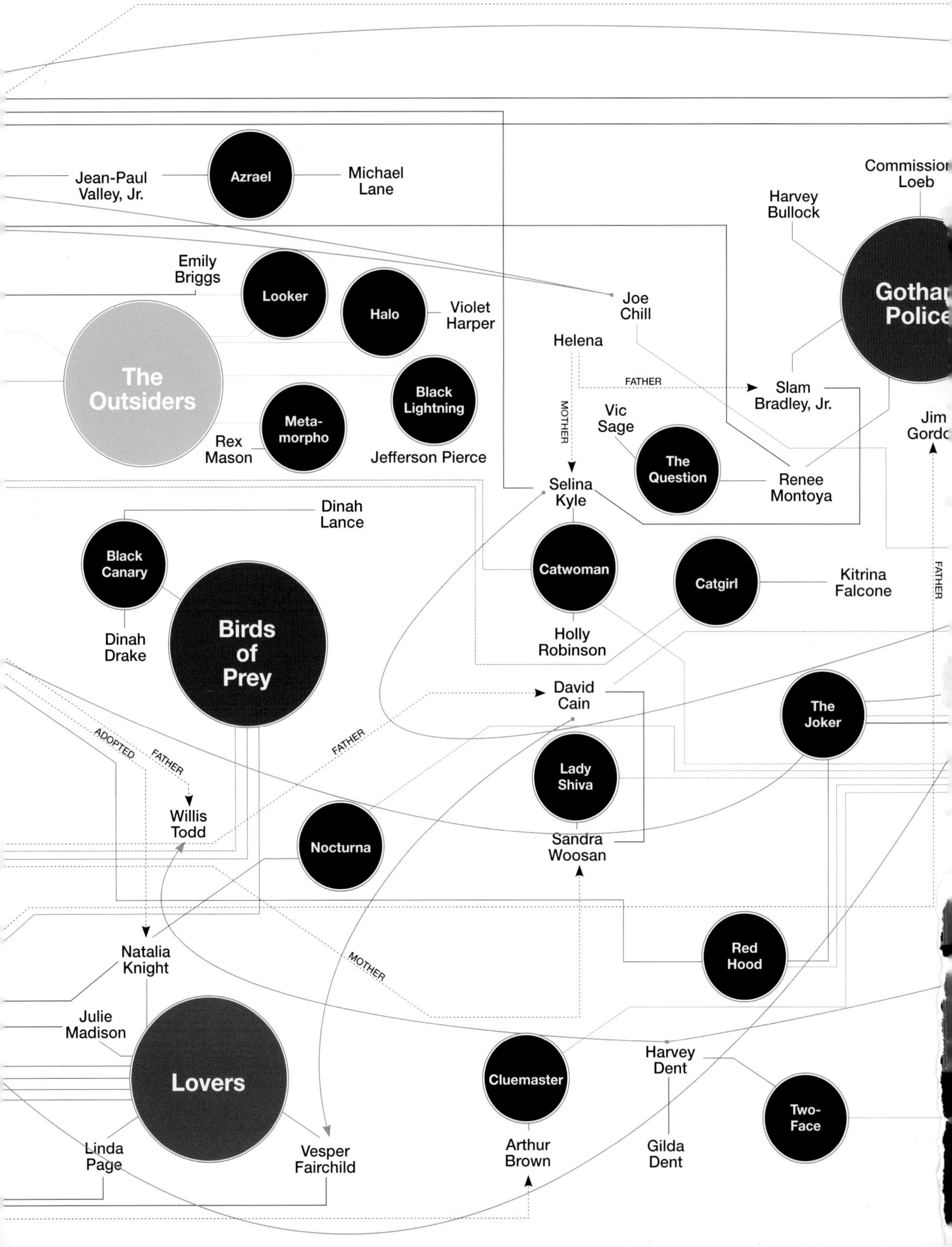
Jean-Paul Valley, Jr.
Azrael
Michael Lane
Commissioner Loeb
Harvey Bullock
Gotham Police
Emily Briggs
Looker
Halo
Violet Harper
Joe Chill
Helena
The Outsiders
Black Lightning
FATHER
Slam Bradley, Jr.
MOTHER
Vic Sage
Jim Gordon
Rex Mason
Metamorpho
Jefferson Pierce
The Question
Renee Montoya
Selina Kyle
Dinah Lance
Black Canary
Catwoman
Catgirl
Kitrina Falcone
FATHER
Dinah Drake
Birds of Prey
Holly Robinson
David Cain
The Joker
ADOPTED
FATHER
FATHER
Lady Shiva
Willis Todd
Nocturna
Sandra Woosan
Natalia Knight
Red Hood
MOTHER
Julie Madison
Lovers
Cluemaster
Harvey Dent
Two-Face
Linda Page
Vesper Fairchild
Arthur Brown
Gilda Dent

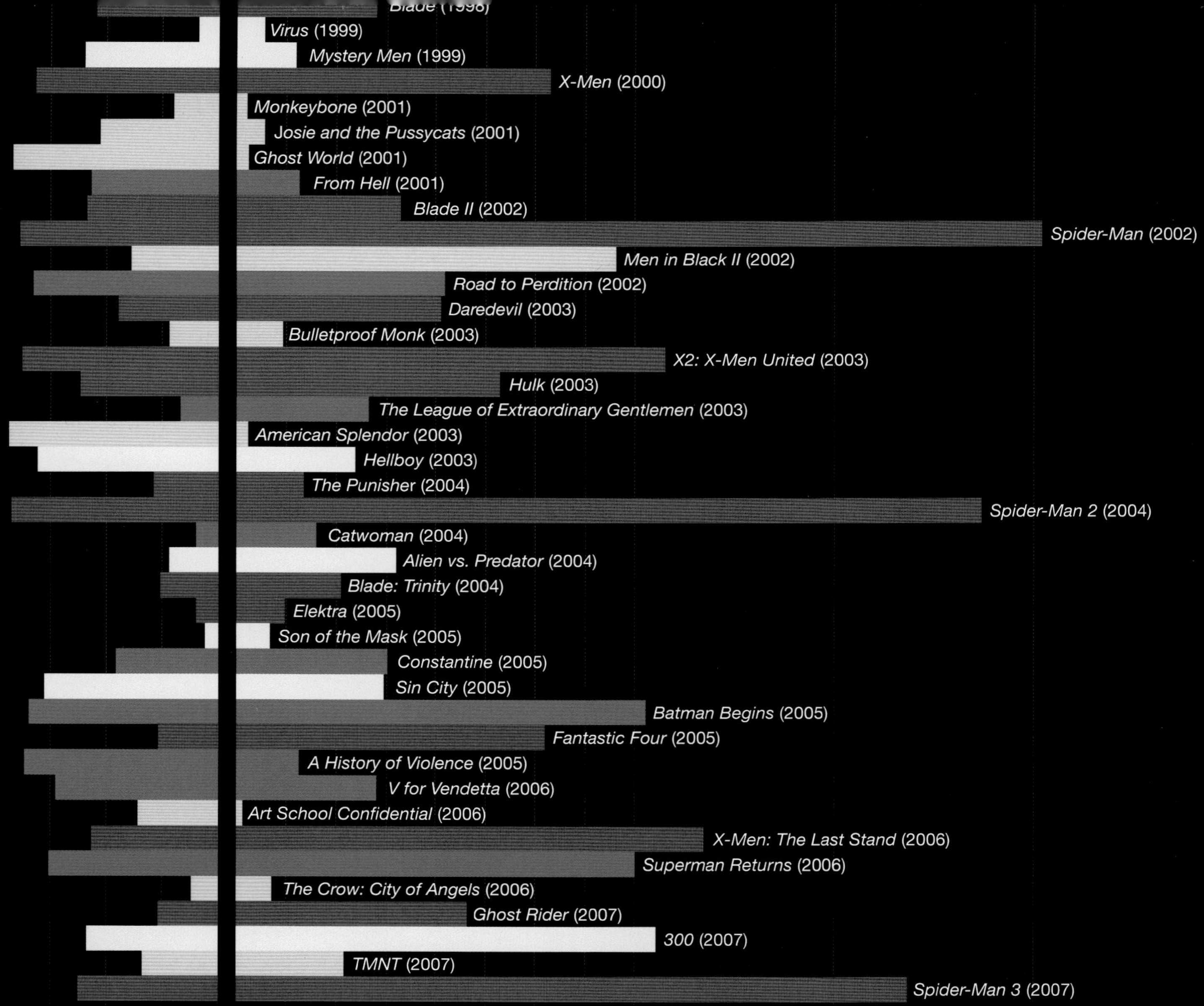

Blade (1998)
Virus (1999)
Mystery Men (1999)
X-Men (2000)
Monkeybone (2001)
Josie and the Pussycats (2001)
Ghost World (2001)
From Hell (2001)
Blade II (2002)
Spider-Man (2002)
Men in Black II (2002)
Road to Perdition (2002)
Daredevil (2003)
Bulletproof Monk (2003)
X2: X-Men United (2003)
Hulk (2003)
The League of Extraordinary Gentlemen (2003)
American Splendor (2003)
Hellboy (2003)
The Punisher (2004)
Spider-Man 2 (2004)
Catwoman (2004)
Alien vs. Predator (2004)
Blade: Trinity (2004)
Elektra (2005)
Son of the Mask (2005)
Constantine (2005)
Sin City (2005)
Batman Begins (2005)
Fantastic Four (2005)
A History of Violence (2005)
V for Vendetta (2006)
Art School Confidential (2006)
X-Men: The Last Stand (2006)
Superman Returns (2006)
The Crow: City of Angels (2006)
Ghost Rider (2007)
300 (2007)
TMNT (2007)
Spider-Man 3 (2007)

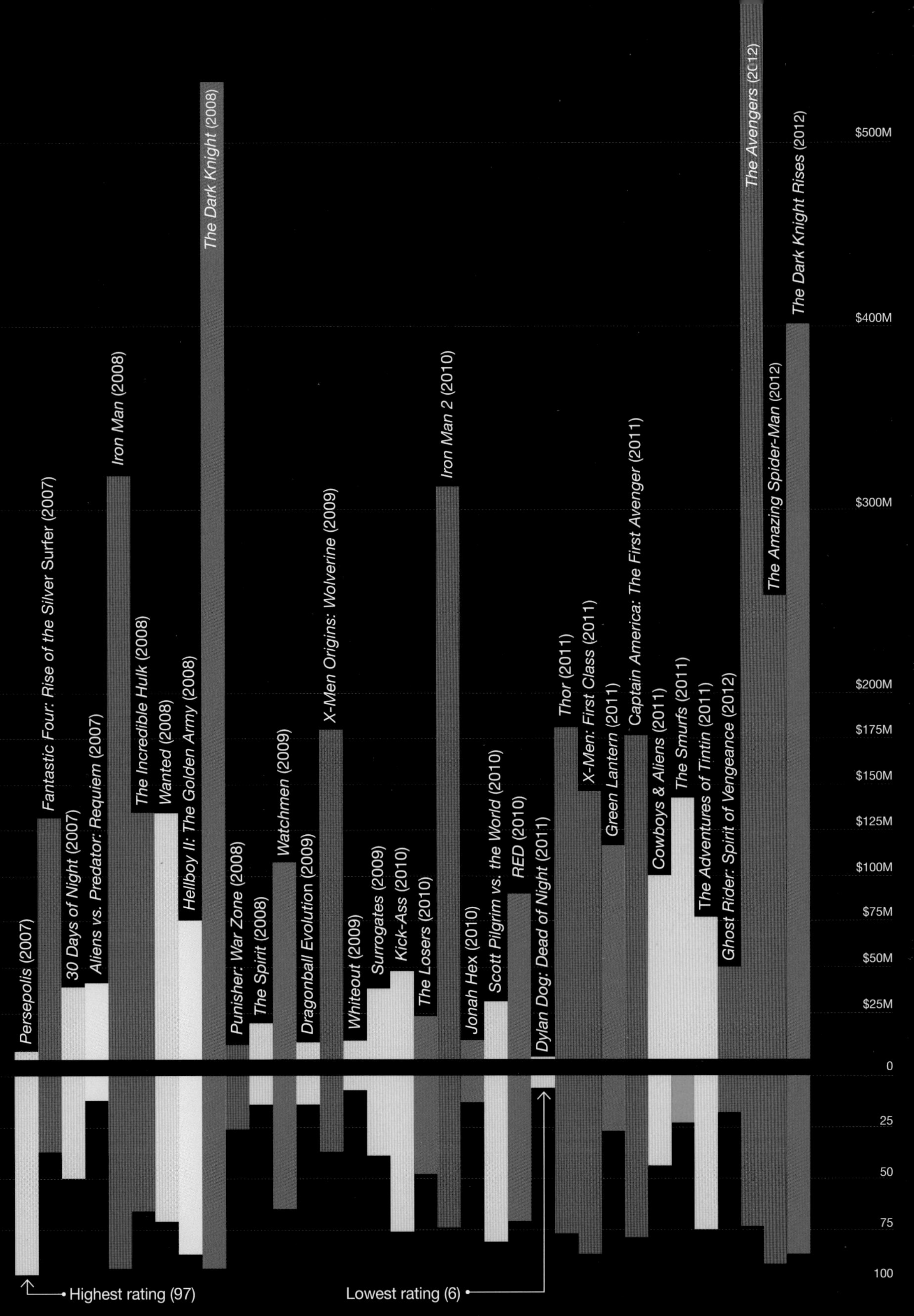
Persepolis (2007)
Fantastic Four: Rise of the Silver Surfer (2007)
30 Days of Night (2007)
Aliens vs. Predator: Requiem (2007)
Iron Man (2008)
The Incredible Hulk (2008)
Wanted (2008)
Hellboy II: The Golden Army (2008)
The Dark Knight (2008)
Punisher: War Zone (2008)
The Spirit (2008)
Watchmen (2009)
Dragonball Evolution (2009)
X-Men Origins: Wolverine (2009)
Whiteout (2009)
Surrogates (2009)
Kick-Ass (2010)
The Losers (2010)
Iron Man 2 (2010)
Jonah Hex (2010)
Scott Pilgrim vs. the World (2010)
RED (2010)
Dylan Dog: Dead of Night (2011)
Thor (2011)
X-Men: First Class (2011)
Green Lantern (2011)
Captain America: The First Avenger (2011)
Cowboys & Aliens (2011)
The Smurfs (2011)
The Adventures of Tintin (2011)
Ghost Rider: Spirit of Vengeance (2012)
The Avengers (2012)
The Amazing Spider-Man (2012)
The Dark Knight Rises (2012)
$500M
$400M
$300M
$200M
$175M
$150M
$125M
$100M
$75M
$50M
$25M
0
25
50
75
100
Highest rating (97)
Lowest rating (6)

The Letter V in *V for Vendetta*

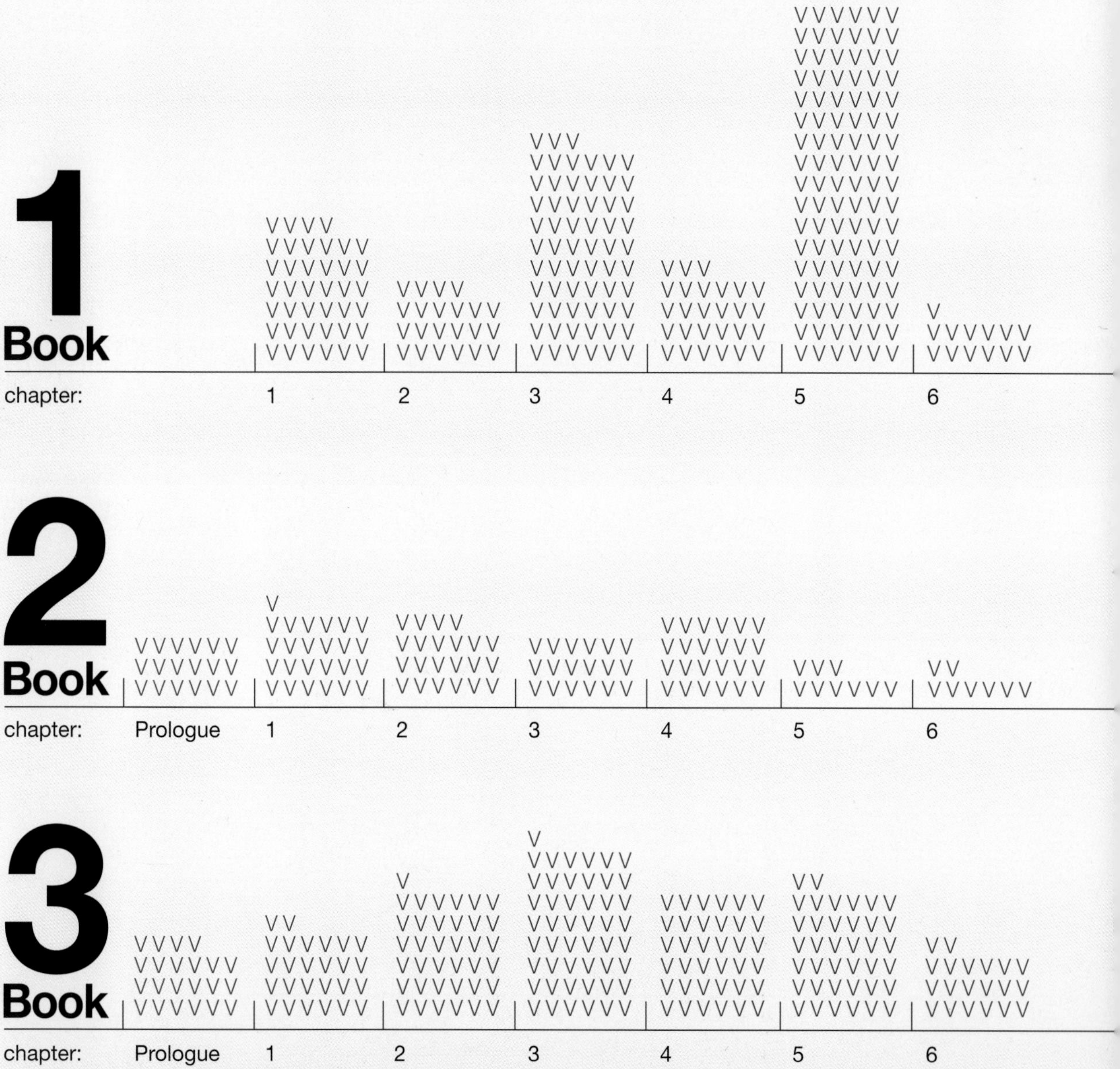
1
Book
chapter:
1
2
3
4
5
6
2
Book
chapter:
Prologue
1
2
3
4
5
6
3
Book
chapter:
Prologue
1
2
3
4
5
6

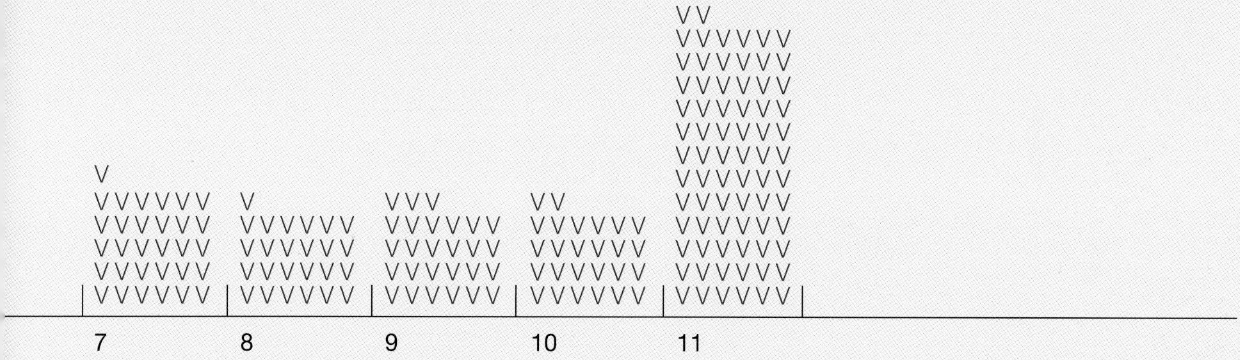

Plot 1:

```
                                        V V
                                        V V V V V
                                        V V V V V
                                        V V V V V
                                        V V V V V
                                        V V V V V
V                                       V V V V V
V V V V V     V                         V V V V V
V V V V V     V V V V V     V V V        V V V V V
V V V V V     V V V V V     V V V V V   V V        V V V V V
V V V V V     V V V V V     V V V V V   V V V V V  V V V V V
V V V V V     V V V V V     V V V V V   V V V V V  V V V V V
```

| 7 | 8 | 9 | 10 | 11 |

Plot 2:

```
                                        V V                              V V
                                        V V V V V            V V V V      V V V V V
                            V V V        V V V V V            V V V V      V V V V V
                V V V V V   V V V V V    V V V V V            V V V V V    V V V V V
V V V V V  V V V  V V V V V   V V V V V    V V V V V   V V V    V V V V V    V V V V V
```

| 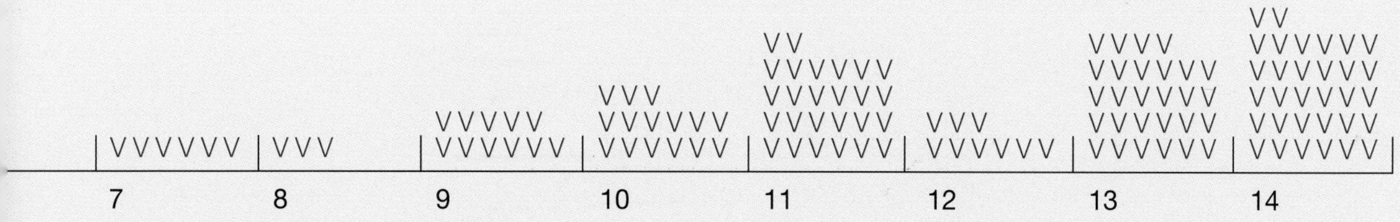 7 | 8 | 9 | 10 | 11 | 12 | 13 | 14 |

Plot 3:

```
                            V
                            V V V V V
                            V V V V V
                            V V V V V
                V V V V V    V V V V V                 V V
V           V V V V V V      V V V V V    V V V V V   V V V V V
V V V V V   V V V V V V      V V V V V    V V V V V   V V V V V
V V V V V   V V V V V V      V V V V V    V V V V V   V V V V V
```

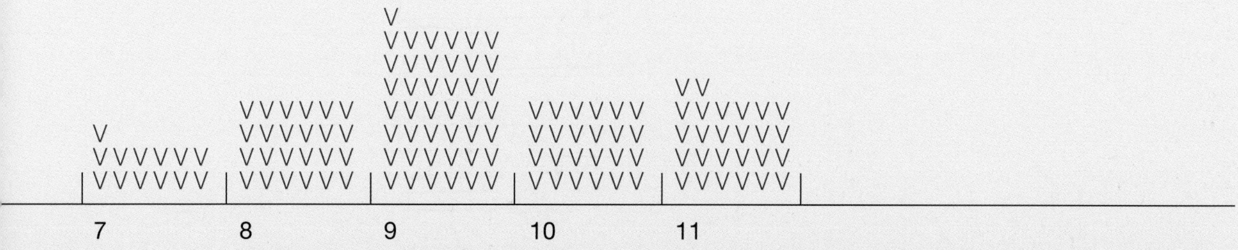

| 7 | 8 | 9 | 10 | 11 |

The Evolution of the Green Lantern Oath

The very first Green Lantern was introduced in 1940. He neither received his powers from a dying alien, nor was he a member of the intergalactic peace-keeping force, the Green Lantern Corps. The earliest Green Lantern was railroad engineer Alan Scott, who, like the modern Green Lantern, sports a ring that transforms his thoughts into real world manifestations. Over time, though, the ring loses power. Recharging requires a power battery and a recited oath. While battery tech has stayed the same, the Green Lantern's oath has evolved over time.

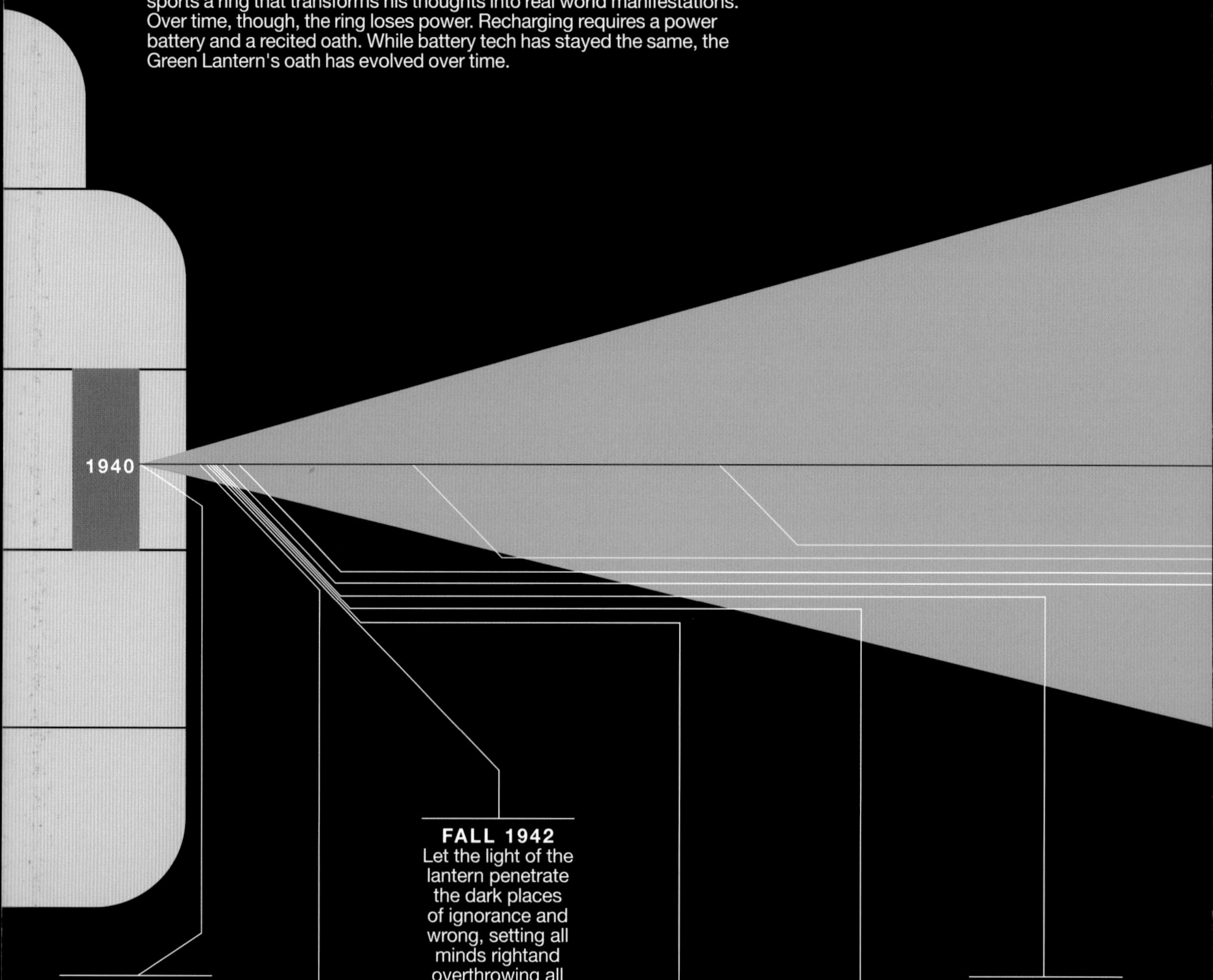
1940

JULY 1940
And I shall shed my light over dark evil, for the dark things cannot stand the light, the light of the Green Lantern!

SUMMER 1942
I shall shed my light upon dark evil,For evil cannot stand the light of Green Lantern!"

FALL 1942
Let the light of the lantern penetrate the dark places of ignorance and wrong, setting all minds rightand overthrowing all servants of evil! I shed my light upon the darkness! Evil has no place to hide itself! Green Lantern goes forth to conquer!"

DEC. 1942
My rays strike the darkest corner, banishing all wickedness!

WINTER 1942
"Let all power and triumph be mine in whatever right I do!"

WINTER 1942
The light of the Green Lantern pierces darkness and mystery, and its radiance will strike at the heart of evil!"

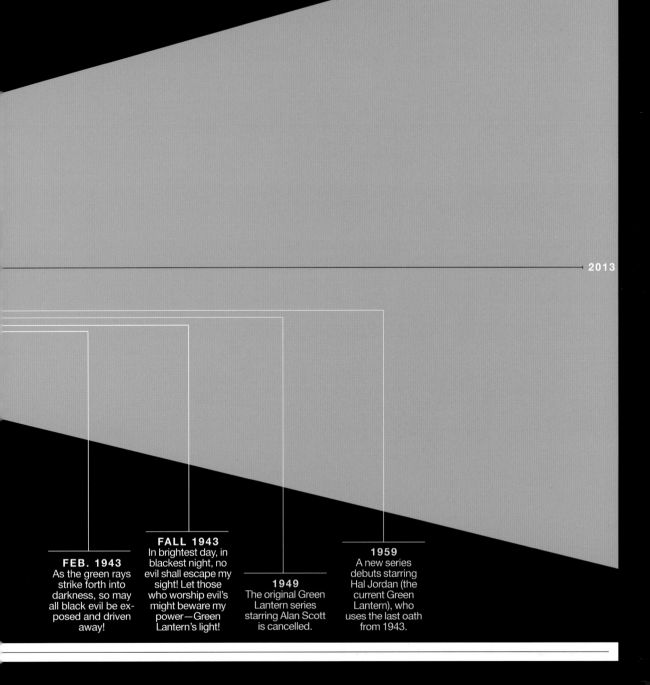

FEB. 1943
As the green rays strike forth into darkness, so may all black evil be exposed and driven away!

FALL 1943
In brightest day, in blackest night, no evil shall escape my sight! Let those who worship evil's might beware my power—Green Lantern's light!

1949
The original Green Lantern series starring Alan Scott is cancelled.

1959
A new series debuts starring Hal Jordan (the current Green Lantern), who uses the last oath from 1943.

2013

Overlapping Interests

SOME OF MARVEL'S MOST PROLIFIC WRITERS: 2000–2010

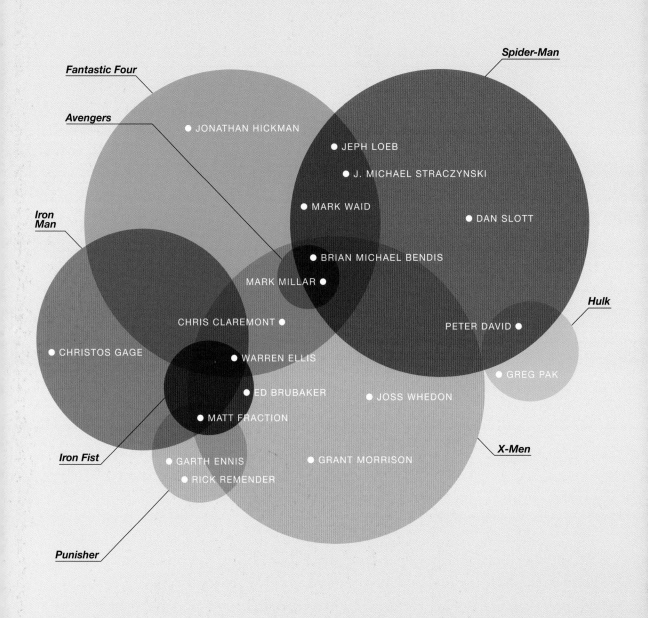

Fantastic Four

Avengers

Spider-Man

Iron Man

Hulk

Iron Fist

X-Men

Punisher

- JONATHAN HICKMAN
- JEPH LOEB
- J. MICHAEL STRACZYNSKI
- MARK WAID
- DAN SLOTT
- BRIAN MICHAEL BENDIS
- MARK MILLAR
- CHRIS CLAREMONT
- PETER DAVID
- CHRISTOS GAGE
- WARREN ELLIS
- GREG PAK
- ED BRUBAKER
- JOSS WHEDON
- MATT FRACTION
- GARTH ENNIS
- GRANT MORRISON
- RICK REMENDER

SOME OF DC'S MOST PROLIFIC WRITERS: 2000–2010

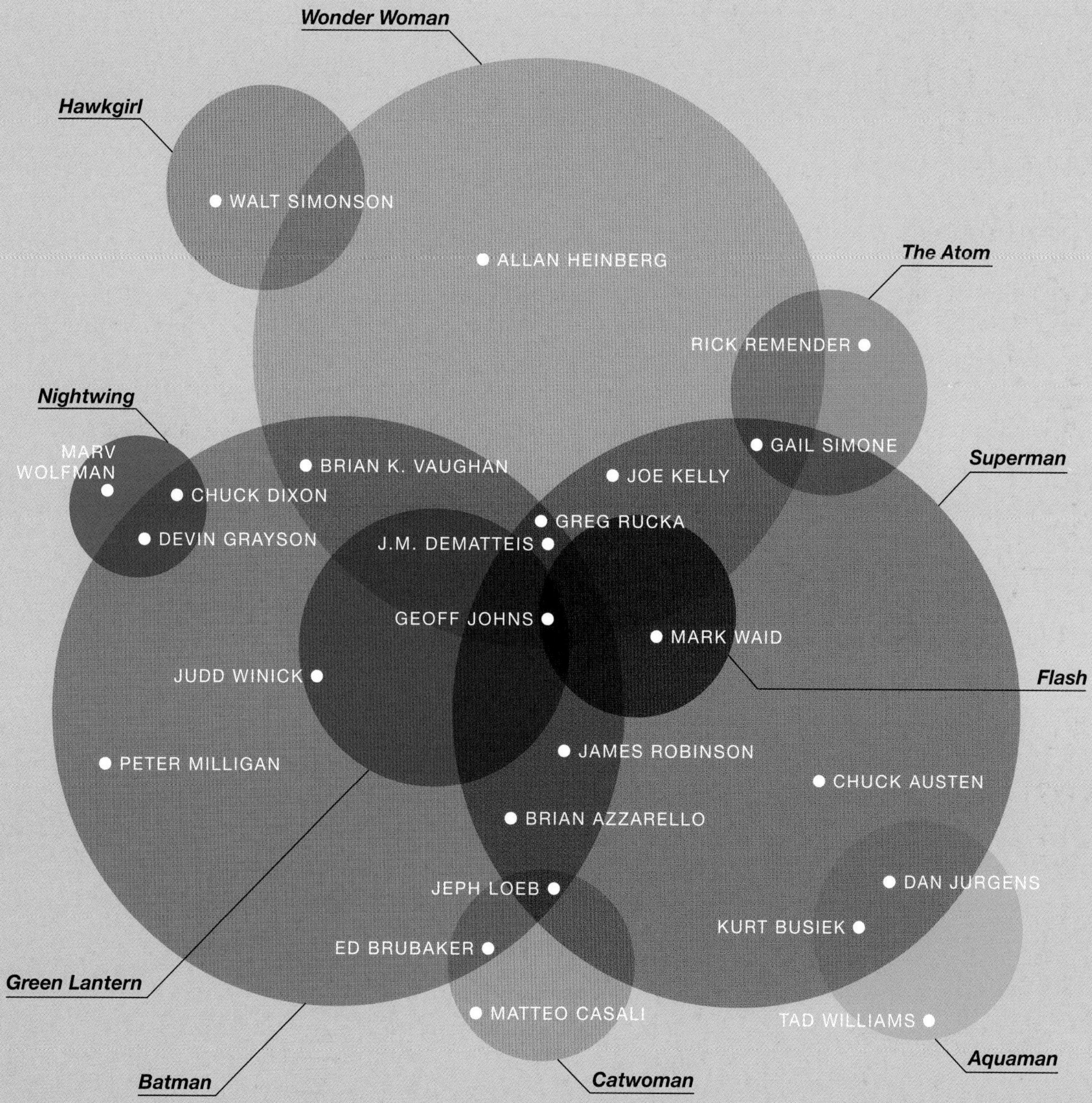
Wonder Woman
Hawkgirl
WALT SIMONSON
ALLAN HEINBERG
The Atom
RICK REMENDER
Nightwing
MARV WOLFMAN
GAIL SIMONE
Superman
BRIAN K. VAUGHAN
JOE KELLY
CHUCK DIXON
GREG RUCKA
DEVIN GRAYSON
J.M. DEMATTEIS
GEOFF JOHNS
MARK WAID
JUDD WINICK
Flash
JAMES ROBINSON
PETER MILLIGAN
CHUCK AUSTEN
BRIAN AZZARELLO
DAN JURGENS
JEPH LOEB
KURT BUSIEK
ED BRUBAKER
Green Lantern
MATTEO CASALI
TAD WILLIAMS
Aquaman
Batman
Catwoman

Rating the Characters in the Marvel Comics Universe

To keep track of the thousands of characters in their library, Marvel Comics catalogues each one and rates them according to their attributes. Heroes, villains, and even civilians are given a score in the following categories: fighting ability, intelligence, strength, speed, durability, and energy projection. Use the key to the right to see how the characters on the next couple of pages measure up.

Use this key with the next few pages to compare character ratings.

Fighting ability

PROFICIENCY IN HAND-TO-HAND COMBAT

Poor 1
Normal 2
Some training 3
Experienced fighter 4
Master of a single form of combat 5
Master of several forms of combat 6
Master of all forms of combat 7

Intelligence

ABILITY TO THINK AND PROCESS INFORMATION

1 Slow/impaired
2 Normal
3 Learned
4 Gifted
5 Genius
6 Super-genius
7 Omniscient

Energy projection

ABILITY TO DISCHARGE ENERGY

None 1
Ability to discharge energy on contact 2
Short range, short duration, single energy type 3
Medium range, duration, single energy type 4
Long range, long duration, single energy type 5
Able to discharge multiple forms of energy 6
Almost unlimited command of all forms of energy 7

7
6
5
4
3
2
1

Strength

ABILITY TO LIFT WEIGHT

1 Weak: cannot lift own body weight
2 Normal: able to lift own body weight
3 Peak human: able to lift twice own body weight
4 Superhuman: 800 lbs–25 ton range
5 Superhuman: 25–75 ton range
6 Superhuman: 75–100 ton range
7 Incalculable: in excess of 100 tons

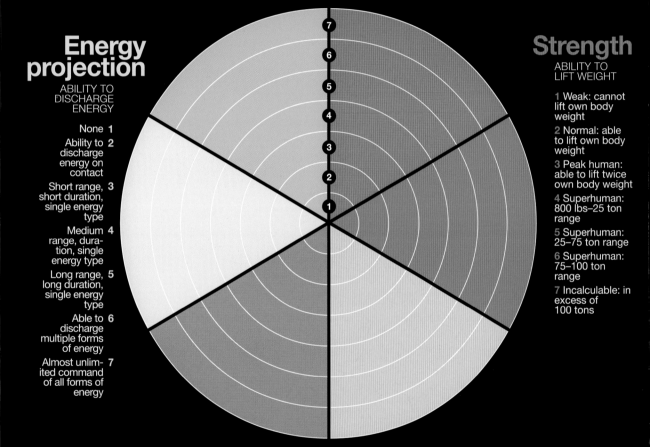

Durability

ABILITY TO RESIST OR RECOVER FROM BODILY INJURY

Weak 1
Normal 2
Enhanced 3
Regenerative 4
Bulletproof 5
Superhuman 6
Virtually indestructible 7

Speed

ABILITY TO MOVE OVER LAND BY RUNNING OR FLIGHT

1 Below normal
2 Normal
3 Superhuman: peak range: 700 MPH
4 Speed of sound: Mach 1
5 Supersonic: Mach 2 through orbital velocity
6 Speed of light: 186,000 miles per second
7 Warp speed: transcending light speed

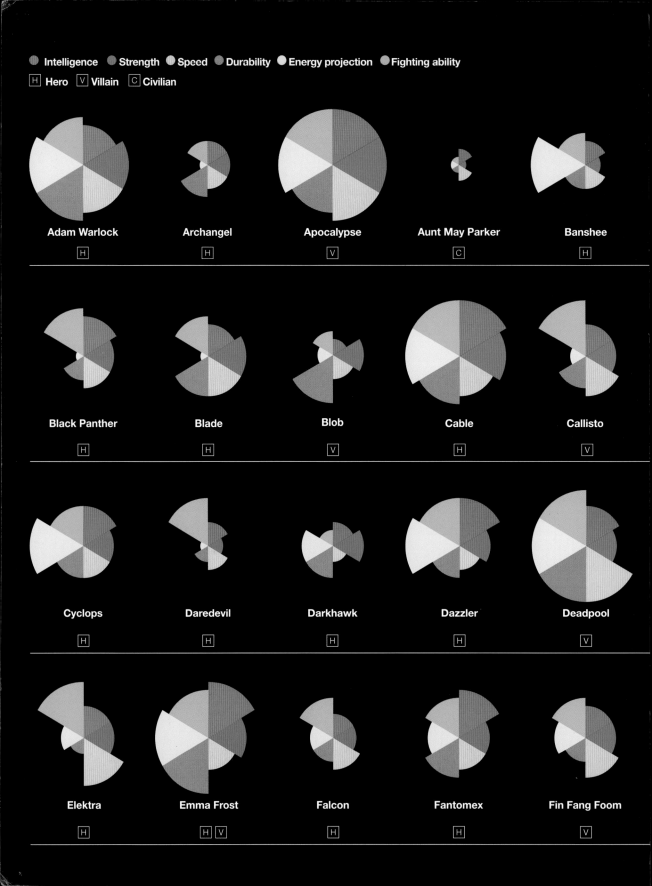

Intelligence ● Strength ● Speed ● Durability ● Energy projection ● Fighting ability

H Hero V Villain C Civilian

Adam Warlock
H

Archangel
H

Apocalypse
V

Aunt May Parker
C

Banshee
H

Black Panther
H

Blade
H

Blob
V

Cable
H

Callisto
V

Cyclops
H

Daredevil
H

Darkhawk
H

Dazzler
H

Deadpool
V

Elektra
H

Emma Frost
H V

Falcon
H

Fantomex
H

Fin Fang Foom
V

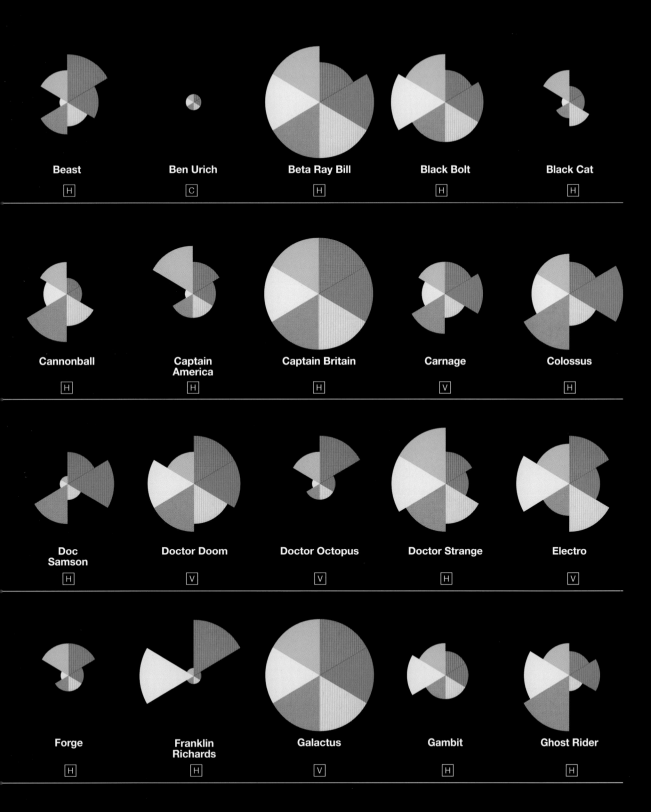

Beast

C

Ben Urich

C

Beta Ray Bill

H

Black Bolt

H

Black Cat

H

Cannonball

H

Captain
America

H

Captain Britain

H

Carnage

V

Colossus

H

Doc
Samson

H

Doctor Doom

V

Doctor Octopus

V

Doctor Strange

H

Electro

V

Forge

H

Franklin
Richards

H

Galactus

V

Gambit

H

Ghost Rider

H

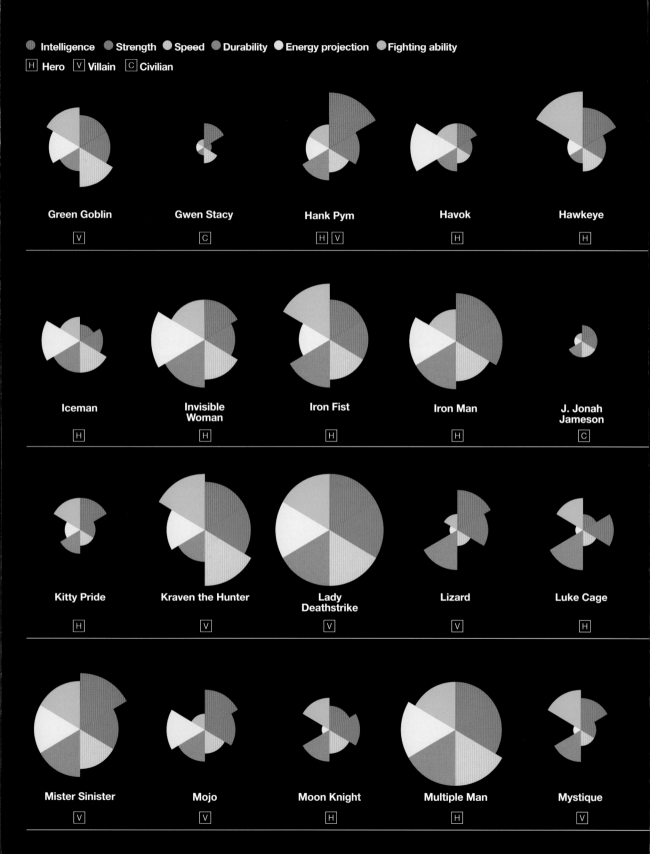

Intelligence Strength Speed Durability Energy projection Fighting ability

H Hero V Villain C Civilian

Green Goblin
V

Gwen Stacy
C

Hank Pym
H V

Havok
H

Hawkeye
H

Iceman
H

Invisible
Woman
H

Iron Fist
H

Iron Man
H

J. Jonah
Jameson
C

Kitty Pride
H

Kraven the Hunter
V

Lady
Deathstrike
V

Lizard
V

Luke Cage
H

Mister Sinister
V

Mojo
V

Moon Knight
H

Multiple Man
H

Mystique
V

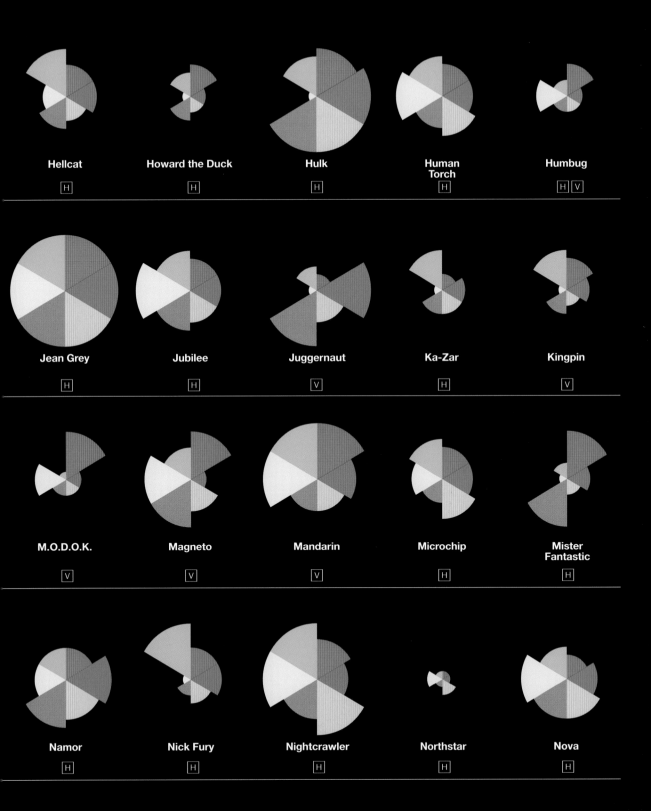

Hellcat
H

Howard the Duck
H

Hulk
H

Human Torch
H

Humbug
H V

Jean Grey
H

Jubilee
H

Juggernaut
V

Ka-Zar
H

Kingpin
V

M.O.D.O.K.
V

Magneto
V

Mandarin
V

Microchip
H

Mister Fantastic
H

Namor
H

Nick Fury
H

Nightcrawler
H

Northstar
H

Nova
H

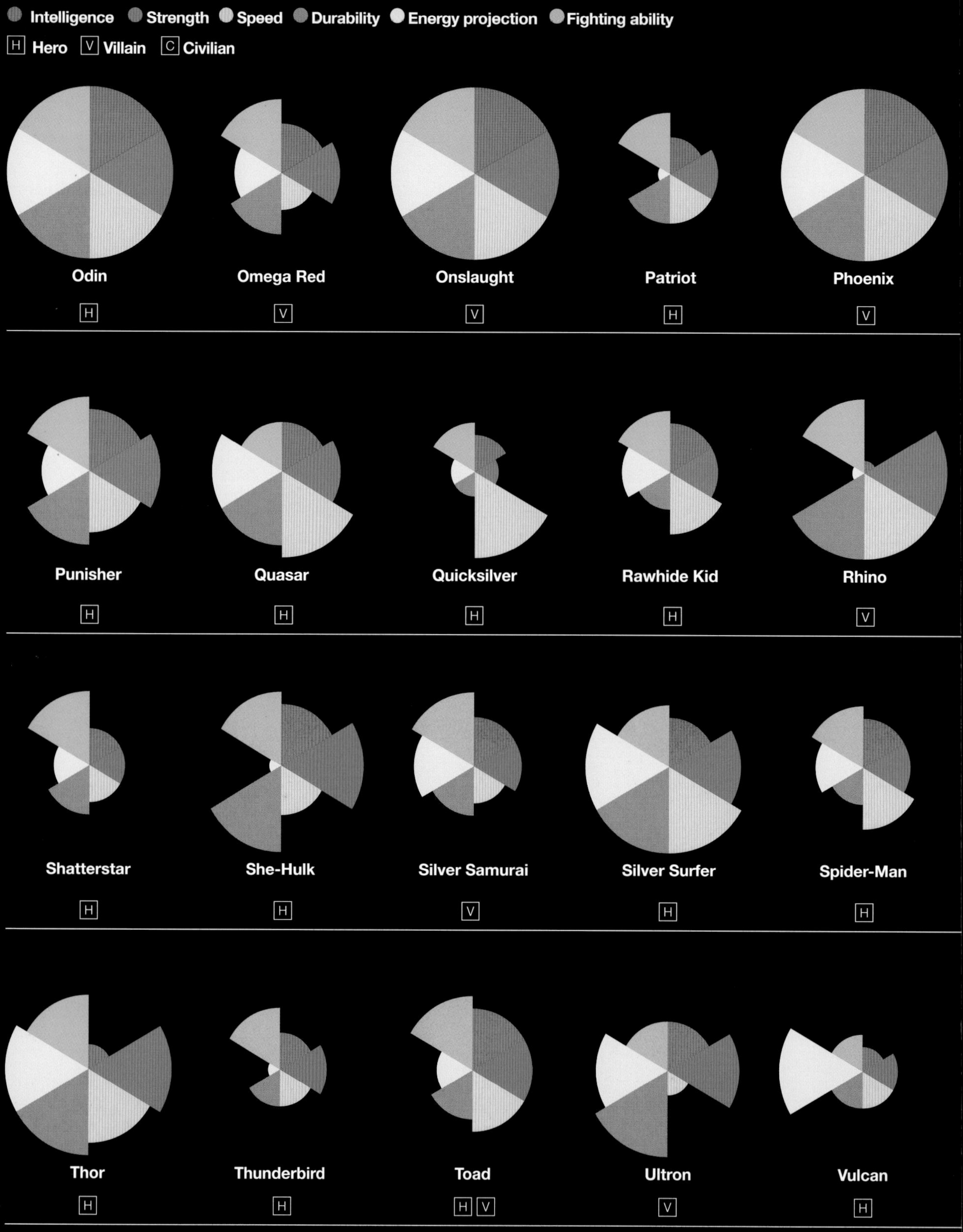

Intelligence
Strength
Speed
Durability
Energy projection
Fighting ability
H Hero
V Villain
C Civilian
Odin H
Omega Red V
Onslaught V
Patriot H
Phoenix V
Punisher H
Quasar H
Quicksilver H
Rawhide Kid H
Rhino V
Shatterstar H
She-Hulk H
Silver Samurai V
Silver Surfer H
Spider-Man H
Thor H
Thunderbird H
Toad H V
Ultron V
Vulcan H

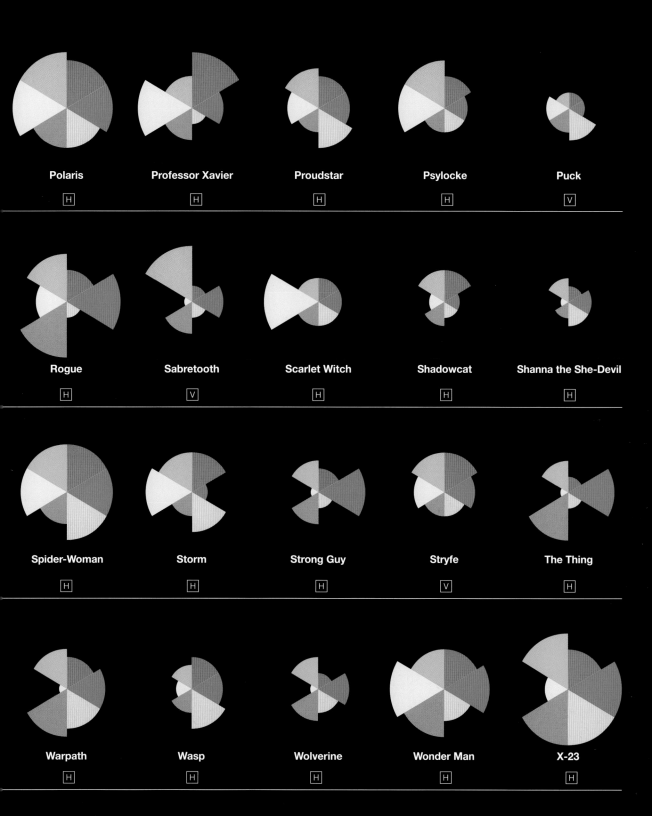

Polaris
H

Professor Xavier
H

Proudstar
H

Psylocke
H

Puck
V

Rogue
H

Sabretooth
V

Scarlet Witch
H

Shadowcat
H

Shanna the She-Devil
H

Spider-Woman
H

Storm
H

Strong Guy
H

Stryfe
V

The Thing
H

Warpath
H

Wasp
H

Wolverine
H

Wonder Man
H

X-23
H

Index

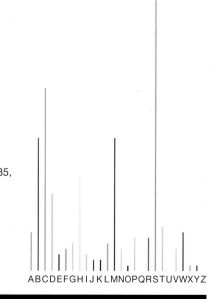

**Most popular letter section
by sub-category**

ABCDEFGHIJKLMNOPQRSTUVWXYZ

Acknowledgments

HUMANS

Chris Anderson

David Brothers

Alice Cho

Neil Egan

Thomas Goetz

Emily Haynes

Laura Hudson

Erica Jewell

Adan Jimenez

Brandon Kavulla

Alan Kistler

Rina Kushnir

Suzanne LaGasa

Andrew Lawrence

Nancy Leong

Rich Leong

Jason Michelitch

Wyatt Mitchell

Caitlin Roper

Peter Rubin

Chris Sims

Rachel Swaby

Jacob Young

Everyone at
WIRED Magazine

SUPERHUMANS

To Rachel, for not breaking up with me during this long process, but also for supporting me through it with incredible love, enthusiasm, and inspiration. Thank you for pointing out when I got things wrong in the book, though I still don't know why you took so much pleasure in doing so. You made this book, and my life, so much better, and I love you so much for it. I could not have done this without you, nor would I have wanted to.

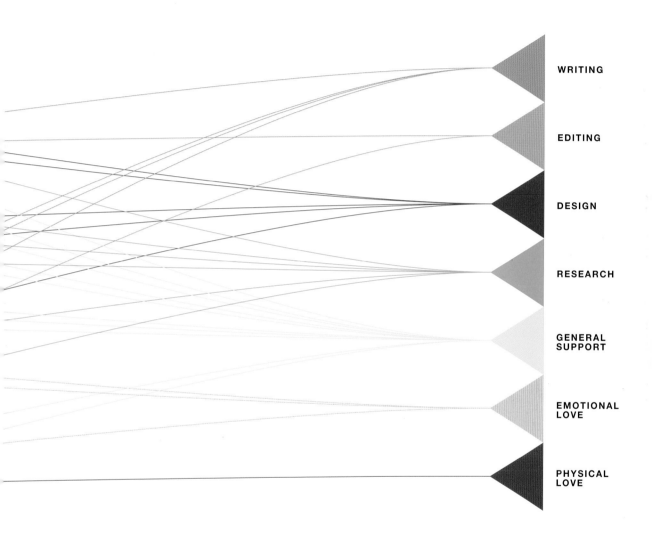

WRITING

EDITING

DESIGN

RESEARCH

GENERAL
SUPPORT

EMOTIONAL
LOVE

PHYSICAL
LOVE

Thanks to everyone at *Wired* for teaching me so much about infographics and being so over-whelmingly supportive.

To all the former readers of *Comic Foundry*. Your support still means the world, and pushed me to take on this project.

NON-HUMANS

To comic books and everyone that makes them and reads them. This book is a love letter to the medium, and hopefully a way to give back to the industry that I owe so much to.

Tim Leong founded and edited the Eisner Award–nominated magazine Comic Foundry and has served as the Design Director at Complex Magazine and Director of Digital Design at WIRED Magazine. He organizes his graphic novels by color and lives in San Francisco, California.

Library of Congress Cataloging-in-Publication Data

Leong, Tim.
Super graphic : a visual guide to the comic book universe / Tim Leong.
pages cm
ISBN 978-1-4521-1388-3
1. Comic books, strips, etc. I. Title.

NC1340.L46 2013
741.5--dc23

2012042335

Manufactured in China

MIX
Paper from
responsible sources
FSC® C016973

10 9 8 7 6 5 4

Cover design by Tim Leong

Chronicle Books LLC
680 Second Street
San Francisco, California 94107
www.chroniclebooks.com